W9-BPK-095

BEHIN

Code

362.11
Wil

Blue

A writer's guide to hospitals

Dr

Other fine Writer's Digest Books are available from your local bookstore or direct from the publisher.

Visit our Web site at www.writersdigest.com for information on more resources for writers.

To receive a free weekly E-mail newsletter delivering tips and updates about writing and about Writer's Digest products, send an E-mail with "Subscribe Newsletter" in the body of the message to newsletter-request@writersdigest.com, or register directly at our Web site at www.writersdigest.com.

04   03   02   01   00   5   4   3   2   1

Library of Congress Cataloging-in-Publication Data

Wilson, Keith D.
    Code blue: a writer's guide to hospitals / Keith Wilson and David Page; with introduction by Michael Palmer.
        p.   cm.—(Behind the scenes)
    Includes bibliographical references and index.
    ISBN 0-89879-937-6 (pbk.: alk. paper)
    1. Hospitals—Popular works. 2. Fiction—Authorship. I. Page, David W. II. Title.
    III. Behind the scenes (Cincinnati, Ohio)
RA963.W54   1999
362.1'1'0248—dc21   99-047591

Editor: Jack Heffron
Production editor: Bob Beckstead
Production coordinator: Rachel Vater
Interior designer: Sandy Conopeotis Kent

About the Authors

DR. KEITH WILSON is the author of *Cause of Death*, one of the most popular books in the Howdunit series. His medical thriller, *Life Form*, was published in 1994 by Putnam Berkley and has been optioned by a film production company. He is now completing his second novel, also a medical thriller. Specializing in diagnostic radiology, Wilson is a board-certified internist and runs a private medical practice in Toledo, Ohio. He is also the medical director of the Harris McIntosh Tower medical facility in Toledo.

DR. DAVID PAGE is the author of *Body Trauma*. A board-certified surgeon and a Fellow of the American College of Surgeons, Page has published over twenty scientific papers and has written two chapters of textbooks for medical students. He is the Director of Undergraduate Programs in Surgery and is Service Chief at Baystate Medical Center, the western campus of Tufts Medical School. He, too, is completing a medical thriller. He lives in Southampton, MA.

– TABLE OF CONTENTS –

.

I love to read.

I understand the richness reading can bring to life as I understand little else. Even with the demands of fatherhood, my medical job, my writing career and an unsettling passion for duplicate bridge, I make time, nearly every night, to pick up one of the books on my nightstand and treat myself to a few dozen pages—more if the prose is stimulating and I can keep my eyes open.

Gratefully, I am not alone in my ardor. And sales figures suggest that the number of folks turning (or returning) from videos and the boob tube to the printed word is growing—heartening news for all of us writers.

I belong to the subset of readers who almost exclusively seek out fiction. Richard Ford, Richard North Patterson, Richard III. It doesn't really matter to me, as long as I know the writer, the story sounds interesting or the book has been recommended by friends who know my tastes. Newspapers and magazines keep me up with what *is*. At all other times, when I read I want to settle in with tales of what might have been.

And therein lies a problem.

In fiction, the story is made up, but the facts must never be. Nothing is more unsatisfying for me than to be yanked from the world in which I have chosen to immerse myself by a "fact" I know is simply not so. The head-injured victim is rushed into the emergency ward and given a shot of painkiller. Next book, please! No ER doc in his right mind would ever administer a drug that might alter the consciousness of such a patient. If the author (and in fact there *was* one in this instance) was going to deal with something as arcane to most writers as emergency medicine, why couldn't she have asked a doc to check her accuracy?

Well now, at least when it comes to life in modern day hospitals, you won't have to impose on your family sawbones (or on me) for a reading of your manuscript. You have the ultimate alternative resource right in your hands. Drs. Wilson and Page have done for you what an entire multispecialty group practice probably couldn't. In clear and concise prose, augmented by high-octane vignettes, excellent photographs, carefully constructed chapter headings and subheadings and a detailed index, they have successfully performed the demystification of hospital medicine.

Now, dear writer, you have no excuse for putting your patient under general anesthesia when clearly an epidural is called for. If your protagonist's girlfriend is shot in the shoulder, let's not have him reach into the entry hole blind and seconds later pluck out the slug with a pair of tweezers—or even a hemostat. You may not need to know about the inner workings of HMOs for every book you write, but if I'm reading that particular novel, you had better get it right.

Well, the hot-breaking news is that now you can.

The good doctors Wilson and Page have put together a worthy reference book that can be taken in small doses *prn* (as needed) or read pleasurably *QID* (four times a day) from cover to cover.

So, what are you waiting for? Conjure up the most diabolical ICU murder, then check out chapter six of *Code Blue: A Writer's Guide to Hospitals* and make it happen in a way that will have the setting, the jargon, and the pharmacology that even the pickiest medical expert (quite possibly me) will applaud.

Michael Palmer M.D.

Misery and suffering have always lingered in humankind's deepening shadows, a sordid background on the stage of human drama, shifting in intensity across *homo sapien* time. Disease is never quite out of sight for anyone, always on the fringe of experience. Few individuals, even in the modern era, travel through their lives without at least once stumbling into injury or contracting an infectious illness.

Unexpectedly, disease may leak joy from one's existence and alter the course of one's intimate relationships. This is the stuff of real life. It also ought to form a portion of the foundation of characterization, as well as offer plot (mis)direction.

Throughout history, illness, like its fellow tormentor, war, has defined humankind's folly. The hopeful protege of this painful history, our species remains a tortured learner. Limping through varied and uncertain existences, we seem confused by the thorn in our heel.

Today disease often brings a trip to the hospital. The young suffer outrageous ravages of trauma, often self-inflicted; the elderly slip insidiously into the waiting arms of age-related deterioration and chronic illness. While highway trauma and inner-city violence wound and maim youngsters, over 75 percent of our elderly suffer at least one chronic disease and often several, with heart disease, cancer and stroke leading the hit parade of causes of elder death. The very aged are admitted to the hospital twice as often as youngsters and stay twice as long. When discharged they often require further institutionalization.

Regardless of their age, it seems hospitalized patients are treated with equal aggressiveness and are discharged before healing is complete. More and more beds in the modern hospital are dedicated to medical and surgical intensive care units, intermediate care areas and floors that offer complex specialty care, and all of these areas house complex technology and specially trained staff.

Some hospitals specialize in only one type of medical problem such as cancer treatment. Some hospitals emphasize research and teaching; others on the periphery of populated geography provide only the most basic type of acute care, with systems of referral for complex patients.

More important than any other feature of modern hospitals is the dedication to doing things to patients, performing diagnostic and therapeutic interventions and complex surgical procedures. These intense treatments include radiation therapy, chemotherapy, hyperbaric oxygen therapy, dialysis and other organ-specific treatments. Physicians who practice in the hospital setting may also be active in community practice, or they may run hospital-based clinics or limit themselves to in-house (hospital) care. A few doctors have elected (or have been directed) to no longer work in the hospital at all.

Procedures which require catheters, needles and other hardware to be inserted into body cavities carry well-defined risks. Some doctors are better at specific procedures than others. Many surgeons limit themselves to a few operations, while others, particularly in smaller hospitals, must perform a wider range of surgical procedures.

In this environment where risky and intense care is delivered to a carefully selected number of sick patients, the stakes are high. Bad things may happen to good people. Excellent doctors may have horrible complications befall their patients. All of these statistics are now available to patients but, as with all statistics, the numbers don't tell the whole story.

And the question which no one wants to ask today is always there for the writer to grab and wrestle to the ground: Who should be treated? In a society wracked by impossible health costs, the issue of rationing of precious but scarce medical resources will not go away. And even if the American people and the federal government quietly turn their backs on the disaster lurking for Americans in the twenty-first century, surely writers will not.

The Writer's View

Few stories have been written without at least one character suffering an element of illness or disability. Most of your characters will have been in the hospital at one time or another in their back story, or may find themselves hospitalized during your current story. Fiction and nonfiction writers alike must understand how the high-tech hospital works, know the changes which have occurred over the last three decades and be able to seamlessly integrate this understanding into their prose.

Wonderful opportunities to create conflict and deepen characterization lie in the modern hospital and in the unpredictable, irrational progression of disease. The popularity of television programs such as *ER* and *Chicago Hope*, as well as movies like *Malice*, emphasize the public's interest in medical issues. But get it wrong and they will not forgive you.

This book is written for writers. Rather than assembling a compendium of data, we have attempted to cull from the exponentially growing mass of medically related literature those interesting facts that will not only inform your prose, but also provoke you to search for new relationships in your material. We believe there is behind-the-scenes information in this book that is not available elsewhere, information that you may expand in your own fictive world.

Just as important as the factual data is the information that does *not* appear in lists and sidebars, but that represents the intimate narrative of the book. It is the hidden taproot of the hospital. This truly unique approach to telling it the way it is provides you with material not published elsewhere and not commonly discussed by doctors. Amid the facts and photos there also lies a minefield of information distilled from untold observed physician interactions and overheard hospital dialogue.

It's the brandy in the hospital eggnog.

Is there a point in your character's life where illness becomes a sheer wall of impedance past which your story must progress? Can you get your hero into trouble in the hospital? Do you know how to get him out of trouble? Or in deeper?

Recently one of us served briefly as a consultant on a major movie (*In Dreams*) where a scene involved a woman waking up from a coma in an intensive care unit. The initial script dialogue for the physician seemed woody and unreal. When changed slightly the scene flowed smoothly, emphasizing the awakening woman and not the doctor. A small adjustment in dialogue based on an understanding of how doctors really talk to patients in the hospital setting and a few suggestions about the doctor's demeanor made the scene more believable.

The history of the hospital's origins is really the story of the evolution of medical care. Every writer should understand the basic elements of this often-sordid tale. As a backdrop to the detailed information provided in the remainder of the book, the historical sketch in the first chapter will enrich your understanding of medicine's recent successes. It provides a starting point for your research for a historical novel, or may expand your basic understanding for a character who lives in a given era.

From there you will learn details of hospital function that will authenticate your own nonfiction work, novel, stage play or screenplay.

Dr. Richard Selzer once said every patient is a short story. Thus, the modern hospital is a many-volume collection of plot material. In the acrid-smelling corridors and behind closed doors and *Restricted Access* signs, terrible things may be happening.

Story conflict lies waiting. But you've got to get it right.

Finally, this book is about the generic modern large-city hospital. It does not attempt to describe every hospital, nor does it describe a specific hospital. Rather, we have written about hospitals in general. Hospitals are different in architecture: Some were built at the turn of the century; some of the newest represent a sophisticated modern blend of function and design. Hospitals are unique in age and design, just as city libraries or schools are different.

However, the overall function and operation of all modern hospitals are similar. New hospitals may have laminar airflow operating rooms, computerized medical records and digital imaging, whereas older hospitals may not have any of these. But the general operation and daily function of all hospitals are the same. We haven't tried to describe the most modern, technically advanced hospital as a standard. But we have tried to point out some of the newest developments within hospitals, and to describe trends for the future.

CHAPTER ONE

The Origins of the Modern Hospital

Humankind learned early in its belligerent history how to dress wounds. Unpredictable traumatic events were commonplace in a hostile world where survival depended more on ingenuity than on strength. Man preyed on all life forms, and death and mutilation were the by-products of the struggle for existence in Early Pleistocene life. When early man began to develop the concepts of possessions, boundaries and ownership of land, he ruthlessly descended upon his own kind to defend them and began the expansive history of warfare, a brutal activity of swords and hatchets that set the stage for the evolution of surgical practice.

Injuries and wounds led humans to experiment with herbal poultices, mudpacks and bark bandages, and to eventually discover the basic principles of primitive medical care. All manner of practitioners populated the convoluted nascent history of medicine and thus contributed to the story of the modern hospital's evolution. The history of medicine informs the story of the hospital. As political, social and economic factors changed in various locales in the world, so did the face of the institution eventually known as the *hospital*.

Early Hospitals

Cure wasn't always the mission of the hospital.

By 600 B.C. hospitals in India employed the principles of basic sanitation and surgery and were built with a regional plan to serve the destitute and the infirmed. Arab hospitals also served as teaching centers where pharmacy and chemistry originated and where classic Islamic learning was preserved. Not only did the Arabs establish asylums for the insane centuries before the Europeans, but their hospitals were characterized by such modern concepts as separate wards for different diseases and different locations for convalescent patients who were less ill and more ambulatory than others.

The cyclic nature and rhythm of human knowledge is reflected in the Middle Ages when all intellectual pursuits, including those already applied to the practice of medicine—as well as any notion of progress—were eradicated. Nursing care, ignorance of sanitation and the absence of reasoned treatment brought medical care to a shuddering halt between the fourth and fourteenth centuries. Medieval houses for the sick provided shelter for pilgrims and other destitute citizens as well as marginal medical care for the poor.

The famous thirteenth-century Hotel Dieu in Paris offered succor to the poor with only occasional physician coverage and was staffed by members of the religious community. It was common before the twelfth century for hospitals to have minimal physician input, as doctors seldom included the hospital in their practices. And even the Hotel Dieu often assigned two or three patients to a single bed; meals were also less than nutritious and heating often nonexistent! It must be said that a few medieval hospitals provided physician and surgeon services and aimed at cures for certain diseases rather than mere comfort care until death—the hospital's mission at that time.

Hospitals in Colonial America

American medicine, borrowing from English, German and French influences, vaulted from primitive bleedings, bandages and purges to the sophisticated interventions that characterize the modern era. The history of the American hospital marks the development of notable medical careers, the nourishment of improved scientific principles with which to practice and the expansion of medical knowledge and technology. It also includes a rancorous vein of disagreement and bickering among doctors and significant distrust by the public. From the beginning, American hospitals were founded and supported by private citizens, at first by contributions from merchants and farmers, and only later by the affluent.

American medicine in general and hospitals in particular lagged behind European accomplishments, despite the trend for Americans to seek medical knowledge in Germany, France, England and Scotland. American doctors eschewed the stethoscope and clinical thermometer when these clinical accoutrements first became available, and resisted new medical knowledge from overseas for quite some time in the nineteenth century.

Doctors were exclusively men until 1853, when Elizabeth Blackwell became the first woman to earn a medical degree. Men who possessed a college degree, read what medical literature was available and gained some experience with patients were as close to a physician as was to be found in the Colonies before the 1760s. Magistrates and clergymen read and practiced the healing arts, such as they were, and competed with "doctors" trained by apprenticeship. These two groups undoubtedly represent the beginnings of the "town versus gown" conundrum of modern times, the confrontation of practical, experienced physicians with their academic, research-based colleagues. The dilemma is reflected in Richard Harrison Shryock's observation in his book *Medicine and Society in America: 1660-1860* that Oliver Wendell Holmes wrote essays praising the practical practitioners and others ridiculing them. Overall, colonial medicine between the early 1600s and 1730 was primitive and disorganized.

Early medical practitioners in America would have been considered ignorant in Europe. Shrylock states that before the Revolutionary War, "It has been estimated that on the eve of that conflict there were about 3,500 established practitioners in the colonies and that not more than 40 of these had received any formal training. Of the latter, only about half— or barely more than 5 percent of the total—held degrees." Laypeople often wrote medical guides focused on hygiene and quackery. And in 1721 in Boston there was only one practitioner who held an M.D. degree!

The early American hospital shared in the ignominy of the slave trade. In 1707, a "pest house" or *lazaretto* was built on Sullivan's Island in South Carolina where the newly arriving Africans were required to remain for ten days, and as long as three weeks, until a health inspector had examined them. According to Edward Ball in his book, *Slaves in the Family*, "Those who had survived the Middle Passage—the second leg of the triangular travel for British ships, which sailed from England to West Africa to America, and finally back to England—stayed under guard in the pest house. People who died during the quarantine were evidently buried in mass graves." The idea was to let any illness contracted at sea run its course before the slave, unseen in a crude brick building set near the marshes of Sullivan's Island, a despicable hospital forerunner, was allowed to set foot in America.

As American cities grew and prosperity increased, so did the wish for improved education. Young men were returning from abroad with degrees, and these practitioners began to insist on improved standards of care by the 1760s. From then onward in both British and American medical practice, serious attempts were being made to admit only those possessing an M.D. degree to the legitimate practice of medicine. It was at this time that the first true hospital appeared in America.

A succession of foreign-trained American doctors formed the spine of quality care in early American medicine. A sequence of distinguished American physicians included Drs. Benjamin Rush, John Morgan and Thomas Bond, who contributed to the parallel development of Pennsylvania Hospital in 1751. New York Hospital was erected later, in 1771. Modeled on the British voluntary hospitals, Pennsylvania Hospital was designed to care for the poor and indigent: Some private patients were admitted and charged fees, but most practitioners cared for their charges without compensation. Shryock states the mortality rate at Pennsylvania Hospital was a remarkable 10 percent, but the so-called "hospitals" sprinkled about the colonies at this time were anything but death-free.

These original "true" hospitals became engaged in medical education, and instruction in gross anatomy began for the first time in America in Philadelphia and New York. Midwives were encouraged to attend lectures along with medical students, and thus a sliver of science insinuated itself into early American medicine. Pushed by John Morgan, the College of Philadelphia established a medical faculty, and the tradition of fusing the university with the hospital began at that time and persists—with only a few exceptions along the historical way—today. Joining the two medical schools mentioned above, Harvard College moved its fledgling medical school to Massachusetts General Hospital in 1821, and thus established the third major teaching center in the colonies. Hospitals and medical schools were beginning to become juxtaposed, a relationship fought for and won in the 1890s as *the* paradigm of the future for medical education in America.

At the beginning of the nineteenth century, American almshouses cared for the destitute, the poor, the blind and the crippled, the alcoholics and prostitutes and anyone else suffering from venereal diseases. These impoverished houses also cared for the working class who suffered from pleurisy, pneumonia and arthritic illness. They existed in overcrowded conditions, in filth and with inadequate ventilation, food and plumbing. Often more than one patient shared a bed, and foraging for food was a constant activity. But America's first true hospitals admitted only those citizens of known respectable character and moral worth.

Charles E. Rosenberg states in his book, *The Care of Strangers: The Rise of America's Hospital System*, "The origins of the American hospital began as much with ideas of dependence and class as with the unavoidable incidence of sickness and accident." Physicians of that era believed that a direct connection existed between personal responsibility and disease: You became sick because of something you did or failed to avoid. Thus, as Rosenberg points out, great care was taken to discriminate between those who deserved hospital care and those who ought to be shipped off to an almshouse. He describes philantrophists as haunted by the prospect of too much medical care creating *the specter of pauperization*—the idea that medical aid might remove any will or moral capacity of those receiving help. This attitude appears to have emerged along with a conviction that suffering was somehow good.

Admission to a nineteenth-century American hospital was based on one's social standing, and often a recommendation from a prominent community member (including religious leaders and physicians themselves) was needed before admission was allowed. And, in contrast to our modern high-tech institutions, patients in the antebellum hospital were not terribly sick. Critically ill patients were not encouraged to enter the hospital, and most surgery was limited to setting broken bones or dressing wounds. Those suffering from the ravages of alcoholism or venereal disease were not permitted the luxuries offered to other hospitalized patients, as punishment was inexorably woven into the fabric of the medical care provided for these irresponsible victims.

In the almshouses, on the other hand, there seemed little concern for the "presumed blunted sensibilities of working-class life," according to Rosenberg.

Even having curtains between patient beds was deemed an unnecessary luxury, and dead bodies were often left on the wards until placed into coffins, while the family looked on in horror. Putrid smells permeated the almshouses, overcrowding was common, beds were shared and some patients slept on the floor. The medical staff visited the almshouses infrequently, and house physicians often viewed their patients with condescension. And when doctors attempted to charge their patients for some services, the trustees of the institution balked. At Pennsylvania Hospital the famous John Morgan resigned. This conflict between physicians and administrators gained momentum in subsequent decades—and is alive and well today.

This was the beginning of the medical care system of an emerging democratic country proud of its devotion to equality!

Nineteenth-Century American Hospitals

The practice of medicine in American in the nineteenth century did the profession little credit, characterized as it was by recrimination among its members, failure to accept growing scientific evidence as the basis for practice and the predominant role of money in physicians' education and professional activities. Between the end of the Revolutionary War and about 1820, the number of medical schools in America exploded. In the vacuum expanding from a rapidly growing population, the so-called *proprietary* medical schools emerged in large numbers, each school sponsored by a handful of enthusiastic young doctors, many of whom had little or no formal education. Although motivated to teach, these neophytes had served an apprenticeship for only two or three years themselves.

Laboratory investigation and the availability of a medical library were usually considered unimportant in the early medical schools, as only practical knowledge was considered useful to the early American doctor. Attempts to develop anatomy courses based on human dissection caused public resentment and resulted in the burning down of more than one medical school building. Grave robbing by the "resurrectionists," or "sack-em-up men" as they were called in newspaper reports of the time, further discredited early American medical education. In fact, in 1830 Massachusetts became the first state to legalize the granting of bodies to medical schools. Nonetheless, more and more proprietary schools appeared.

According to John Duffy, author of *From Humors to Medical Science: A History of American Medicine*, "While medical schools had been slow in appearing during the first thirty years of the new nation's history, their numbers increased rapidly after 1810. No less than twenty-six schools were founded between 1810 and 1840, and another forty-seven between 1840 and 1875."

The school year for these various medical schools—which consisted of little more than a practitioner base of six or fewer individuals and a lecture hall—lasted for two *4-month* terms, and when attempts were made by the more prestigious schools to lengthen each term to six months, enrollment dropped precipitously, forcing the schools to return to two 4-month programs. Little or no actual hospital teaching was involved in these early medical school curriculae, and few patients were actually examined. Patients, women in particular, did not as yet accept a physician's hands and fingers prodding what was otherwise personal—and concealed—body anatomy. Duffy states, "The ease with which medical colleges could be established and the fact that many professors were more concerned with collecting fees than with providing a medical education led to keen competition for students."

An exception was the New Orleans School of Medicine, which in 1856 emphasized clinical teaching, insisting students evaluate hospitalized patients and record their findings. This was, in fact, the very first *clerkship*. Clinical clerkships would only become established later in the century when Johns Hopkins School of Medicine became established, and William Osler would take credit for beginning this effective method of teaching medicine. Overall, the medical curriculum remained lean and unscientific for many more years. Duffy states, "Whether or not the level of medical education declined in the antebellum years, clearly the move to reform medical schools came to nought."

Another contentious matter embroiling the medical profession in the nineteenth century was the issue of licensure. Various states legislatures and medical societies attempted to establish themselves as the primary body involved in the examination of candidates for licensure. Conflict with medical schools and the lack of any real power to enforce penalties left the system impotent. By the end of the Civil War, notes Duffy, not a single state was making any serious attempts at regulating the practice of medicine. Little wonder Abraham Flexner's renown report of 1910 severely criticized proprietary medical schools and their lack of affiliation with universities.

In the late nineteenth century, three classes of physicians practiced in America: The top group held medical degrees from reputable American schools; the second group held degrees from second rate schools or were awarded them after apprenticing with a doctor; and the third group consisted of the virtually illiterate doctors with minimal training who practiced in rural areas and often supplemented their incomes with farming. Repeated blood-letting, the use of dangerous drugs and a paucity of medical knowledge—all overlaid by the constant bickering and in-fighting among the various doctors groups and often in print—left the populace skeptical of the medical profession and leery of entering a hospital.

Entering the Twentieth Century

Most medical care was administered in the private home in the late nineteenth century, and this trend of avoiding hospitals carried into the twentieth century. Hospitals served the poor and the destitute. American doctors paid little attention, for example, to developments in Europe in the field of bacteriology led by Louis Pasteur and Robert Koch. Frightening is the revelation that *twenty-five years after* Pasteur demonstrated conclusively that no bacteria ever arose spontaneously—a formerly cherished theory of ignorant practitioners—a medical graduate from Tulane Medical School based his thesis on a series of diphtheria and typhoid cases which were said to have developed in isolation! This "doctor," as well as those who entered proprietary medical schools with the sole requirement being the ability to read and write, continued to employ bleedings, severe emetics to induce vomiting, purges and a variety of formulations based on opium and alcohol.

According to Kenneth M. Ludmerer in *Learning to Heal: The Development of American Medical Education*: "When a brave Union surgeon general, William Alexander Hammond, banned the use of two toxic drugs, calomel and tartar emetic, because of their severe side effects (profuse salivation and putrid gangrene of the gums, mouth and face) he was court-martialed and condemned by the AMA."

But these pockets of ignorance were about to be dissipated. By the end of the nineteenth century, steam sterilization, bacteria as the cause of disease and anesthesia were about to be coupled with Wilhelm Konrad

Roentgen's discovery of X rays. These four helped form the basis of scientific care and led to the Americanization of hospital care.

We now come to the most significant change in American medicine.

In 1893, Johns Hopkins School of Medicine came into existence, and science and research became irrevocably enmeshed in the culture of American medicine. Johns Hopkins became the first medical school to require an undergraduate degree as a condition of admission. Laboratory studies in chemistry, physics and biology necessitated more than a passing knowledge of grammar. And by 1900, chemistry had been moved to the undergraduate curriculum for good, permitting more advanced courses to be added to the medical school program. Inexorably, an elitist flavor entered medical education and left a bad taste in the mouths of many practitioners.

Johns Hopkins Medical School required two rigorous years of basic sciences followed, as every medical school does today, by two clinical years spent in the hospital. Bedside teaching and hands-on learning from real patients became of paramount importance. The physical plant consisted of a new hospital as well as buildings for research and for teaching the bulk of the medical school curriculum. The new school combined the best traditions from Europe with the finest American medical educators.

During the first half of the nineteenth century France was the medical Mecca for the world, advancing physical diagnosis and the field of pathology as well as employing statistics in the assessment of clinical problems. Clinical observation at the bedside in the hospital dominated the French approach to patient care and influenced the many Americans who studied in Paris in the first half of the century. But French doctors distrusted laboratory investigations and did little to study disease. They were primarily observers, and as such lost their international edge to the Germans, who moved into laboratory research, making it an essential part of medical education in Germany.

The list of German investigators who gave the world a sound grasp of cell biology, bacteriology and a host of experimental approaches to physiology, biochemistry, etc., runs long and deep. Americans flooded German medical schools after the Civil War, bringing to America a new appreciation for the role of laboratory investigation in diagnosis and treatment. The names of these American medical giants subsequently populated Johns Hopkins, Harvard, Cornell, Michigan and other rising American medical schools.

Yet, all was not well. The majority of practitioners remained troubled by the aristocratic posturing of these new medical schools. These schools were accused of becoming unegalitarian, restricting opportunities for young men who were seen as likely to succeed by sheer willpower if given a chance, a chance now taken away by the severe premedical requirements of a broad education.

The new curriculum, elitism aside for the moment, demanded more topics and thus a much more demanding academic load. Also, medical students were required to spend more time at the bedside in the hospital. Rounds with students and residents became common, and the flavor of the hospital now was clearly educational.

The Twentieth-Century Teaching Hospital

As we progress through the history of medicine in the twentieth century, we will note that hospitals became more numerous, growing in size and complexity. In academic circles an unresolved argument centered on whether or not the modern hospital followed an industrial model of organization as it emerged in the twentieth century. The end-product nevertheless was inexorable medical specialization with a horizontal division of clinical areas by organ system diseases and populations, as well as by vertical division of labor by procedures that, according to Barbara Bridgman Perkins, are " . . . assigned to a hierarchy of institutional-based personnel." Perkins goes on to note the medical profession's leadership in recognizing this horizontal organization as representing a monopoly in the same sense as trademarks and name brands. This fragmentation was the beginning of competition of specialties for recognition as full departments.

Before specialty departments became well established, patient care areas were shifting in size and configuration. The concept of open wards with multiple beds in rows slowly gave way to the concept of hospital floors with semiprivate and private rooms. Medical and surgical floors with nurses trained in the nuances of specialty care became commonplace, as did a shift toward more private care. Reimbursement squabbles and an explosion of new knowledge existed together in a much more complex medical environment. Small hospital laboratories eventually gave way to huge collections of chemistry, bacteriology and pathology labs as well as burgeoning blood banks. Novel surgical procedures necessitated more operating rooms at the same time medical care became increasingly complicated and invasive.

Hospital space proved to be a growing priority.

New hospitals were built. More interesting was the expansion of existing facilities. The space problem was often solved by adding wings. A cursory examination of most modern hospitals reveals a succession of old, new and yet newer wings jutting out in all directions. It becomes clear with inspection of many hospital floor plans that strategic planning for the most recent additions amounted to aligning new additions with old buildings, or building completely new hospitals next to the old (which often became the site of administrative offices or a rehabilitation facility).

Not all hospitals grew at the same rate. Not all hospitals served the same mission. And not all hospitals survived the reforms dictated by the Flexner Report in the early part of the century. Hospital closures have punctuated modern medicine's march toward technological complexity and economic streamlining. In many hospitals in the late 1990s, emergency departments have closed because of inadequate reimbursement, and hospitals have merged with other larger institutions in order to remain solvent. One neglected aspect of modern hospital care was the attention paid to intimate patient concerns.

In the 1980s several studies were done to assess how patients felt about being *inside* a modern hospital. One such report demonstrated a significant preference by many patients for rooms with windows where contact with nature—visual contact with trees, flowers, etc.—was possible. In an article in *Literature and Medicine* (Spring 1996), David B. Morris reviews many of these reports and quotes one, " . . . patients whose windows faced a natural setting fared much better than patients whose windows faced a brick wall: They had shorter postoperative hospital stays, received fewer negative evaluations from nurses and took fewer potent analgesics." Morris refers to the great biologist Edward O. Wilson's hypothesis of *biophilia*, or the intense connection humankind makes with nature, presumably due to our genetic and cultural co-evolution.

There may be a built-in genetic preference for certain settings, and particularly those associated with what we affectionately call "the great outdoors," the component missing from early hospitals as well as from our modern specialized care units. Morris quotes writer-surgeon Richard Selzer, who stated that if he were to build a hospital, he would include a large fountain. Selzer writes in his autobiography, *Down From Troy: A Doctor Comes of Age*, "There can be nothing so consolatory to the sick as a fountain."

Florence Nightingale

Perhaps no one knew as much about the ideal hospital environment as Florence Nightingale. Her experiences in the Crimea and elsewhere helped to convince Nightingale that the hospital environment might well contribute to disease as much as assist in regaining health. These notions are elucidated in her *Notes on Hospitals*, presented to the National Association for the Promotion of Social Science at Liverpool, England, in 1858, regarding sanitary conditions of hospitals and defects in hospital construction. In the same publication she addresses the Royal Commissioners on the state of the army in 1857; her remarks to both groups were published in 1859.

Florence Nightingale was perhaps the first person to make a distinction among different hospitals' mortality rates, addressing the issue of different disease mixes and thus the misleading nature of these statistics. In her case, Nightingale was looking at the effect of sanitary conditions; today, mortality rates for various surgical procedures have replaced grime as the statistician's grist. Of paramount importance to creating a healthy hospital environment as outlined in 1857 by Nightingale were:

- an appropriate number of sick patients within a given hospital
- adequate space for each patient—e.g., avoid overcrowding
- adequate ventilation with fresh air
- adequate light

Nightingale was convinced the absence of any of these factors represented a major deficiency in hospital construction. But she went on to deny the existence of a "contagion," a possible organism that would cause an illness. Nightingale opines, "There is no end to the absurdities connected with this doctrine. Suffice it to say that, in the ordinary sense of the word, there is no proof, such as would be admitted in any scientific inquiry, that there is any such thing as 'contagion'." And yet she agreed that infections occurred, particularly in crowded conditions, and that large groups of patients could "infect" each other. By what mechanism? By fouling the air.

Nightingale continues, " . . . if they be shut up without sufficient space and sufficient fresh air, there will be produced not only fever, but erysipelas, paemia, and the usual tribe of hospital-generated epidemic diseases." Indeed, in the next decade such organisms would be proven to exist. Nightingale did predict and identify what we now call *nosocomial infections*—infections occurring in the hospital from hospital sources. What she attributed to purely sanitary conditions—the spread of disease within the hospital from one patient or attendant to another—was correct, but the agents were bacteria and viruses, a concept she rejected.

Nightingale nonetheless made many other recommendations for hospital construction, including references to patient location and windows, anticipating the twentieth-century studies previously quoted. Modern hospitals have addressed a majority of Nightingale's concerns, but there was a time at the turn of the century when conditions remained marginal in many facilities. Education again led to reform.

Developing the Modern Hospital

The reorganization of American hospitals during the first two decades of the twentieth century wasn't new, but rather a return to the principles of sanitation learned and relearned over the centuries. Still, the scramble to survive in a chaotic environment of cost containment today seems tame compared to the revolution in hospital management experienced immediately after Abraham Flexner dropped his critical "bomb" in 1910 regarding the inadequacy of many existing medical schools and their associated hospitals. No doubt a significant deficiency existed in basic patient care as well as in the educational inadequacies Flexner documented.

Kenneth Ludmerer describes the seminal fusion of three medical schools with nearby hospitals in or just after 1910 as a reflection of the national trend toward a tighter affiliation between hospitals and medical schools. Today, we assume they are one. It wasn't always that way. Leading the movement were Harvard Medical School bonding with the new Peter Bent Brigham Hospital, the College of Physicians and Surgeons (Columbia) with Presbyterian Hospital, and Washington University Medical School with Barnes Hospital. The three unions were modeled after the Johns Hopkins program, which had redefined academic medicine in America. The boards of trustees for each of these institutions (medical school and hospital) overlapped to a considerable extent, permitting a relatively smooth merger. As momentum grew and more medical schools joined the movement toward steadfast hospital associations, conflict expanded exponentially between the schools and the hospital staffs.

Three duties eventually became recognized as the reason for these mergers: improved patient care, improved medical student and resident teaching, and expanding research. To accomplish these goals specialized faculty were needed. Scientifically trained clinicians were hired, and a new paradigm for the modern teaching hospital fell into place. Replacing the era of solitary private practitioners examining their patients in the company of respectful nurses who dutifully carried charts and promptly answered the physician's queries, walking respectfully behind the doctor as he made rounds, was a new breed. Boisterous and energetic, the young doctors and students visited their patients in clusters.

Thus, the teaching hospital began to develop all of the characteristics to which the private doctors had originally objected. Noise and inconvenience from successive waves of students examining patients at mealtime and at night annoyed patients and the hospital staff alike. Rounds became an endless procession of white coats accompanied by noisy bursts of questions and answers. And through it all the assumption, never proven or discarded, was that patient care had improved in the intense learning environment of the teaching hospital.

On the heels of improved patient care in the United States there arrived the issue of creating great teaching centers. Board of trustee members, medical school deans and clinicians all agreed that carefully selected faculty members, doctors known for their expertise in a specific field, all drawn together under one roof with common goals, would redefine excellence in American medical schools. Indeed, this has occurred. But the third piece of the equation threw a perfectly good educational system into disarray, a condition that persists today.

New medical knowledge required research.

Thus, another reason for medical schools to affiliate with specific hospitals was to encourage basic research that could be translated into clinical problem-solving—the creation of immediate, dramatic cures. The trustees saw international fame as another by-product of medical school association: Reputations were built in laboratories in close proximity to the clinical facility on the medical school campus. Complex patients would be referred to predominantly urban medical centers where expertise with specific diseases was entrenched and where an awesome array of basic scientists and clinicians focused on the identification and treatment of one or more illnesses was assembled.

Finally, the merger of hospitals and medical schools made economic sense. The elimination of duplication permitted more funds to be poured into specific programs focused on solving a particularly mysterious clinical conundrum. Ludmerer adds, "In each case, hospitals made available to the universities superb teaching facilities that the university could not have afforded on their own. In return, the universities equipped and maintained the hospitals' laboratories and provided the hospitals with scientifically distinguished staffs." These initial mergers were driven by the fact that they were well financed and the hospitals possessed sizable patient populations.

Eventually other medical schools joined with local hospitals. The public seemed to like the idea of medical specialization as science infused more and more aspects of American life. Voters and local legislative bodies followed suit and approved similar public institutions, and so around the country funds were appropriated for the joining of medical schools with new hospital teaching facilities. But not all cities went along with the modern order. Some forced the universities to build their own hospitals. And the schools that were marginal to begin with often closed—this the final stake in their agonized hearts. Scientific teaching had arrived for good, and those schools unable to provide the "new" curriculum, which included high-quality, hospital-based clerkships, went out of business. Because most of the larger medical schools were to be found in the city, medical education as a consequence became more and more urban.

The Modern Hospital

Within a test tube throw away—or at least within the city limits—the mother institution is most often found. Behind the historical trail of white coats exists a story of discovery, medical evangelism and no small degree of strife. The evolution of the American medical school still isn't over. We are stuck in a thick educational batter consisting of an unequal measure of teaching, patient care and research. And as it is stirred and nurtured, we discover the overpowering odor of research.

Foremost in the minds of today's medical educators is the crusade for ever more funding. Expertise in writing grants for pet research projects far outweighs the energy spent on teaching tomorrow's doctors. No one would argue with the contributions made by twentieth-century research: Only a foolish person would suggest we rediscover the nineteenth-century French penchant for clinical medicine to the exclusion of new science. No one would venture to suggest the complete unveiling of the human genome is worthless, not even to suggest it's only tangentially valuable to clinical medicine. Apple pie and all of that.

But as you view the ramparts of the modern hospital and enter into its sacred halls, brushing past hurried young men and women in white, you must realize the extent of the system's deficiencies. Just as apprenticeship-trained practitioners in the late nineteenth century gave way to more scientifically oriented physicians trained in academically sophisticated medical schools, now those very clinicians are stepping back from the teaching podium, replaced by Ph.D.s, laboratory-trained specialists in any science with a remote bearing on medical practice. Now teaching the first two years of medical schools are these research-obsessed professors who view teaching as an annoyance and who, anyway, do not understand what a clinician needs to know in order to care for patients. To a large degree we have lost our way in the maze of evolving scientific data. The task of selecting what is clinically relevant has fallen on the medical school deans, who have manipulated the curriculum with varying amounts of self-interest and reason.

From a century of medical practice characterized by virtually no science, where ancient treatments carried forth from previous centuries and myth and astrology served as the profession's high watermark, we arrive today at a teaching menu stuffed with bits and pieces of high-tech research. Succulent morsels by themselves, curious if not intriguing, these hors d'oeuvres have little to do with curing patients and nothing at all to do with caring. The medical school curriculum is in danger of becoming modeled after an adver-tisement, with out-of-context sound bites flashing forth as real information. Curriculum committees struggle like intellectual chefs, constantly rearrang-ing their plateful of goodies, unsure which to feed to the dog and which to save for their "culinary" curricular presentation.

And while the academic deans create ever new menus for tomorrow's doctors to master, still more novel interventions and procedures arrive on the scene, created and refined by hospital specialists who are not permitted to set the agenda for the curricular table. Everyone has something they want in the program. "Leave this stuff out and our students will suffer grievously" is the implication.

At one time medical professors fought with surgeons to get more of their own material in the curriculum. Among the medical experts a new divisiveness arose: Pulmonary medicine was slighted in the third year by too much endocrine material. Now the dean must listen to the endocrinologists argue among themselves. Why so much on diabetes? Why not more on thyroid disease? We are no longer cutting up the pie; we've begun picking out apple slices.

How much of this is actually learned by the modern medical student? What is truly important? Consider that the primary care physician who is now the gatekeeper—the doctor who assesses each and every disease to determine if referral to a specialist is necessary—never sets foot on a surgical service after ten or twelve *weeks'* exposure to surgery as a third-year medical student. How can a doctor evaluate a disease he's never seen?

Of course, with fiscal restraints on hospitals and individual doctors these decisions have become even more critical. It is curious that the snowballing scientific revolution that began at the turn of the century, the impetus for improved patient care, now seems to be melting. The very specialization which draws patients to America from all over the world is being subjugated by limited resources and an army of primary care doctors who cannot possibly know enough to direct patients to all of the proper experts. Americans seem to have lost sight of an overarching query: If it takes a doctor four or five years to become expert in a specific area of medical care, how can the primary care physician judge the need for that care if she has little comprehension of the complex clinical issues involved?

Categories of Hospitals
Rural Clinics
Rural clinics are little more than first-aid stations with basic equipment such as bandages, antiseptics, basic instruments for diagnosis and treatment, including a minimum of surgical instruments for suturing, cast materials for fracture treatments and basic drugs for the treatment of

insect-sting reactions (anaphylactic shock), antibiotics, cardiac drugs, drugs for the treatment of acute asthmatic attacks and so forth. An examination table, instrument cabinets and a small sterilizer in a single examination/treatment room constitute the majority of rural clinic setups, and may be expanded to two or more exam rooms with a small office for a traveling physician.

Free-Standing Daystay Surgical Units
These are small or large specialized clinics that provide same-day surgical service to a variety of specialties including general surgery (hernia repair, lumpectomy, proctologic procedures), gynecology (D&C, laparoscopic procedures, exams under anesthesia), plastic surgery (various tissue transfers, cosmetic surgery, uncomplicated grafts), pediatric surgery (hernias, lumps and bumps), ENT surgery and urological surgery (cystostomy, bladder fulguration, hydrocoele excision, minor excisions) to mention common procedures.

Small Community Hospital
The community hospital serves a defined local population and offers many of the services and procedures mentioned under the daystay heading above, as well as uncomplicated but major surgery such as colon removal, hysterectomy, thyroid operations and other head and neck operations. Also, some basic radiological interventions and tests such as CT scans may be offered, as well as uncomplicated medical treatments for acute cardiac, pulmonary and kidney disorders. Complex care is referred to larger institutions. These hospitals offer Level III trauma care, which is limited to the treatment of simple injuries and the referral of all other multiple-trauma victims to a larger institution.

Community Medical Centers
These medical centers vary in sophistication, from extended community hospitals, with more staff and services with small residency training programs, to complex medical centers. The latter offer open-heart surgery, transplant surgery, complex radiological interventions including biopsy of internal organs, interventional cardiology such as coronary angioplasty, specialized pediatric and adult intensive care services, Level I trauma care, large multiple-specialty residency training programs and clinical research.

University Medical Centers

These larger hospitals include all of the services offered by the large community medical center plus specialty care in specific diseases (the best-of-the-best clinicians and basic researchers in one building or unit) and specialty surgical services for the treatment of common illnesses such as breast cancer, where the doctors only treat a single disease and are recognized as world experts. An example is Duke University Medical Center, which is a two hundred-acre complex with eighty-six buildings, which include hospitals, specialty clinics, research labs, a nursing school, a cancer center and a children's health center.

Money and Mergers

As we reach the end of the twentieth century, a new phenomenon has once again threatened to change the hospital landscape: *merger mania*. The once-mighty medical centers affiliated with prestigious medical schools now find themselves in need of fusing their names and identity in order to survive in the heated battle for shrinking health care dollars. It's all bottom line. Yet one hears the incessant echo of meek voices in the background, emanating from the leadership of managed care, insisting they are still offering quality care. Perhaps they are; let's hope so.

In the foreground the battle bloodies and washes over the landscape to the bugle blasts of *vanishing medical resources, rationing* and *clout*. The reality is that Americans are having their health care traded on Wall Street by insensitive capitalists whose sole interest is profit. Referring to a recent splash of community hospital acquisitions by large corporate entities, Robert Kuttner in an article in *The New England Journal of Medicine* (August 8, 1996) stated, referring to these deals, " . . . are notable for the speed, secrecy and legal ingenuity with which they are accomplished. The company has flying squads of acquisition specialists backed by financial analysts, accountants, lawyers and consultants, and can negotiate a binding letter of intent with a hospital's board of trustees in a matter of weeks."

Are we back to the motivating medical bugle blast of the unscientific nineteenth century, the allure of filthy lucre in the care of the sick? Is there a shred of difference between the preoccupied, marginally trained post-Civil War doctors intent on upping their fees and the granite-hearted capitalists squeezing HMOs for one more drop of profit today?

It seems the start of the new century is bringing with it unhappiness for hospitals, patients and doctors alike. Health insurance premiums remain high as services shrink. Access to physicians and other health care providers is blocked by a system where those with little training in the nuances of specific illnesses are positioned to permit or deny consultation with specialists. And whether the managers of care like it or not, rationing *is* occurring. Fortunately, the U.S. Congress is stepping up its consideration of bills to protect consumers of health care. A patient "bill of rights" will provide patients with recourse to restrictive managed-care policies.

In the end, two chores seem to remain for medical educators who ultimately determine what will occur in the modern hospital, where so much of the learning and practice of medicine takes place. The first task is clearly to define the medical school's role: Is it primarily for research or teaching? If the education of doctors is the singular goal of medical schools, then teachers must be sought and rewarded as teachers, with no hidden agenda regarding research output.

Most medical students today are taught in the first two scientifically oriented years by postdoctoral candidates focused on their own research, Ph.D.s who have little or no teaching experience—or interest. In the clinical years a major portion of the students' instruction comes from residents who are students themselves. This begs the question: What are all of the highly esteemed, highly paid professors doing?

Research?

One need only query a few disgruntled patients to discover the loopholes in the knowledge of some of today's physicians. How many diagnoses are missed? How many antibiotic and other prescriptions are scribbled with no apparent connection to the patient's chief complaint? Why are these fundamental clinical problems insoluble by our medical graduates?

Could it be the great ideals of Johns Hopkins University and the goals set for undergraduate and graduate medical education, lofty ideals that are as valid today as they were in 1893, are simply being ignored?

In the hospital-based practice of medicine, as well as in the clinics where educational efforts are being shifted, teachers are attempting to meet the needs of students as well as to cure the illnesses of the sick. Technology permitted the bar to be raised to a higher level. There can be no question patient care has reached a new level of expertise overall. Still, there seems to be a dissonance between the character of high-tech specialty practice and primary care medicine. This is seen in such crucibles as the Emergency Department, where treatment and teaching often reach extremes in disharmony and disrespect, reflected, for example, in the instance of a physician assistant student glibly disagreeing with the opinion of a board-certified surgeon.

Yet in the end, the modern hospital serves the sick in ways never anticipated, even as late as the mid-twentieth century. Kidney dialysis and transplantation of vital as well as supportive organs and tissues have become commonplace. Organs failing in the face of overwhelming disease are supported in the intensive care setting with steely certainty by knowledgeable doctors dedicated to curing—and often untrained in the art of letting go. Hearts regularly receive new plumbing and sagging skin is removed, repaired in the name of beauty and the American denial of aging. Cancers are cured and infectious diseases wiped out—with the spectacular exception of AIDS. Arthritis has been tamed, along with asthma, diabetes and a host of childhood illnesses.

Money is thrown at these illnesses until there seems to be little left. A significant number of people admitted to the hospital have no insurance; many children cannot receive appropriate medical care. Personal responsibility lags as an issue in medical economics, and automobile trauma, cigarette, drug and alcohol abuse and domestic violence continue to thrive in a culture distracted by an all-devouring media.

And through it all our hospitals persist, a testimony to man's creativity, his industriousness and triumph over disease. Left to solve are the multitude of social and ethical dilemmas spreading across the hospital's floor, painting us into a corner. In the final—and as yet unwritten—chapter of the hospital we will undoubtedly discover the fallout of our reluctance to face our human natures. We must resolve to allow a measure of true freedom in choosing how we will die and how much care we will give and receive.

We must face our religions, our politics and our conflicted souls.

In the following chapters you will learn more about the modern hospital and why this intense healing environment deserves your creative attention. The medical staff, nursing personnel, students and ancillary workers all contribute to the functioning of the hospital.

CHAPTER TWO

The Emergency Center

S udden illness or unexpected body trauma propels patients to the modern hospital's emergency room. Life-threatening catastrophes bring patients to the ER via ambulance, with red lights ricocheting off of the hospital's ER double doors, or by helicopter, with prop wash distorting crouching figures in white coats and blue scrubs.

From gang warriors with chest wounds to gasping grandmothers choking with phlegm-riddled lungs, from adrift and depressed midlifers to croupy kids, the emergency room rings with the sounds of anguish and the odor of incontinence and damage. In ones, twos and threes, victims limp or drag themselves through the admitting doors, some wheeled into treatment stalls and rooms on stretchers or in wheelchairs. All bleat for attention.

The Emergency Room

Before the 1960s, most community and midsized hospitals had emergency rooms that were in fact basically made up of rooms for advanced first-aid treatment. Suturing lacerations, X-raying injured limbs, dispersing medications and casting broken bones constituted most of the care given in the ER. Anything more serious was admitted. Staffing was provided by the entire medical staff, usually without special training in emergency medicine, on a rotational basis. A pediatrician would do a great job with the babies he saw during his rotation in the ER, but would be very limited in dealing with trauma, adult myocardial infarctions or stroke patients.

During the 1960s, new ways were developed to help people survive their first heart attack with CPR, cardiac defibrillators, pacemakers and new medications. At the same time, MAST trauma suits, rapid-response surgical teams and medical-evac helicopters also began to save lives. All of this medical advancement and technological development gave rise to the modern large, sophisticated Emergency Centers, complete with their own trauma rooms and physicians trained and skilled in emergency medicine.

These large, complex areas are far advanced from the early "emergency rooms." In larger hospitals, they are now called either the *Emergency Department* or the *Emergency Center*, which reflects the sophistication and complexity of the modern emergency care centers. However, the modern Emergency Department or Emergency Center is still referred to simply as the *ER* by doctors and nurses alike.

For the rest of this book, we will use either the term *Emergency Center* or the abbreviated *ER* to mean the same thing.

The Emergency Center

Just as the operating room changes in character between elective and emergency surgery, the ER is a chameleon, shifting its colors between the blood reds of Saturday night and the subdued pastels of early light on Sunday morning.

On a busy Saturday night, EMS personnel, sirens and lights, police, sick or injured patients in wheelchairs and gurneys, nurses, doctors and concerned family members demanding immediate attention create a war-zone-like atmosphere of chaos. Mixed with the sounds of overhead pages, pagers and monitors are the sounds of coughing, screaming, moaning and often yelling.

ER Sights on a Busy Saturday Night

- **AT THE ER UNLOADING DOCK (AMBULANCE ENTRANCE)** a row of parked ambulances, others leaving and more arriving with their crimson lights bouncing off ER doors as they back in; people straggling about outside waiting for their significant others who are being treated; ambulance stretchers enter through a sliding double door directly into the ER; others walking into a reception area
- **AT THE RECEPTION AREA** secretaries behind (bulletproof) glass

Admitting can seem interminably long and painful as patients wait their turn. Once their name has been called, an admitting clerk will get all the necessary information, fill out an admitting sheet to begin a new chart, and have the patient sent by wheelchair or cart to the floor.

windows take information . . . name, problem, urgency, insurance, etc.

- **THE WAITING ROOM** is growling with injured, sick and unhappy folks in varying degrees of discomfort: blood-soaked bandages on arms and legs; people bent over in pain; folks walking and muttering, with many languages used to express fear, annoyance and anger at the patients and the hospital; kids screaming in real or imagined pain

- **THE MAIN EMERGENCY CENTER** represented by a large central room and smaller rooms off of the main room, as well as cubicles formed by *U*-shaped tracks on the ceiling and hanging curtains, as in other hospital areas; the size of the hospital determines the size of the ER; the components of the main ER that are *seen* include:

1. a huge central desk with multiple stations with computers, phones, chart racks, shelves, etc., where doctors and nurses review labs, write in charts, call other consultants, call hospital floors about new admissions, call the admitting office, etc.

A ward clerk answers the phone, does important paperwork and keeps charts in their proper filing area in the nursing station. A physician at the desk is writing orders on the chart of one of his patients, while a nurse adds information to the nurses' daily sheet. Charts are located on the desk for easy access.

2. equipment ready for use, such as IV poles loaded with bags of fluid, blood pressure cuffs on wheels, stretchers, open cubicles ready for use with monitors on back shelves, oxygen source, suction, etc.

3. big erasure board with patient's name, room or cubicle location, diagnosis, time of arrival, nurse's name

4. ER charts on desks, on stretchers and within doctors' grasp in varying stages of being assembled and being read by consultants

5. crash carts for sudden Code Blue calls in the ER

6. equipment bins on wheels much like the OR, with instruments, tubes, laundry hampers, hazardous wastes hampers, etc.

7. special rooms—*trauma room* with central operating room table and other surgical equipment and resuscitation equipment, making it a true OR for procedures that cannot wait for the patient to be taken to the OR because of a life-threatening event such as bleeding or a bullet hole in the heart; *endoscopy* performed as an emergency for patients with massive upper or lower intestine

hemorrhage, using endoscopy cart with scopes, light source, suction, etc.

8. the elements of an examining room include combinations of the following equipment, some permanently in the room, some brought in from other departments: sutures, gauze, basic surgical instruments, various tubes, drains, IVs, cast material, oxygen source and masks, plastic airway; physical exam equipment including ophthalmoscope, otoscope, tongue depressors, Q-tips, GYN vaginal speculum, reflex hammer, flashlight, anoscope, sigmoidoscope, stethoscope

9. personnel include ER physicians, ER residents, PA students, nurses, nursing students, medical students, technical assistants, orderlies, clergy, police, firemen, paramedics, housekeeping staff and patients' relatives

ER Sounds

- an ambulance's siren in the distance, closing on the hospital
- excited voices in the waiting room, angry voices, weeping or screams of anguish
- different languages used in the waiting room and attempts by others at interpretation
- in the treatment area the sounds of sickness prevail, with moans and groans and pleas for medication or attention; also the verbiage of anger, rage, irritation, fear and outrage ring out at unpredictable intervals from behind drawn curtains
- machines add to the background sound procession, including ventilators, suction machines, EKG monitors with beeps and alarms, computers "clacking" as information is entered, X-ray machine in use, intercom squawking, a paging operator's omniscient voice pleading for "Respiratory therapy, ER stat!" or "Doctor Grim, East five . . ."

ER Smells

- "unwashed" body odor is more common among homeless and other disadvantaged people
- uncontrolled bowels as related to diarrheal disease rather than (as in the OR) gangrenous tissue

- gangrenous extremities (usually legs) from ischemic or diabetic vascular disease
- the smell of "rot" from nursing home patients with large decubitus (*sacral* or "fanny") ulcers; may be several inches wide and two or three inches deep . . . literally to the bone
- the stench of fresh vomitus, including a mixture of booze and food; in patients with bowel obstruction, feculent ("bowel movement") vomiting is seen
- the stench of cigarette smoke on clothing
- foul-smelling sputum in patients with bronchitis or pneumonia, including uncouth folks who spit on the floor
- the "meat-locker" smell of a massive upper or lower gastrointestinal bleeder; the combination of feces and blood creates an objectionable odor that cannot easily be described
- the "good scents" of perfume and deodorant

The ER Scene

But you would not see the separate components mentioned above. What you would see is the combined effect of everything mentioned, mixed together into sickening smells, loud noises and a sea of people.

A ruptured abdominal aortic aneurysm is rushed to the OR with no blood pressure and no pulse, the wailing family trailing the flying stretcher as it leaves the ER. Two kids scream with infected ears; their mothers demand care for their charges—now! Five hunched-over people, three with arm slings, sit outside X ray which is backed up with an obstructed bowel case who just vomited on the X-ray table.

In Cubicle Seven a seventeen-year-old is having a spontaneous abortion, and the paging operator screams overhead for the OB resident for the umpteenth time. The mother of the kid with a facial dog bite refuses to let the ER doctor sew up her child, demanding a plastic surgeon. A surgical resident threatens to chew the phone and screams at someone in the lab. Paramedics called in with a four-car accident on Route 91, the triage nurse just went home with the flu and no one's shown up to remove the DOA from the trauma room. . . .

Sunday morning.

An ambivalent sun peeks out from behind a row of maples behind the Emergency Center, uncertain if it's time to start all over again. The

33

waiting room is empty, except for Mrs. Finn, whose cab hasn't arrived yet. The shifts change; new faces grin at the warriors leaving the battle zone, knowing they'll be back on the night shift next month. Only two patients to sign out to the fresh team. The aroma of coffee drifts like incense through the big room, where hushed conversations are punctuated with occasional cackles of hilarity. It's all so absurd.

IV poles with new bags of fluid and tubing hang in expectation, monitors are ready and floors are clean and mopped, with no sign of last night's ambush. Soft music fills the cubicles and rooms and slides out to the waiting room. The guarded double doors of the ER are uncharacteristically open this Sunday morning. Mrs. Finn's taxi races from the ambulance zone and disappears into the city.

The Emergency Center sits in stillness: A deception, a sense of order, prevails, suggesting something is done and recovery is complete. In reality, the interlude is savored by the staff this beautiful Sunday morning because they understand the cyclic nature of chaos and the dark side of human behavior.

The ER and the Hospital

The Emergency Center is described in detail in both Doctor Wilson's book, *Cause of Death*, and Doctor Page's *Body Trauma* in the Writer's Digest Books Howdunit Series. We will present only the essentials here, and instead expand the discussion of emergency care to the hospital's overall role. The broader concerns regarding security, disaster management and caring and protecting celebrities such as the President will be covered in some detail.

The essential difference between patients admitted to the hospital electively and those evaluated in the Emergency Center is that the latter have potentially unknown and life-threatening illness. Acute asthma attacks, internal or external bleeding, heart attacks, coma, convulsions and uncontrolled infections are reasons why the ER bustles with an electric atmosphere of uncertainty and despair. Most will survive. But a definite number will die.

ER doctors and nurses are trained to triage patients, sorting them into those in dire need of care (in the act of dying), those who need treatment quickly (will die within thirty to sixty minutes) and those who may wait until the smoke clears from the first two groups. Hospital size determines who treats what diseases. In a large urban medical center ER, doctors, Physician Assistants (PAs) and residents of various specialties all interact, sorting out "big crunches" from those who can wait: Surgical residents care for trauma victims; pediatric residents and Attendings treat severe infections, asthmatics, etc. Medical teams swarm in and begin sorting out massive myocardial infarctions and congestive heart failure patients. Everyone determines who must be admitted and to what specialty unit. And of course this includes patients transferred by ambulance or helicopter from smaller outlying hospitals.

Smaller hospitals must have emergency room coverage, but the level of expertise varies tremendously. One doctor and a team of nurses may see all of the above, triage the worst cases and decide who they can safely treat and who must be transferred to "St. Elsewhere." As mentioned earlier, the really small rural clinics are little more than first-aid stations, offering splints, bandages, IV fluid and a trip to a larger town for major trauma or illness. Somewhere in between are community hospitals, which provide a considerable amount of quality care in all areas.

Shock can't wait. Hemorrhage must be halted. Babies insist on being born at weird times. Kids need patent airways, STAT.

Writers often want to set up an Emergency Center scene in which chaos rules, not unlike many of the episodes in the successful TV show *ER*. To craft such a scene, one must understand the elements that underlie the surface disorder so that *order* (the basic elements of dramatic structure) nonetheless form the spine of the scene. Thus, when writing a scene in which someone is dying, severely traumatized or experiencing an exacerbation of an existing illness (e.g., an acute asthma attack), keep in mind the following *life-threatening body function disruptions*:

- **CARDIAC (HEART) FAILURE** from damage to the heart muscle from a blocked coronary, direct trauma to the heart muscle (blunt chest trauma), laceration of the heart muscle or coronary from penetrating trauma (chest stab wound), failure of the heart muscle from diffuse coronary disease or damage to the heart muscle from specific causes (cardiomyopathy)
- **PULMONARY (LUNG) FAILURE** lungs fill with fluid from pneumonia (infected fluid), congestive heart failure (uninfected fluid), secondary to nonlung causes such as overwhelming infection anywhere in the body (called *Adult Respiratory Distress Syndrome*) or from

Triage Challenges in the Emergency Center

- *How many victims are there?* Answer: Includes what the issue is; e.g., a disaster with multiple victims, a gang fight, murder-suicide or food poisoning at a wedding.
- *How sick is each individual patient?* Answer: This varies from in the act of dying, in shock and in danger of dying soon, or relatively stable.
- *What is the medical problem?* Answer: Direct patient to proper specialist; e.g., pediatrics, surgery, obstetrics, cardiology or neurosurgery
- *What immediate life-saving maneuvers must be employed?* Answer: Start evaluation of airway, breathing and circulation while the first three questions are being addressed

direct blunt trauma; or from airway disease such as asthma, allergic bronchitis or smoking, causing spasm and blockage of small airways, which results in wheezing and difficult breathing

- **MASSIVE BLEEDING** from any major blood vessel or from the heart itself from penetrating trauma or a "blowout" after a massive heart attack (myocardial infarction)
- **SHOCK** from heart failure or bleeding or from diffuse loss of tone in the vascular system resulting in too little blood for the volume; this results from anaphylactic reactions to insect stings, allergic reactions to drugs or high spinal cord injuries
- **"BRAIN FAILURE"** various states of unconsciousness, lethargy, coma or behavior disruption from true organic brain disorders or psychiatric causes; these threaten the patient in many ways, including dangerous behavior, the risk of stopping breathing or choking
- **TRAUMATIC INJURIES** may produce any of the above catastrophes but usually involve a severe head injury, major chest trauma, massive abdominal injury with hemorrhage or a complex pelvic fracture with massive bleeding and disruption of major organs

The location in the ER or in the hospital in general where acute care is provided doesn't shift the awesome responsibility burdening each medical professional who becomes involved.

Let's see how the system works by examining what might go *wrong*. For the most part this discussion assumes we're working in a large hospital with significant resources. However, with the increasing mobility of the American public, *anything* can happen *anywhere*.

Patient Identification and In-Hospital Tracking

Patients who are admitted to the hospital through the ER are provided with a specific identification number. Of course, this system is used for elective admissions as well (see chapter two). In the latter instance the patient registers at the admitting office, where information is gathered and entered into the new hospital record via a computer. Because the setting is unrushed, the secretary in the admitting office is usually able to receive and record all pertinent information simply by asking the patient appropriate questions. Family members or significant others are permitted to be present during the registering (admissions) process and may assist in providing information. In chapter three more information on the admitting process will be covered.

Often no one knows the victim's name when he arrives *in extremis* in the hospital's ER. Family, friends and significant others are not permitted through the double doors that swallow the patient on arrival. For those in shock, or those whose lives are similarly threatened and in need of swift treatment, there is no time to ask questions. The traditional order of evaluating an elective patient by first taking a medical history and then performing a complete physical examination is reversed in the acute evaluation process.

Treat now, ask questions later!

What if two dozen casualties arrive at the ER simultaneously with no identification? Or two hundred? How do you track these patients as they are treated and discharged or sent out of the ER to other areas of the hospital? What if they all need different IVs and medications? How do you avoid confusion and error?

The biggest mistake made by personnel in the acute care setting (as well as with elective workups and therapy) is giving the wrong medication or doing the wrong thing to a patient. An entire chapter (chapter ten) has been devoted to mistakes and complications within the hospital.

Avoiding Mistakes

Recently a nurse attached an intestinal feeding solution to a patient's intravenous catheter, resulting in liquid food instantaneously flushing into the woman's circulation, killing her within minutes.

Before moving on, it is necessary to defend nurses in what sounds like a parade of inexcusable mistakes. The errors used as examples are real enough, but the nurses who make these errors are often new and inexperienced. And quite frankly, they are less expensive to cash-strapped hospitals determined to survive with fewer and less-skilled RNs if that's what it takes to balance the bottom line. Overworked, frustrated and bound by their sense of duty to provide the best care possible, nurses plow ahead and on occasion miss things—make mistakes. Not unlike doctors.

What about the more complicated issue of mass casualties with no names?

Most hospitals use a two-number system for patient identification. One number is the patient's unique identifier number. The second number is different for each admission and serves to track the patient through a particular hospitalization or series of sequential admissions. Thus, both numbers are registered on the patient's information sheet in the front of the hospital chart. When a procedure is performed—a surgical operation, for example—the surgeon refers to the unique identifier number when dictating the operative report. When transcribed, the operation note finds its way into the appropriate chart via the special patient number. The patient wears a wristband that records his name, age, the hospital numbers just mentioned and the name of the physician of record.

The simple identification protocol the nurse or other health care personnel are supposed to follow when administering to a patient includes:

- Ask the patient their name.
- Confirm it is the same name on their wristband.
- Confirm the patient's name and unique identifier number on the wristband matches the name and number on the bag containing blood, antibiotics or digitalis.
- Administer the drug, blood product or IV, or draw a blood sample or other body fluid specimen.

These steps should be followed whether drawing blood, giving medications, starting dialysis, providing respiratory therapy treatment or providing physical therapy. The connection must be made. Avoid clerical errors! This litany is tossed at nurses and house officers all the time. And yet there they are: shattered bodies piling up in the ER after a mass injury situation or a terrorist bombing of a city building. How is identification handled?

Prepackaged *John and Jane Doe kits* are ready to be used when unidentified single or multiple casualties arrive in the ER. Each kit has admission paperwork ready with wristbands labeled with a unique patient identifier number. Even for single unidentified victims, these packages are used until the proper identification can be made. A significant number of patients arrive in the ER with altered mental states or are frankly unresponsive. The differential diagnosis of coma is well known to ER physicians and includes drug overdose, head trauma, metabolic disorders such as diabetic ketoacidosis, psychiatric illness, stroke and shock. But the proper documentation of each John or Jane Doe—the traditional name used to signify a patient whose identity has not yet been established—must occur on admission to the Emergency Room in order to ensure a clean line of care.

Tracking patients in the modern hospital may be straightforward or remarkably complex. The common denominator that bonds a patient to all aspects of her care is the written or printed medical record, which also has its electronic shadow in the hospital's information system. When a patient travels around the hospital during elective or even a semi-emergent workup, the (physical) medical record must accompany her. It contains a distillation of the care provided and the doctor's diagnostic and treatment plans, to mention just a few aspects of immediate importance. A three-ring binder is used in most cases for the physical or paper record. Computer terminals are present on all floors and in all treatment areas.

Access to patient information begins when the physician or nurse uses his special code number to enter the system, and uses the patient's unique provider number to access the patient's orders. Some hospitals have special tracking software to determine where (in, for example, a separate surgical or endoscopy unit) the patient may be located. A floorplan of the unit or separate building permits the doctor to click on a room, whereupon more information about who is in that room comes up on the screen. The nurse or doctor may thus search to see if their patient is in pre-anesthesia holding, in the OR or in the post-anesthesia recovery area.

Assessing Patients

Now let's return to our critically ill patients in the ER. We have an acute problem in Room Five. The immediate dilemma is: How sick is this

> ### *Steps in the Assessment of a Critically Ill Patient*
> **AIRWAY** Establish a clear airway after removing any foreign material by lifting the chin or thrusting the jaw forward: In some situations, an endotracheal tube is needed or a surgical airway may be necessary; e.g., tracheotomy or cricothyroidotomy.
> **BREATHING** Make certain that the victim is actually moving air in and out of the lungs; may necessitate artificial ventilation, or a mechanical ventilator.
> **CIRCULATION** Check pulses to ascertain blood is being pumped by the heart: If there is no pulse at the wrist, for example (the groin for the femoral artery or the neck for the carotid artery); chest compressions are required if the patient is "pulseless."
> **DISABILITY** Next check the patient's level of consciousness and ability to move all four extremities and to respond to questions and stimulation (if unconscious).
> **EXPOSE** Remove all clothing and inspect the patient from head to toe, particularly trauma victims and those suffering potential penetrating trauma (a gang member after a shootout now in shock may have been shot in the back); turn the patient—with appropriate in-line traction on the neck if a cervical injury is suspected—and examine all anatomic areas; scrapes, bruises, lacerations and "imprints" all help make the proper diagnosis and may have forensic significance.
> **FLUIDS** The most critically ill patient needs a "bolus," or initial large volume of IV fluid, particularly if in shock; the exception to this general rule is the heart attack victim, who should not receive intravenous fluid resuscitation but must have an IV placed for access to the central circulation for the administration of cardiac drugs.

patient? Someone must decide. That individual is usually a triage nurse who is trained to sort out the unending stream of victims of trauma and disease. Who needs to see a doctor immediately? Who can wait?

Once the victim has been sorted out as someone in dire need of medical intervention, the Emergency Center physician enters the picture. The ER doctor follows a time-honored sequence of steps (see sidebar above) to determine what life-saving intervention may be needed. Three or more of these assessment tools are employed, and the patient is stabilized. That means any malfunctions such as shock, blood loss, heart attack, cardiac rhythm abnormalities, etc., are addressed before any attempt is made to sort out the exact diagnosis.

When the patient is stable and the major medical problem has been identified, the ER physician either begins treatment or calls the appropriate specialist to come to the department to further evaluate and treat the patient. Both major and minor trauma figure in the daily bread-and-butter cases seen in the ER. But, it is multi-organ trauma and the threat of sudden death in one or more victims that really lights the burners in the Emergency Center.

Three Levels of Trauma Cases

The size of the hospital determines the extent of the services available to victims of extensive body trauma. Three levels of trauma care are recognized by the American College of Surgeons in an effort to coordinate the provision of services in various states. While most violent attacks on humans and accidental injury occur in the urban setting, the system must also account for the care of victims of rural trauma.

Level Three Trauma Center

This community hospital level of care is the *least* comprehensive, if one ignores the outpost clinics and small hospitals in the rural setting—which are mere first-aid stations. The latter, Level Four, center provides splints, bandages, IVs and immediate transport for any trauma case of consequence. A Level Three center also provides uncomplicated surgical care for single-system trauma or simple two- or three-system traumas. If a victim of a fractured leg also demonstrates evidence of an intra-abdominal injury, the general surgeon in the community hospital will explore the abdomen and correct the problem. Complex neurosurgical surgery and neurosurgical ICU followup with intracerebral pressure monitoring is available in a Level Three facility.

Surgeons practicing in smaller communities routinely care for single- or two-system traumas, including nonoperative neurosurgical and chest trauma, uncomplicated fractures and abdominal trauma. For patients requiring extensive monitoring, even if a neurosurgeon is available in the community, the patient may be transferred to a Level Two facility for more advanced monitoring postoperatively.

Level Two Trauma Center

Trauma care provided in this institution includes a diverse team of surgical specialists and intensive care specialists. Most two- or three-system traumas and all single-system traumas are kept local and managed appropriately. Specialists in orthopedic, plastic, urologic, maxillofacial and thoracic surgery work as a team to manage multisystem trauma. What they lack is a cardiac (open-heart) surgical team and members of the above specialties who perform very complex procedures in their specialty; e.g., complex orthopedic total joint replacements, plastic procedures such as rotation flaps and the care of large injuries such as massive burns.

Level One Trauma Center

At the top of the expertise heap is the Level One trauma center, which provides all aspects of trauma care. Not only are the specialties mentioned previously well represented, but the hospital has a cardiac surgery service capable of providing bypass capabilities for disrupted hearts (penetrating cardiac trauma), torn aortas with massive hemorrhage and peripheral vascular surgical care (torn leg arteries after fractures or penetrating trauma).

A Burn Service is available in a Level One trauma center and requires numerous personnel, including dedicated surgeons, rehabilitation services (including tank facilities) and specially trained nurses. A special Wound Care Service including the provision of hyperbaric medicine is needed in a large medical center, as many of these trauma victims have poorly healing wounds. Complex trauma patients often must be operated on several times to clean wounds and replace or remove hardware.

Full-time surgical personnel characterize the difference between a large urban medical center Level One Trauma Center and the smaller centers providing basic trauma care. Surgeons in private practice cannot care for these multi-organ patients and run a separate practice. Too much time is needed to care for victims who are often indigent. The urban medical center serves the purpose of caring for all victims of trauma and violence.

Hospital Security

Hospitals are not prisons, and for the most part are open and friendly to the public. The difficulty is to find the balance between security and need of accessibility for the public. The size of the hospital has a lot to do with how much security is needed. Obviously, large urban medical centers, often located in, or near, ghetto conditions, must protect not only their patients but also the personnel employed by the hospital. Smaller facilities may get away with a security guard in the ER at night and random visits by the local police, who cruise in for a cup of coffee in the wee hours. But in the urban hospital, security has become an expensive part of providing safe medical care.

We will discuss several aspects of hospital safety and what is involved in planning and executing a comprehensive security program. Included are:

- control of access to the hospital
- workplace violence
- the use of weapons by security guards
- the use of metal detectors
- methods of physical security
- handling VIPs
- the role of different cultures in the hospital
- issues of restraint

A number of tragedies in ERs around the country in the last several years focused attention on the need for increased security. Most outbursts of violence and episodes of patient emotional crisis occur in the ER. Thus, security directors focus their attention and personnel in the Emergency Center and, in fact, smaller hospitals may have their only visible security presence in the ER. This cross section of concerns ranges from a concern for a "hard" physical presence to the softer educational and cultural sensitivity issues that make the ER a complex social arena.

Of paramount importance to hospital security personnel are the many issues of access. What entrances are left unguarded? Which doors must be locked at all times? Who has access and when? Which doors are open twenty-four hours a day? What system of identification and card access is best for doctors, nurses and other personnel who arrive and depart at odd hours?

Incidents of violent assault in the ER have been documented over the last ten years, and new national OSHA guidelines are designed to address these tragedies. Several years ago a disgruntled patient in Los Angeles fired a pistol at three doctors. In Springfield, Massachusetts, about ten years ago a deranged man grabbed a boy and held the waiting room hostage, eventually cutting the youngster's throat and killing him. In

January 1989, a female physician, Dr. Kathryn Hinnant, was raped and murdered in her hospital office by a man who had been "co-oping" (living) in a vacant space in the hospital without being detected. He wore a scrub suit, a stethoscope and a stolen hospital ID without being challenged. The hospital was found not liable in the subsequent $25 million lawsuit. But it subsequently added security personnel and additional patrols for out-of-the-way places, increased access control measures and implemented tighter controls over who received scrub suits.

Fights still occur sporadically in the ER and other hospital waiting areas where dysfunctional families wrestle with the possible demise of critically ill loved ones. But the staff also bring their own problems to work. For security personnel the task includes not only controlling violent behavior, but also doing so in a manner that doesn't terrorize other patients and staff. The possible sources of workplace violence include:

- violent patients attacking staff
- a patient's family attacking staff
- families fighting with each other
- staff with personal issues who mistreat patients

Obviously, the solutions to the multiple faces of workplace violence must be creative and must vary in intensity with each situation. Sexual harassment is addressed with information—meetings and discussions, with followup memos on appropriate behavior—and disciplinary actions if needed, including loss of job. Staff members who abuse patients or other staff may be more difficult to ferret out and identify. Subtle elder abuse, for example, may occur through delayed provision of basic needs and concealed physical abuse such as pinching and "roughing up" patients unable to defend themselves. The ultimate abuse, killing patients with intravenous injections, repeatedly raises its ugly head.

When families, patients and/or staff indulge in physical attacks on one another, the job goes directly to the security staff of the hospital. If a major crisis occurs—for example, a distraught, dysfunctional family who decide to start a knife fight with each other in the ICU waiting room—local police may be asked to intervene as well. A violent event such as a fight raises the issue of how much firepower security personnel need.

The use of weapons by hospital security officers has been debated for years. Large urban teaching hospitals do permit armed officers on the premises; these private, multibuilding facilities include Massachusetts General Hospital in Boston, Henry Ford Hospital in Detroit, and Johns Hopkins Hospital in Baltimore. Also, sprawling state and federal institutions such as large Veterans Administration facilities may have armed guards, as do city hospitals like Bellevue in New York. For the most part, private hospitals use armed city police and keep their own guards unarmed, while in the federal system it's a matter of what rank the assigned officer holds and what the perceived threat seems to be.

Tom Lynch, Director of Security at Baystate Medical Center, feels weapons are not needed in the provision of adequate security in most hospitals. He fears the consequences of a firefight in the ER waiting area or in treatment rooms. Lynch quotes an ill-fated experience at Yale-New Haven where a restrained patient took a weapon from an officer and fled in a stolen car. According to Lynch, struggles between armed corrections officers guarding patients have resulted in shots fired during the ensuing struggle, with bullets piercing the walls of adjoining treatment areas of the hospital.

To ensure weapons aren't being smuggled into the hospital, metal detectors are being used more and more in the ER. Problems arise with this additional layer of security because more staff are needed to man the station; besides, stretchers cannot easily pass through the blockade created by the metal detector. Perhaps of even more concern is what to do if a weapon is indeed discovered. Lynch states that the only hospital security officer killed in his eleven years working in New York occurred at the VA hospital in the Bronx when a metal detector was set off by a man carrying a gun who subsequently shot the officer before fleeing. One alternative is to use handheld metal detectors—for example, in the psychiatric holding areas and on high-risk persons identified by the staff—to screen new admissions.

The recommendations made by OSHA to "harden" the Emergency Room include:

- glass at the registration area
- bulletproof glass at the triage area
- closed-circuit TV in the ER waiting room
- bulletproof closed-circuit TV in the ER parking garage
- universal use of access control systems

> **Typical Security Measures for Access Areas**
> - placement of a greeting officer to screen and route arriving patients
> - require photo ID to be worn by all staff
> - lock all doors to the triage areas
> - lock all doors to the treatment areas
> - restrict access to ambulance entrance areas
> - require ID card access control systems on all doors leading into the hospital
> - require visitor passes for the patient's family and friends

- the provision of a "safe room" within the treatment area that staff may retreat to in the event of a major violent incident

The key to providing good security is the prevention of a violent person from gaining access to the hospital in the first place. Once inside the treatment area, the disturbed individual compounds all of the issues providing safe care. The Emergency Center therefore presents the security people with the biggest challenge, and specific planning is needed to keep the ER under control. Security directors concentrate their energies on the following kinds of emergency plans:
- the management of violent disturbances
- the protection and supervision of VIPs
- how to properly restrain patients (as well as others)
- how to intervene in a major crime event in the hospital

Because of the inherent threat of physical injury to all parties in the scenarios mentioned above, a paramilitary flavor exists in most hospital security services; the larger and more urban the medical center, the more entrenched the system. In the last twenty years security personnel have become younger and better trained. In some hospitals the security guards are armed; in others they carry only "sticks" or batons. Some use stun guns as an intermediate level of preparedness, and aerosol weapons—pepper sprays in particular—are becoming more popular.

Pepper sprays provide a number of advantages over handguns, stun guns and even batons. The downside of any aerosol weapon includes spraying unsuspecting people in the vicinity, particularly outside at hospi-

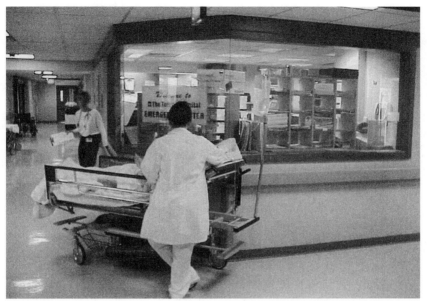

The reception area of the emergency center is surrounded by bulletproof glass.

tal entrances in windy conditions. Also, in the hospital the spray may enter the ventilation system and create problems at a distance from the zone of initial attack.

Pepper sprays have the following advantages:
- relatively inexpensive
- can be effective at distances of up to ten feet
- the effect is over in less than ten minutes and is not life-threatening
- deters violent behavior—the bad guys know it's around
- gives the officer a choice: use or don't use; show it as a deterrent
- the hospital is less liable (no severe injuries to bad guys)
- results in fewer injuries to security personnel

How to Handle VIPs

In some urban areas such as Los Angeles and New York where celebrities require hospitalization, the issue of security is heightened. Many VIPs have their own security personnel, and these young bucks may or may not see the hospital's security force as colleagues. Conflict arises when the paparazzi flood a hospital seeking, for example, the very first *exclusive* photograph of Demi Moore's baby: The media must be corralled off to one area to permit mother and child privacy.

Religious leaders, movie stars and international dignitaries all must be protected from the mindless marauding of the media. At the top of the list of VIPs is the President of the United States. When the President visits, a lot of preliminary legwork is done.

Memorial Community Hospital has been selected as a stopover on the President's trip through the Midwest. You are the Director of Security at Memorial and "suits" from the state department arrive and walk through your facility. What do they want to know? The major issues the President's security team wants to know before arrival include:

- What are the major access routes to the hospital?
- Is there a helicopter landing zone? (If not, make one.)
- Where are all of the entrances to the hospital?
- Which entrances are secured and which are not?
- Who are the security forces and who will be here?
- What are the Emergency Center resources; e.g., doctors, nurses, equipment, access, equipment?
- Where is the operating room and what are its capabilities; e.g., trauma care? Cardiac surgery? (The President will have his own blood "brought in" for transfusion if needed.)
- Where are the intensive care units and what are their capabilities?

The President will have his own security force, which will form the inner "circle of protection" regardless of where the President goes—including the hospital's ER or OR. American presidents have an extensive history of getting shot, and information is available on the resuscitation efforts that saved Reagan's life as well as the nature of the fatal bullet that claimed John Kennedy. To appreciate the speed and selfless abandon with which the President's security forces react, you need only revisit the film of Reagan's assault.

Imagine the same circumstances occurring inside a hospital.

The final security measures used outside of the hospital are *emergency telephone towers*, which also are used on some college campuses. About ten feet tall, emblazoned with the word *help* and blue in color, they have emergency phone buttons. When the button is pushed a strobe light goes on and the security personnel monitoring the system receive a signal that tells them which tower is calling and its location. The high-powered light will not go off until the security command center turns it off.

Closed-Circuit TV

Two critical areas in the hospital's emergency room where the added vigilance of closed-circuit TV provides improved patient care are the trauma room and the acute psychiatric care rooms. In this regard the system isn't only a part of security. It's also a matter of watching and recording treatments and patient's responses and, in the case of suicidal psych patients, looking for behavior that must be stopped or that can be used to justify admission and more aggressive treatment.

But who watches the monitors? Who is trained well enough to know when a teenager is about to use his belt to end his life? And where do these observers sit? Where are the cameras, and where are the monitors?

Does the hospital have two systems? One for security monitored by that staff, and one smaller local system to watch the ER?

Security measures often include video monitoring of the ER as well as other high-risk areas, including the newborn nursery, critical care areas and the psychiatric units. This added precaution permits not only identifying undesirable behaviors as they occur, but also recording them for future use. Not all hospitals use closed-circuit TV—and you may set up your fictional ER anyway you wish.

These closed-circuit TVs are also used to monitor parking garages and the ER loading dock.

Lethal Infections

The worldwide AIDS epidemic has changed the way health care workers view body fluids. No longer are bare hands seen in the hospital (or even in the boxing ring, for that matter). The ascendancy of drug abuse and multipartner recreational sex makes everyone suspect, and if an injury (needle stick, blade cut, spilled blood on a hospital worker) occurs in the hospital, the doctor of record must request that the patient involved undergo an HIV and hepatitis blood test. Nobody knows who's carrying what these days. The lethality of HIV infection makes the safe handling of body fluids critical.

Certainly the problem goes far beyond aggressive retroviral infections. So-called "flesh-eating" bacteria have made the scene along with individual virulent *E. coli*, staph and strep infections, not to mention the old standbys such as salmonella, staph food poisoning and botulism.

Supposedly sophisticated health care consumers stumble badly on the issue of infections, pressuring doctors to provide more and more prescriptions for antibiotics—often when the problem is clearly viral. What happens? The antibiotics become resistant, developing enzymes to combat new (ever more expensive) drugs.

The public assumes that the pharmaceutical industry is ready with yet another generation of "gorilla-mycin," a new chemical cure to be used when moms try to force pediatricians to order drugs for Billie's sniffles.

In the hospital, the lesson has been learned and is struggled with daily. Impossible bugs such as VRE (*vancomycin-resistant enterococcus*), MRSA (*methicillin-resistant staphylococcus*) and PRSR (*penicillin-resistant staph pneumonia*) terrorize intensive care units. Critically ill patients with devastated immune systems, a secondary consequence of a variety of diseases, become infected and die of what is called a *nosocomial*, or *hospital-acquired*, infection.

Isolation

How are these patients isolated in the ER and elsewhere in the hospital? How are patients with terrible infections isolated from other patients? The following principles apply to patients already in the hospital when the infection was identified and patients returning to the hospital who have already been labeled with one of these hospital-acquired infections.

• All patients identified with VRE, MRSA or PRSP (we'll call them "bad bugs" from now on) must be placed in a private room or in a room with another patient with the same infection.

• The patient can only be removed from the room after a full course of (intravenous) antibiotic treatment and when all repeat cultures of appropriate fluids are negative—specific cultures are sampled according to the hospital's infectious disease protocol.

• Only a member of the Infection Control Team can remove a patient from isolation.

• If the patient is readmitted to the hospital, he must be placed into isolation unless the followup cultures are on record as being negative.

• A special *Alert* sign must be posted outside of the patient's isolation room door.

- The patient should wear a special colored wristband, containing no written information, by which the staff will identify the patient.

Specific rules of conduct must be followed for infected patients during their care, and this applies to the medical staff, nurses, family and visitors. Obviously the number of visitors is severely restricted, and family members must adhere to the infectious disease rules employed for any patient with the "bad bugs."

The guidelines for managing a patient in isolation with bad bugs include:

- Gloves must be worn by everyone entering the room and these gloves must be removed before leaving.
- Hand washing using antimicrobial soap and a waterless alcohol product is mandatory after glove removal.
- Gowns and masks may be indicated as well (masks when suctioning a patient or performing intubation, or with a patient with severe pulmonary secretions; gowns when working close to the patient: bathing, lifting, transferring, etc.).
- Dedicated instruments such as stethoscopes, reflex hammer, blood pressure cuffs and thermometers which remain in the room must be identified. No doctor should use personal equipment; the dedicated instruments are disinfected weekly and at the time of the patient's discharge.
- Wheelchairs, stretchers and anything else that leaves the room must be disinfected.

Although the issue of serious infections is not unique to the ER, it is worth reviewing these principles here. The associated concerns regarding HIV and hepatitis infections highlight the need for health care workers to constantly be vigilant about who may harbor bad bugs or virulent viruses. Thus, *universal precautions* must be followed.

The concept of considering all patients at all times as potential sources of lethal infections is captured by the term *body substance isolation* (*BSI*), which mandates the following precautions:

- Gloves must be worn whenever contact with body fluids (e.g., urine, feces, pus, serum, blood or sputum) is anticipated.
- A gown should be worn whenever one's clothes might come in contact with or be contaminated by a patient's body fluids.

- Masks and glasses or goggles must be worn if the patient has fluids that may be splashed on the health care provider.
- For patients with tuberculosis, respiratory isolation with a special tight-fitting mask is required.

Psychiatric Emergencies and Lockdown Units

What happens when a wild, emotionally deranged patient arrives at the Emergency Center? Where is the patient placed? How is such a patient restrained? How much force is permitted?

These psychiatric patients are a threat to themselves and to the people around them. This includes their own acquaintances and the medical team charged with their care.

What is the defining line between a psychiatric assault and a criminal assault? Where is the interface between appropriate medical care by the treating team in terms of medical and physical restraints and the patient's rights? These are questions writers should address in exploring the world of the mentally challenged.

If medical restraints are used and the patient harms himself, does it mean the medication was inadequate? Should physical restraints have been used? In a northeast hospital some years ago three patients committed suicide: The first was a teenager who hanged himself. A lawsuit for wrongful death ensued—as did two more suicides. How vigilant must the hospital be?

Mass Casualties

The Oklahoma City bombing and the New York Trade Center bombing reminded us that our world has changed remarkably in the last three decades. And while gang wars continue to challenge trauma teams, there is a new threat that seems unlikely to disappear in the near future: international terrorism. What ghastly numbers of blast and burn victims will next reach an unsuspecting hospital? Are we prepared? Is any hospital truly ready to handle fifty, a hundred or three hundred casualties?

Some years ago at Memorial Hospital in Martinsville, Virginia, a hostage drill took place at 4 A.M., which served to prove two points: It's difficult to actually train for this once-in-a-lifetime catastrophe, and even the hospital personnel weren't cooperative—some of those involved complained that the exercise was too intrusive. Local police refused to participate in the exercise. That alone should have set off a warning in the organizers' minds. Is it possible to handle a real situation with terrorists without local and state law enforcement officers?

The conclusions from this drill were that better communication among the principals was needed, and that these exercises must not be abandoned: The threat of assault in the ER especially is a real part of our violent modern world.

In this regard mass transportation and crowd events such as professional sports present local hospitals with a possible mass casualty situation. Can there be a life-threatening situation more tenuous than multiple casualties? More rift with potential for loss of life?

Can it get any worse?

There's always the time-honored litmus test for any city hospital: What happens when the President of the United States comes to town? Inquiring about a presidential visit shows how hospital administrators, medical staff and federal officials interact in the (potential) heat of battle. There is a real record of how life-threatening injuries to the President have been handled. And because anticipatory planning always precedes the President's visit, we can use this theoretical event to look at the modern hospital's emergency services in all of their complexity.

Handling Mass Casualties

Hospitals have an inherent responsibility to be prepared for *mass casualties*, disasters involving large numbers of injured victims, some of whom will require major resuscitative and treatment efforts. The unanticipated catastrophe may occur in the community, in the immediate geographic area or at a distance at which a given hospital must accept overflow patients from a primary hospital closer to the scene. Victims may arrive by ambulance or by helicopter, in large numbers, simultaneously.

Also the hospital must be prepared to handle any multiple-casualty event that occurs within the hospital's walls, an *internal disaster*. This might involve fire, explosions of various types or acts of terrorism such as a bombing. Disruption of electrical power along with failure of the auxiliary system would create life-threatening scenarios throughout the hospital when electrically powered medical equipment shut down. Major hospital food contamination and the subsequent gastrointestinal illness would flood the ER with dozens of victims, burdening the system and leaving the hospital unable to feed its patients.

The third category of disaster that can result in mass casualties is *natural catastrophes*, particularly those related to severe weather. Some geographic areas suffer from repetitive hurricanes in the late summer; others suffer from tornadoes, floods and earthquakes. In the Northeast major snowstorms are a constant threat in winter. Two problems arise from each of these scenarios: first, the need to treat injuries specifically related to the weather event, such as hypothermia, frostbite and other cold injuries during blizzards; and second, to deal with hospital staffing difficulties with isolation and lack of access to the hospital because of the weather.

Baystate Medical Center (BMC) in Springfield, Massachusetts, sits at the crossroads of two major highways near several large and small airports, and is surrounded by a variety of industrial plants, including a gun manufacturer, and many colleges. Civil disobedience, spills of transported materials, aircraft crashes, multiple-car crashes, industrial explosions and fires all pose potential mass-casualty threats to the medical center.

The following material is excerpted from BMC's disaster plan. It typifies the identification of levels of preparedness, the need for a chain of command and a method for mobilizing hospital personnel. The elements of this plan are intended to be flexible and to serve as guidelines.

The Medical Center's CEO has sole responsibility for instituting the Disaster Preparedness Plan; in his absence, the Administrator on call assumes this responsibility. Each department head will remain in charge of her unit until someone higher up in the chain of command relieves her of her duties. Three levels of readiness are outlined below:

- **PLAN D: STANDBY** This means the hospital has received unconfirmed reports that a mass casualty situation may have occurred and an influx of a large number of victims may follow; the response to this level of alertness is to organize and prepare staff and to assess availability of supplies and personnel.

- **LEVEL ONE ALERT** A predetermined call sequence is executed to notify departments that a number of casualties are expected but the casualties should not exceed the hospital's capacity to manage them, or that a major weather event or natural disaster is anticipated; the response at this heightened level of preparedness is to establish a Disaster Command Center, which is then responsible for further responses; also, appropriate adjustments for staffing and the provision of added supplies must be set in motion.

- **PLAN D: NOW IN PROGRESS** This is Baystate's highest level of disaster preparedness and is immediately set in motion if any of the following is proven: a nuclear disaster, radiation spill, commercial or military plane crash or any catastrophe resulting in greater than thirty casualties; the response is the immediate implementation of the Disaster Preparedness Plan, including alerting all staff and ascertaining appropriate equipment and supplies availability.

As soon as the hospital has been notified of a possible disaster, the CEO or administrator on call must obtain the following information:
- name and telephone number of caller
- location of disaster
- type of disaster
- number of casualties

Next, the following sequence is followed by the CEO:
- Call the emergency room and provide above information.
- Verify disaster by return phone call or the arrival of casualties.
- If unable to verify, remain on "Standby" for two hours and then cancel.
- If disaster is verified and the number of casualties does not exceed usual capacity (in BMC's case, thirty), proceed to Level One Alert and implement Level 1 call list.
- If disaster is confirmed and the number of casualties exceeds usual capacity, announce "Plan D Now in Progress" and implement Plan D call list to set in motion a full-disaster response.
- When Plan D is set in motion at BMC, the CEO/administrator on call must personally call the following people: CEO, senior VP, VP for medical/professional services, Chief of Security, Chairman, ER, VP of nursing, Director of Communications and Chairman of the disaster committee.
- Establish command center, activate phone system and maintain contact with the ER.
- Verify that all special areas are prepared.
- Monitor events related to disaster management.

> ## *International Coding System for Patient Identification*
> **RED PRIORITY** shock/hypoxia present or imminent with high probability of survival with rapid transportation and immediate care
> **YELLOW** injuries with possible systemic effects which will tolerate up to an hour delay in the field
> **YELLOW PRIME** catastrophically ill
> **GREEN** localized injuries with no systemic threat and which will tolerate several hours of delay before treatment with no loss of life or limb
> **BLACK** dead or unsalvageable victim

The Command Center continues a liaison with other regional hospitals while ensuring adequate personnel are available to provide the hospital's services. These include a physician pool, personnel pool and a nursing pool. Other specialized areas controlled by the Command Center are

- triage
- major trauma
- fractures
- ambulatory care
- medical emergencies
- security
- a family center
- a Press and Information center

Finally, all casualties should be wearing a colored tag that was placed in the field by an emergency medical technician using an international coding system. Each victim will be triaged at the Emergency Center according to the tags as well as any changes in the casualty's condition or a perception by the triage doctor that the injury is either more salvageable or worse than labeled.

CHAPTER THREE

Admission to the Hospital

B eing admitted to a hospital may seem like a relatively simple process to the patient, but getting admitted is actually a complex procedure that involves a series of medical, financial and legal issues. This chapter will sort out those various issues and take you step by step through several different scenarios as patients are admitted.

The first question to understand is whether a hospital has to admit you as a patient. The answer is no. A hospital is not required to admit you and may choose not to for a variety of reasons, most commonly because of restrictions placed by insurers.

What about emergencies? Can a woman in labor or a man with an acute heart attack be sent away without treatment? Are hospitals required to treat them? Emergencies cannot be sent away: They must be treated and at least stabilized. Hospitals are required by law to treat any emergency that arrives.

Hospitals have to *treat* any emergency that is seen in the emergency department. However, since they are not required to *admit* everyone, a hospital's emergency center may treat someone to stabilize them, but instead of hospitalizing them for long-term expensive testing and treatment, will transport the patient to another hospital for admission.

Sending patients to another hospital for admission is a daily occurrence among hospitals and happens for a variety of reasons. The most common reason patients are transferred is because the patient's insurance carrier or HMO plan determines which hospital the patient must be admitted to, and these plans usually refuse to pay for admission to an unapproved hospital.

In some cities, transferring patients may be because of "dumping."

Dumping

Dumping occurs when one hospital sends indigent or uninsured patients to another hospital for admission, requiring the second hospital to absorb the high cost of the patient's hospitalization. Dumping usually occurs because most for-profit hospitals have no way of recovering the cost of admitting these patients. Health and Human Services (HHS) passed a law preventing hospitals from delaying care while awaiting insurance company approval, or even denying treatment if a patient's coverage is in doubt.

The once-frequent occurrence of transferring uninsured patients now happens only rarely. Today, most modern hospitals have a charity fund and also receive some aid from the city, county and state to help defray the cost of treating indigent or uninsured patients. Almost all hospital-to-hospital transfers now happen because HMOs will only authorize payment to a particular hospital, requiring patients to be moved.

There's also a more subtle form of dumping. Rather than blatantly transferring a patient to another hospital, a maneuver that is now illegal, the doctor at the "subtle-dumping hospital" decides he doesn't want to have to take care of the patient for any of a number of reasons, including:

- The patient has no insurance.
- The patient is on welfare.
- The patient has a disease that will require tedious medical or surgical care over a protracted time frame.

Recognizing the long profile of anticipated treatment for nominal monetary return, the dumping doctor claims the patient would be better served at a (usually) larger, often urban, medical center. He may tell the patient he hasn't done many of the procedures the patient needs performed: He's not comfortable with it. Unfortunately, these dubious and ethically repugnant behaviors do occur all the time, and the flow is almost always from smaller hospitals to bigger institutions.

Types of Admissions

Admission to a hospital can be for a variety of reasons and circumstances. There are three broad categories of admissions:

1. Standard Admission (more than twenty-four hours)
   Medical evaluation/treatment

    Obstetrics (labor and delivery)
    Elective pre-operative admissions
2. Short Term (Less than twenty-four hours)
    Referred to as "23:59" admits
3. ER—surgical/medical emergencies (see chapter two)

Standard Admission

There is nothing routine about being admitted to a hospital, but *routine admission* refers to patients who are processed through Admitting rather than through the Emergency Department and who are staying longer than twenty-four hours. These patients are admitted for the following:

- scheduled surgery (pre-op evaluation, testing and preparation)
- labor and delivery
- medical/surgical problems of adult and pediatric patients requiring treatment and extensive diagnostic testing

The term *standard* or *routine* is used to differentiate these admissions from acute, life-threatening emergency admissions that are automatically admitted through the ER, or from "short" admissions that are hospitalizations of less than twenty-four hours. Routine full admissions are for twenty-four hours or more and may extend for several days or weeks.

Admission to most hospitals follows a standard procedure. The Admitting Department fills out a form when interviewing the patient that provides very valuable and specific information. This is called the *face sheet* (or *admission sheet*) and constitutes the first page of every chart.

The face sheet is often the first thing a consulting physician or resident reviews to get a quick overview of the patient prior to going into the room to see the patient for the first time. For instance, a new doctor reading a face sheet might learn that the patient is an eighty-year-old moderately overweight woman with a history of diabetes and recurrent congestive heart failure, recently widowed and who now lives alone. The consulting doctor now has a general profile of the patient before he even enters the room to meet her. It's the same information the primary care doctor who admitted the patient has in her office records.

Short-Term Admission

These are admissions that are less than twenty-four hours in duration. These admissions are sometimes referred to as *twenty-three fifty-nines*

(23:59s), meaning 23 hours 59 minutes or less in duration. They have a shortened admitting process, with a face sheet, a limited history and physical on the chart and a shortened discharge process at the end of the treatment period.

Under the 23:59 rule, third-party payers pay for the shortened hospital stay as a percentage of the procedure; they do not have to reimburse for a whole day of hospitalization. This allows patients to be seen and treated as outpatients, while utilizing hospital facilities during the short recovery period before going home.

23:59s, or *short admits*, are also called *observations* (or *obs*) by hospital personnel. Short admits are for observation following procedures such as coronary angiograms, some elective surgery such as laparoscopic gallbladder operations, mastectomies, biopsies or complex treatments. This allows patients to be observed closely in a hospital setting to ensure that they are stable before discharging them.

These 23:59 admissions may involve one night in the hospital or day-stay surgical unit. *Daystay surgery* means just that: The patient has surgery and returns home the same day. The term *short-stay surgery* means minor excisions under local anesthesia with no sedation. These excursions are truly in-and-out experiences.

Pre-Certification

HMOs and some insurance companies require that patients be pre-certified prior to any testing, procedure or hospitalization—meaning that the insurer has authorized it and has agreed to pay for it. With any anticipated hospitalization, pre-certification actually states how many days have been authorized for the patient to stay in the hospital. If complications require a longer-than-expected stay, the patient must be re-certified to cover the extra days. To minimize their costs, HMOs often deny extended hospitalization to treat unforeseen complications. Because of this, doctors sometimes "fudge" the records to allow sick patients to stay longer when the doctors know the HMOs would otherwise not approve it.

Some hospitals are beginning to pre-certify patients by telephone. Those who are otherwise healthy with no significant health conditions may be cleared without a paper trail. It's fast and efficient.

When a patient has been pre-certified by the doctor's office, the hospital admitting department has the patient's name listed on a *booking sheet*.

The Face Sheet (Admission Sheet)

The first page of every chart contains the following information:
- full name of patient
- age
- address
- referring (or personal) doctor
- clinical symptoms and working diagnosis
- insurance providers
- pre-certification to authorize hospitalization for a given number of days
- closest relatives to contact
- religious preference
- living will/advanced directive preferences (now required by most states)
- a signed consent for treatment

This sheet contains the names of all pre-certified patients to be admitted, their doctors' names, the working diagnoses and a copy of the insurance card. This greatly speeds up the admitting process.

Living Will

A living will is a declaration of a patient's wishes about extended medical care and allows someone to speak for the patient if terminal illness or a state of permanent unconsciousness renders him incapable of speech. This advanced directive allows a competent adult to state her wishes regarding what resuscitative efforts should (or should not) be performed on her during the hospitalization. A living will is a written statement of personal desires regarding future health care, and is a declaration of the patient's wishes regarding life support. A living will can speak for you when you can no longer speak for yourself. Without a living will, a patient could end up on a life-support system contrary to his wishes. Living wills allow the patient to make decisions on vital issues of treatment. It involves both the treatments he does or does not want, and the conditions under which these might apply.

Who is authorized to make a living will? The law permits anyone to make one if they are of sound mind and at least eighteen years of age, or if they are married.

When considering a living will or an advanced directive, the person should consider which treatments they would accept or reject, and under what clinical conditions those choices would apply. The patient can indicate if she wishes to receive or reject any of the following:

- cardiac resuscitation
- mechanical respiration
- tube feeding or hydration
- blood or blood products
- any surgery or invasive diagnostic test
- kidney dialysis
- antibiotics

The person also should consider specific clinical conditions:

LIFE-SUSTAINING TREATMENT A medical procedure that will only prolong the process of dying or maintain the patient in a state of permanent unconsciousness.

PERMANENTLY UNCONSCIOUS A medical condition of total and irreversible loss of consciousness. Example: irreversible coma or vegetative state.

TERMINAL CONDITION An advanced incurable and irreversible medical condition that will result in death.

What about a patient who has a living will and presents in an emergency room? What happens then? It is presumed that the patient is there for all necessary medical care. Patients who are conscious and able to make their wishes known may refuse unwanted medical care. But a living will should *not* be taken to forbid resuscitation in the emergency room on an unconscious patient. Without prior knowledge of the patient, the physician should not assume that the document belongs to that patient or that it reflects the patient's wishes in that situation.

If there is a reasonable probability that life-saving care will be successful, then it should not be withheld on an unconscious person. For example, an elderly patient in currently good health may have signed a living will out of fear of a lingering cancer death. However, the patient might very well want to be given emergency treatment after an automobile accident. Also, failure to honor a *do not resuscitate* or *do not treat* clause of a living will has resulted in at least one doctor being sued for doing too much.

"Five Wishes" Living Will
- The person I want to make care decisions for me when I can't.
- The kind of medical treatment I want or don't want.
- How comfortable I want to be.
- How I want people to treat me.
- What I want my loved ones to know.

The Florida Commission on Aging With Dignity created Five Wishes, a "living will with heart." Five Wishes is a living will that addresses medical issues such as whether a dying person wants a feeding tube or should be kept alive by artificial means. But it goes further than typical living wills by trying to meet the other needs of dying people, such as family relationships and details of care. It makes it easier for families to know what their loved ones want.

Following the completion of the face sheet, the patient is banded with a plastic wristband for proper identification and is taken by wheelchair to the assigned room.

Summary of the Admitting Process
I. Routine Admission and "23:59" Short Admits
(This also includes Pre-Op, and Labor & Delivery admissions)
- pre-certification
- face sheet filled out
- signed consent for treatment form
- signed living will/advanced directive
- patient banded with I.D. bracelet
- taken by wheelchair to floor
- nurses admission sheet added to chart
- history and physical performed

II. Emergency Admission
- emergency resuscitation or stabilization in the ER
- make diagnosis and institute emergency treatment
- seek identification information for face sheet
- inform family or significant other(s) of the admission and treatment plan

---

Who Pays the Medical Bills?
- self-insured (uninsured)
- traditional fee-for-service insurance
- HMOs
- POSs
- Medicare/Medicaid

Who Pays the Medical Bill?

The construction and upkeep of hospitals includes the cost of utilities, expensive state-of-the-art equipment, funding for research, medical education, salaries of nurses, technologists and support personnel, food services and community programs—and it all takes money. Lots of money. Presidents, kings and dictators from countries around the world come to the United States to receive medical treatment because, under the current system, it is in fact the best in the world.

What about the uninsured in America? Who will pay for them? According to Census Bureau data, the number of uninsured in this country continues to rise. An estimated forty-four million Americans (15 percent of the population in the United States) lack health insurance—some by choice. Unemployed Welfare recipients receive Medicaid. The problem is that when they finally get employment, they lose Medicaid and move into low-wage jobs that carry no insurance for workers. Low-income workers who aren't offered health insurance can't afford it on their own. Congress is still debating how to handle this, since the cost to insure these people would be staggering.

There are several methods of reimbursement for medical care. Traditional health insurance has been _fee-for-service_, where the doctor calls the shots and the patient's insurance company pays the bill. Some patients choose to be _self-insured_, meaning they carry no insurance, but instead pay the doctor directly for office visits, treatments and exams. The government provides Medicaid for those on Welfare, and Medicare to those receiving Social Security benefits.

Managed-Care Programs

Another method that has made its way on the American medical scene is the HMO (health maintenance organization). Basically, an HMO is a group that contracts with employers, hospitals, clinics and physicians to provide medical care for a group of individuals, usually the employees of a company contracting with that HMO. The HMO guarantees a reduced cost of medical care to the employer contracting with them, and the amount allocated per person is determined. That means that if the medical bills of the patient are less than the amount allocated, the HMO has a profit (the company employer has already paid the HMO the allocation up front). Conversely, any amount that exceeds the patient allocation is a loss. The HMO covers most charges for care received within a narrow network of providers. Patients usually have no out-of-pocket expenses.

Because medical costs have skyrocketed as technology grows and as more expensive testing and treatments have become available, companies are turning to HMOs to provide cheaper health care coverage for their employees.

A POS (point of service) plan is generally similar to an HMO except that the plan pays a large share of the cost of out-of-network care. This option is usually more expensive than HMOs.

HMOs (Health Maintenance Organizations)
HMOs are organizations that provide health insurance to employees of companies at a fixed allocation per person, regardless of whether any bills are paid. If less is spent, the HMO has a profit. If bills exceed the allocation, the HMO has a loss for that patient. The term used to describe the money allotted for each covered person is *per member per month* (PMPM) and is called *capitation*—the doctor gets this amount of money whether she sees a patient or not. The motivation? See as few patients as possible. For specialists who will not play this game a *carve out* or reimbursement for special services such as dialysis is covered separately. Young healthy members reduce the risk to the HMO.

POS (Point of Service)
Point-of-service plans are a cross between traditional fee-for-service insurance and an HMO. It defines the payment of each patient, but allows out-of-network care for the patient, giving the patient many more options. This usually costs more than an HMO.

The Problem With HMOs

Health care is changing as large companies dictate how medicine will be practiced based solely on profit—often to the detriment of the patient. The problem is *rationed* care. An HMO is a for-profit corporation with responsibilities to stockholders that take precedence over its medical care of the patient. The HMO directly controls the amount of health care that can be provided to its members and determines which doctors and specialists may be referred to and what treatment may or may not be allowed. Patients are often not allowed to go to the doctor they've had for years, but instead are assigned another doctor within the HMO.

Primary care doctors within an HMO plan are required to act as a "gatekeeper" to keep the cost of each patient to a minimum. Doctors are encouraged to cut costs by eliminating access to specialists and to cut back on the number of tests they order. They are also punished in various ways for ordering too many tests (by HMO standards).

Doctors in managed care feel that the financial incentives and pressures of HMOs are hurting patient care. An article in the *New England Journal of Medicine* described doctors who felt they were pressured by HMOs to see more patients and limit the number of referrals to specialists. Physicians complain bitterly that managed care is interfering with the practice of medicine. Scores of physicians who have worked within certain HMOs dropped out of these plans, and many have retired from the practice of medicine.

Almost every aspect of medical care provided by HMOs is second-guessed by accountants and their hired medical henchmen. In their haste to cut costs and show a profit, HMOs have sometimes made foolish and dangerous decisions, often not allowing critical treatments or tests. As HMO profits grow and medical care is squeezed to a minimum, patients often find themselves the losers.

Length of Hospitalization

The average length of hospitalization in the U.S. is becoming shorter and shorter. Under many circumstances, this is both cheaper for the insurer (HMO or insurance company) and better for the patient. The patient is required to be up and about, often with better results and fewer complications, than if they had stayed in bed longer. And almost all elective testing, no matter how complicated, is performed on an outpatient basis.

For example, four hours after a shoulder operation, the patient is sent home for rest and recuperation. It would have required at least a four-day hospital stay just a few years earlier. Even mastectomies and laparoscopic gallbladder surgery require but one overnight stay in the hospital or special daystay unit.

However, early discharge is not always beneficial, and this approach to save money is abusive and done at the patient's expense. It is the practice of many HMOs to not allow hospitalization more than one day after delivery of a child. Both mother and baby with a normal, uncomplicated birth are sent home the same day, even though studies show that babies discharged within a day of birth face increased risk of developing jaundice, dehydration and infections.

A series discussing HMOs, published in *USA Today*, stated that the guidelines used for HMOs are not grounded in scientific studies, but are merely devised with the intent of reducing health care costs.

Here are some examples:

• Some HMOs cover the costs of epidural pain relief administered for only five hours during childbirth, even though many women have labor pain upwards of twenty hours.

• HMOs require women to be discharged from hospitals within twenty-four hours after mastectomies, even though studies show women receiving outpatient mastectomies have significantly higher risks of being rehospitalized and of having surgery-related complications.

• HMOs have strictly limited hysterectomies, even though there is no medical evidence to justify their guidelines limiting this surgical procedure.

Patients suffer when HMOs set arbitrary limits on medical care. HMOs do not adjust their guidelines for a patient's health complications, and they deny payment for care falling outside the guidelines they have set. The guidelines, including those for length of hospitalization, are a tool for controlling costs and returning a profit; unfortunately, they are not usually made with regard to patient care.

Current HMO Guidelines for Length of Hospitalization

Procedure	*Length of hospitalization (after surgery)*
Hiatal hernia repair	3 days
Below-knee amputation	1—2 days

Mastectomy	outpatient
Removal of kidney	3 days
Vaginal childbirth	6–18 hours following delivery
Hysterectomy	2 days
Coronary artery bypass	3 days

Doctors Lie to Help Their Patients

An article in *USA Today*, November 11, 1998, reported that doctors admitted lying to HMOs so their patients could get proper care. Doctors said they exaggerated patients' symptoms to prevent early discharge from the hospital by HMOs, or changed diagnoses on billing records to make sure patients received medical coverage. HMOs force doctors to make an unacceptable choice: lie or deny their patients the medical care they need. And that's a dangerous signal that clearly states how HMOs' attempts at cost-cutting have gone too far. According to the article, "A health care system based on fraud is dangerously flawed."

HMOs Abandon the Elderly

An editorial in *USA Today* discussed problems the elderly are now experiencing with their HMOs. When HMOs started, they actively sought Medicare patients. They agreed to provide all medical services and medications that Medicare had provided, but at a slight discount. Older and disabled Americans counted on the HMO's promise of a secure, comprehensive and low-cost care. However, as the population has grown older and health care costs to the elderly increase, HMOs have quit or sharply reduced their Medicare coverage. The elderly have simply been abandoned by managed care providers.

HMOs profit because they primarily insure "well" patient populations, such as the work force of companies, and not "sick" patients. The elderly have more medical problems, office visits, hospital days and medications. The HMO's promise to provide affordable, comprehensive health care was broken. And as a result, thousands of older Americans are left with no other managed care options.

The elderly have been dumped and the commitment to them ignored. HMOs bear the blame for this debacle.

The Future of Managed Care

The health care picture is starting to change in favor of the patient. Congress has tried to pass a Patient's Bill of Rights regarding HMOs, making the HMO responsible for the health care of the patient. As it is now, patients have no recourse when HMOs refuse to reimburse medical care. This bill would also allow the patient to contest decisions he felt were unfair. The bill passed in the House of Representatives, but stalled in the Senate. God bless corporate America.

Also, courts have finally taken action against HMOs and have made them responsible for their actions. A lawsuit against an HMO in Texas resulted from a suicidal patient being discharged from the hospital because his coverage had ended, in spite of his physician's objections. Shortly after discharge, he killed himself. The lawsuit states that the HMO committed malpractice.

In Kentucky, a jury found $13 million in damages against Humana. Kentucky doctors hope that the judgment against Humana will send a message to HMOs to stay out of medical decision-making. A Louisville jury found that Humana's denial for surgery to a woman with a pelvic tumor showed "reckless disregard" for the patient's health.

And in a recent case, a California jury awarded more than $120 million to a woman whose husband fought fruitlessly against Aetna U.S. Health Care, the nation's largest insurer. According to an article in *Time* (February 1, 1999), the husband, a prosecuting attorney, found himself battling not just the disease that would ultimately kill him but also Aetna, who refused to pay for the cryosurgery and chemotherapy that specialists urged. Aetna bureaucrats challenged his use of out-of-plan doctors and treatment. He lost his battle to both Aetna and to the cancer. In the stiffest such penalty ever imposed on an HMO, the jury awarded $116 million in punitive damages and $4.5 million in damages, claiming that Aetna had "acted with fraud and malice."

HMOs argue that they shouldn't be liable for medical malpractice because they don't make medical-care decisions. However, doctors say that quite clearly HMOs are practicing medicine. Since HMOs are responsible for everything that happens—or doesn't happen—to a patient, they should also be responsible for their actions. This is particularly true on decisions of whether to admit to a hospital.

There is both public and political backlash against managed care. Doctors are very angry and frustrated, and patients are furious at having to make round after round of inconclusive phone calls and getting no answers. HMOs' bureaucrats are practicing medicine to save money, but it is at the expense and well-being of the patient.

According to the *Wall Street Journal*, HMOs are trying to figure out what it is they do to make people so mad. The HMOs are slowly accepting the fact that their image problem isn't entirely the fault of greedy doctors and simplistic media horror stories. HMOs traditionally prevented doctors from having frank discussions with their patients about treatment options. But in an attempt to repair HMO relationships with doctors, they have dropped the "gag" rule and allow physicians to freely discuss all options with their patients.

Here's the medical dilemma facing the next century.

1. Patients want cheaper health care available to them, while at the same time demanding the best, most up-to-date medical care and technology available.

2. HMOs provide patients with cheaper health care, but continue to reduce services (exams, tests, surgery), thereby seriously limiting the care provided in an attempt to show more profit. Patients pay less but also get less in return.

3. Doctors struggle under the burden of having to see more patients while experiencing yearly deep cuts and having HMO accountants tell them how to practice medicine, often to the detriment of their patients. At the same time, advocacy groups demand that doctors be "perfect," with no mistakes allowed.

Something has to give. Scores of physicians—unable to deal with the incredible intrusion of bean-counters into the practice of medicine—have either dropped out of HMOs or have left the practice of medicine entirely.

Dying in the Hospital

A recent study found that 70 percent of patients died in the hospital, 20 percent died at home and 10 percent died in hospices and elsewhere. The percentage of people dying in the hospital has gone up in recent years: In 1960, less than 50 percent died in the hospital. It is harder for families to cope with care for the dying at home, even though it is generally where most people wish to die, in familiar surroundings. Bringing dying people home assures them they're wanted and won't be deserted. Dying people fear losing control over their lives. Everyone should be afforded dignity and comfort at the time of death. They should be able to expect optimal pain relief, physical comfort and psychological support.

It is generally accepted that in the past, nurses and doctors viewed death as a failure of their skills, and rejected the dying person as a reminder of their inability to sustain life. Recently, attitudes have dramatically improved as health care professionals begin to understand and improve hospital care for the dying. However, doctors and nurses still find it difficult to get close to the dying patient in the hospital, and tend to distance themselves. They withdraw because they feel they have little to offer.

Modern hospitals are not soulless machines; doctors and nurses are not ogres. They are a part of our society's alienation from death. It has been said that we die alone, but there are degrees of loneliness, and the feeling of being unwanted at the end of life may be the most poignant of all human emotions.

The Anxiety of the Unknown by Beckman states that the kind of death one would hope for today—to die in one's sleep, ignorant of the event—was in the Middle Ages only wished upon one's enemies. An orderly death was part of an orderly life, and a number of ceremonies were an intrinsic part of dying. A will was written and psalms were chosen long before death actually occurred.

— CHAPTER FOUR —

Inside the Operating Room

Perhaps no other area of the modern hospital conjures up an image of heroic and at times desperate treatment like the operating room. Even elective operations carry risk and uncertainty. Lay articles on medical topics frequently use photos of the operating room to highlight or dramatize the importance of a medical topic—even if the topic is unrelated to surgery.

But what actually goes on in the OR?

Is it really a private world of sexy surgeons and nubile scrub techs? Is every EKG heartbeat a measure of the tenuous distance between life and death? Do surgeons scream and shout? Is the typical OR awash with Beethoven or Wagner or the Rolling Stones? Do surgeons joke as they remove diseased organs and masses of cancer? Is levity tossed out in the face of despair?

Or is every moment solemn and measured? Is the operating room an oasis of riveting silence? What does this world of disease, damage, (potentially) lethal body fluids and sick body parts do to a doctor, particularly after twenty or thirty years of practice?

As you might anticipate, the operating room is not a homogenous place: Not all OR rooms are alike, nor do surgeons perform their procedures in the same way—even within the same specialty. Surgeons have pet instruments, pet peeves and pet scrub techs. The intrusion of managed care into medicine has also reached the operating room. Cost-cutting includes the quality of gloves and sutures, and the rate of replacement of equipment. If you think the OR is a bastion of individualism protected from the insanity of cost-containment—think again.

Basic Principles In Surgery

First we'll look at the basic elements of what a surgeon actually does, and then look at the way an OR is set up. We'll evaluate the variations in room plans and types of equipment needed by various surgical subspecialists to show how the physical plant serves the demands of the techniques employed.

All surgeons follow basic tenants of surgical science. In their early years of residency, surgeons learn elements of technique that apply to all areas, regardless of whether the specialty has specific maneuvers such as the placement of orthopedic hardware, "reaming" out a prostate or "lifting" a face. The most basic principles of surgery by which competent surgeons practice are

- adequate exposure of the organ of concern
- a knowledge of the specific anatomy of the region
- careful hemostasis or control of bleeding
- gentleness with tissues

All of these principles belong in the *armamentarium* of the individual surgeon, but they also necessitate good lighting, high-quality instruments and proper assistance during surgery. It is worthwhile recalling some issues from the early days of laparoscopic surgery in relation to these principles. Board-certified surgeons with extensive experience with open gallbladder operations suddenly saw the procedure from a different perspective. The first target of minimally invasive surgery, the gallbladder could no longer be touched and could not be assessed by tactile discrimination. Instead, the surgeon used new technology that distanced him from the patient. Some of it didn't work that well.

For example, the cameras often broke or the instruments themselves were faulty. Surgeons struggled until the technology caught up with their skills. Now the issues surrounding laparoscopic surgery have shifted. But it's still tied into what happens in the operating room.

The vital role of the surgeon's motor skills and personality will become apparent. Clearly, these two issues form the heart of what most people want to know about the mysterious place called the OR. Later we will attempt to provide an honest evaluation of surgeon's attitudes and how personality affects everyone working in surgery.

Surgery holds the intrigue enjoyed by professional sports events with the addition of warnings instead of scores, neon numbers listing death

---

How a Patient Is Positioned During Surgery

SUPINE POSITION   The patient is lying flat on the back with arms extended on arm boards or tucked in by sheets at the side; used for many operations, including abdominal and pelvic.

PRONE POSITION   The patient is face-down on the OR table with arms at side or out on arm boards, head turned to one side.

JACKKNIFE POSITION   Same as prone, with the OR table bent or "broken" in the middle to lift the patient's hips; used in proctology.

TRENDELENBERG POSITION   Patient is supine, with the foot of the bed elevated.

REVERSE TRENDELENBERG POSITION   Supine, with the head of the bed elevated.

LITHOTOMY POSITION   "pelvic examination position" with legs in stirrups and buttocks at end of the table for GYN and proctology surgery.

MODIFIED LITHOTOMY POSITION   With legs in stirrups that are less flexed, legs spread; permits access from abdomen and below (perineum) for some gynecological and proctological operations.

LATERAL POSITION   Patient is placed partially or completely on side for access to chest and flank for thoracic and kidney operations.

---

and disability on the scoreboard. In the OR there are no time-outs, no substitutes and no instant replays. As with sports, you never know quite what you're getting into: No one can define the risks completely.

The Operating Room Layout

Before considering surgeon performance, what's the physical layout of the hospital with respect to where the operating rooms are located?

Three issues regarding the OR and the hospital as a physical plant are
- the location of the operating rooms in relation to the Emergency Center
- the floor plan of the operating room
- the configuration of individual (specialty) operating rooms

The matter of locating the operating room in some sort of proximity to the ER applies only to the primary (not daystay) operating rooms, the place where major cases are performed. Daystay surgery and short-stay (minor) surgery are often located at a distance from the ER because they serve no immediate tie-in role in acute patient care. But major trauma

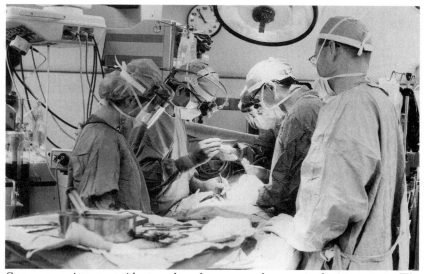

Surgeons, assistants, residents and scrub nurses work as a team during surgery. The anesthesiologist is at the head of the patient behind the drape.

and acute surgical illnesses such as a ruptured aortic aneurysm must be transferred to the OR with the least waste of time, as these patients are often in profound shock and surgery is an essential part of the resuscitation process.

In a well-designed urban hospital, the operating rooms are either around the corner from the ER, down one floor or up one floor, with dedicated elevators for emergency transport. Patients are quickly transferred to the OR after assessment and stabilization in the ER, and this often includes a team of nurses and doctors who must breathe (ventilate) for the patient, pump in IV fluid and/or blood and propel the stretcher down the corridor with dispatch.

For elective surgery and some less urgent acute operations, the patient is taken to a holding area near the OR with corridor connections. Here the patient is prepped for surgery. This includes meeting the anesthesiologist, signing informed consent, inserting an IV if not already done, and receiving sedation, antibiotics and a kiss good-bye from loved ones, who head for a nearby waiting room.

The operating room itself may take several forms, not unlike the critical care areas, where open floor plans and separate isolation rooms vary

The Basic Components of an Operating Room

- a centrally located operating room table
- several stainless steel tables on wheels and draped with sterile sheets
- an anesthesia machine connected to hoses for oxygen and inhalation agents
- suction equipment (hoses from the wall or ceiling and a receptacle)
- a unit-dose pharmacy machine accessed by code
- laundry bins or receptacles for soiled sheets, towels, etc.
- a cautery machine
- shelves and drawers in the walls for equipment
- a telephone
- intercom connections to the front desk and the pathology department
- IV poles, stools, storage carts on wheels
- a desk
- X-ray view boxes on the wall with "whiteboard" and pens (to record sponge, needle and instrument counts)
- storage cabinets on wheels for sutures, mesh, etc.

in configuration. Each operating room is a self-contained unit with a single mechanical or electrical table. The room is functionally connected (messengers bring to the room and take away needed objects, specimens, etc.) to pharmacy, sterilization and instrument-storage areas. A central desk represents the control center where one or more nurses (usually) and an anesthesiologist direct traffic and answer phones. Corridors lead from the holding area to the various surgery suites; stretchers are parked outside the OR room as elective and emergency surgical patients undergo their operations. Elective patients may walk or be transported by wheelchair or stretcher (gurney) to the holding area.

In most hospitals, operating rooms are designed to handle specific kinds of cases. But the key elements in each room are basically the same. Extra equipment and special modifications of the OR table or other equipment are added to the basic furniture in designated rooms.

This additional equipment includes such items as:

- laparoscopic equipment with TV monitors, carbon dioxide insufflation devices with pressure monitors, etc.

The Process of Elective Surgery

- Patient is registered at a central desk in the Admitting Office, in a special registration location for major surgery, or in the daystay hospital.
- Patient undresses, dons a johnny, gets an IV (not for short stay) and sedation—and possibly pre-op antibiotics.
- Patient discusses anesthesia choices with anesthesiologist to confirm what was presented to the patient during the pre-admission consult.
- Patient talks with the surgeon, who reviews the proposed operation and expectations, and answers last-minute questions.
- Patient says good-bye to relatives and is wheeled into the operating room on a stretcher.
- In daystay, a "bed-chair" or wheelchair may be used for transport, or the patient may walk to the OR.
- The patient undergoes surgery.
- Patient is extubated and transferred to PACU, where EKG, oxygen saturation, BP, pulse and respiratory rate are monitored.
- When stable, patient is either: (1) transferred to a surgical floor, (2) discharged home same day (daystay) or (3) for complex cases, transferred to the surgical ICU.

- specific types of lasers for ophthalmology, dermatology, thoracic surgery, etc.
- special machines to freeze tumors (cryosurgery)
- special dissection equipment such as the harmonic (blunt, vibrating) scalpel
- special asepsis devices in orthopedics with hoods, helmets and associated ventilation systems
- heart bypass machine

Many hospitals now have separate daystay operating rooms, and some have separate hospitals dedicated to same-day operations. These units are organized around the principle of getting the patient in and out with the least commotion. Patients follow the same basic sequence of events followed by any elective surgery patient, regardless of the magnitude of the operation.

Daystay operations usually involve a form of conscious sedation—short-acting drugs that permit the surgeon to complete procedures such as hernias with local anesthesia, surgeries that could not be comfortably done with the injection of local medication alone. It's quite remarkable how much dissection can be performed with these novel chemicals blunting the patient's sensibilities. Most folks awake after their operation wondering when it's going to start!

The least complicated surgical unit is called *short stay*. Used for minor "lumps and bumps" removals, only local anesthesia is required and this is administered by the surgeon himself. No sedation is given. The patient typically walks in and undergoes a thirty- or forty-minute operation and walks out. No recovery room time is needed because no sedation was employed.

The short-stay unit is usually located in a place that allows easy access. Some hospitals use valet parking. This is similar to the method of handling large volumes of patients undergoing radiation therapy, who must be processed for a rather short time in the radiation department. Parking sometimes takes longer than the treatment!

Surgical Instruments

Surgical instruments are familiar to most people because of the ubiquitous hemostat, which may be found in a modified form anywhere from the family garage to a trout stream. Actually, a majority of commonly used surgical instruments are based on the hemostat "scissors" principle of two hinged, connected metal arms of various lengths and with sundry tips, edges and shapes. They are used for grabbing tissue, blood vessels and organs (and occasionally the assistant's glove to get his attention).

Instruments are often not used by surgeons in the manner most laypersons might imagine. A specific surgical instrument in competent hands becomes an extension of the surgeon's fingers, a projection of his nervous system. Touch and feel form the foundation of delicate dissection. Different skills are needed for laparoscopic surgery for this reason, and not all surgeons possess them.

In open surgery the surgeon relies on his experience with normal tissue, as well as disease processes such as inflammation and the alteration of tissue caused by it. For example:

• The ever-mentioned scalpel plays a minor role in most operations (used to open or cut the skin and soft tissues; now done more often with

A close-up view of the surgical instrument tray.

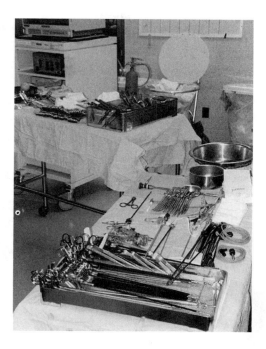

cautery to avoid sharp instrument use (because of the threat of HIV and hepatitis infection).

• The surgeon's fingers perform as much of most procedures as almost any other "instrument" (so-called *blunt dissection* is safer than sharp cutting of tissues and sets up the use of scissors, cautery, etc. by exposing structures).

• Many instruments are used in a manner for which they were not designed (blunt dissection with the end of the forceps, blunt dissection with the nonblade end of the scalpel, dissecting with a hemostat rather than using it to grab tissue, "picking" at tissue with the scissor blades closed).

Also, contrary to a commonly held concept of surgery, procedures are not entirely performed by a surgeon while the assistant passively positions instruments and retracts for exposure. Properly performed surgery requires two or more people working in concert and aware of each other's role, each individual cognizant of her well-defined responsibilities and each person paying attention to detail—not just to the assigned task.

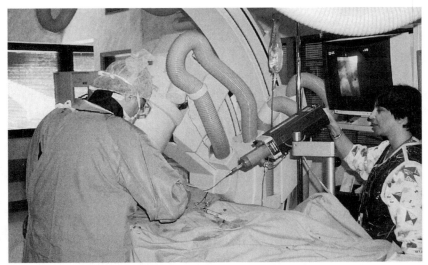

An angiographer prepares to do an angioplasty. To the right is a power injector.

The Surgical Assistant

Surgery is a team sport.

Smaller operations don't always require this high level of cooperation, and in fact the surgeon may elect to not have an assistant for such procedures as hernia repair, breast biopsy, D&C and hardware placement and removal. But major surgery can't be done single-handedly. Sure, surgeons differ in how they employ their help. Some surgeons say "Here . . . hold this," and proceed to ignore the assistant until the retractor is shifted to a new location—where the order is repeated.

Good surgeons engage their assistants.

To give you a sense of where conflict may arise in the process of performing an operation, we will consider a few basic ideas that serve as the most crucial aspects of what a surgeon must be thinking as he completes a dissection. To highlight the cooperative nature of surgery, we will look at it from the assistant's point of view. For example, regardless of specialty, assistant surgeons must adhere to the following maneuvers in order to perform safe surgery.

• Tissue must be placed on traction by the assistant and the surgeon before being cut to avoid excess damage or to avoid cutting the wrong structure.

- Exposure requires the assistant to retract body cavity walls, position overhead lights and stay out of the surgeon's way.
- The assistant must anticipate the surgeon's next move in order to make the procedure a seamless event.
- The assistant must perform certain parts of the procedure because it is easier from the assistant's position.
- Several skills must be employed at the same time by the surgeon and the assistant with sharp instruments without injuring each other.
- The assistant must know when *not* to move so as to not jeopardize the maneuver or get cut.
- The assistant must know which instruments to ask for and when.
- The assistant must learn when to keep his mouth shut when things are going badly.
- The assistant must know when to speak up if he sees that something is not right, knowing the surgeon doesn't see it and realizing the surgeon isn't going to be happy to be informed of the problem.

We will address the psychological and emotional aspects of the operating room and the sort of conflict some of the issues mentioned above may create. The interactions go beyond the surgeon and his assistant.

The Physical Design of an Operating Room

Operating rooms are designed for safety and efficiency. Tile and linoleum cover walls and floors, permitting swift cleansing with antiseptic solutions between cases. The centerpiece of the OR is a narrow table. It may be mechanically or electrically operated and is capable of adapting to the positions required for different operations.

Large electrical outlets are available on walls or as part of special columns which drop down from the ceiling and also contain anesthetic gases, oxygen and suction. Wall cabinets are built in and contain all of the needed equipment not included on the case cart. The case cart is rolled into the room for a specific case and contains the instruments and sutures necessary for that type of case. The usual generic equipment such as razors, tape and gauze is kept in the wall cabinets; most of the specific equipment arrives with the case cart.

An anesthesia machine sits at the head of the OR table and is connected to the overhead gas sources by color-coded hoses, as well as being connected to a (separate from surgery) suction source. At least two huge overhead, multibulb operating lights hover over the table. Stainless steel tables remain in the room and serve the scrub tech's needs when covered with sterile towels.

Outside the operating room are scrub sinks and sterilization equipment (the major sterilization machines are in a central processing area away from but connected to the main OR).

Overview of the Surgical Area

The following sections provide an overview of the surgical area, including pre-op, the OR, and post-surgery-anesthesia recovery areas. These sections describe what is seen, heard, smelled and experienced as one moves through these areas.

The Pre-Operative Holding Unit

Usually a large room with cubicles created by curtains, the pre-op holding area is the staging zone for the OR. It contains:

- large doors at the unit's entry for stretchers
- multiple U-shaped curtain runs on the ceiling with hanging curtains that may be used to encircle each stretcher ("walk-ins" now mount their stretchers)
- rollaway tables where the anesthesiologist reviews the chart, nurses check operative permits and other information, and surgeons re-read the history and physical exam
- multiple wall blood pressure cuffs
- overhead monitors
- storage cabinets with sheets, towels, IVs, etc.
- a workstation with a phone and a posted list of the OR cases for the day
- a posted list of today's patients, their doctors and pre-op holding slot numbers
- special pediatric pre-op with toys, wall pictures of cartoon characters, etc.
- emergency crash cart
- a covey of nurses getting all of the pre-op details together

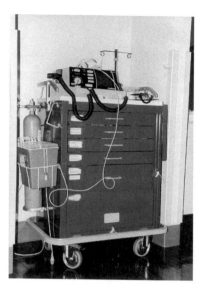

A red crash cart contains all the drugs, needles, airway and cardiac defibrillator for treating an acute cardiac arrest.

The Operating Room Corridors

The patient's stretcher is rolled from pre-op holding down the hall to the operating room to which that patient was assigned. The anesthesiologist pushes the stretcher while the surgeon performs last-minute housekeeping duties such as phone calls and checking with the scrub tech about special instruments. As the stretcher rolls from pre-op holding, the following scene will pass by; let's assume you are the patient and *you see*:

• At the front desk sits a secretary, a nurse and anesthesiologists waiting for their surgeons.

• The "big board" is inscribed with the day's cases listed by room, patient, procedure, anesthesiologist, scrub tech and circulating nurse.

• Down the corridor, as other stretchers pass you going to the PACU, circulating nurses rush by with arms full of equipment; scrub techs move from one room to another to relieve each other for lunch or to go on break.

• You move past stretchers parked outside of rooms where surgeons are at work.

• You pass stainless steel case carts parked outside of rooms.

• You recoil at soiled laundry carts from just-finished cases.

• You move past alcoves where scrub sinks are manned by surgeons and techs talking about anything but the operation about to start, where

---

Equipment in a Special Hospital Unit

MAJOR TO SHORT-STAY SURGERY, ENDOSCOPY, SPECIAL PROCEDURES, DELIVERY ROOMS

- a central operating room table, X-ray table or stretcher
- overhead or side lights
- a monitor with EKG, pulse, blood pressure, O^2 saturation
- rollaway carts with equipment and supplies
- wall cabinets with equipment, laundry, instruments, sutures
- special storage for scopes
- a suction system with hoses and a floor unit with disposable plastic "bucket" receptacles
- a sink; sometimes a scrub sink
- an oxygen source with masks and tubing
- a cautery unit with leg pad, wires, probe
- laundry and hazardous wastes hampers

---

a computer may be mounted on a small table and a wall phone is available.

- The sounds of the individual rooms are not heard—the doors are closed: Instead *you hear* the intercom and the paging system and the rattle of metal containers and used instruments as scrub techs gather soiled kits and roll the used case carts back to a central sterile processing area; voices are muted except in rooms where the doors are open, the case done and the radio notably loud.

- The *smells* in the corridor shift as you progress to your OR; disinfectant, perfume, the stench of a bowel case.

- In the room reserved for emergencies, a bloated body lies on the OR table, the room empty of personnel, the floor a bloodscape of clots and smears, the anesthesia machine mute; it is the night's trauma victim, a gunshot to the belly who died ten minutes earlier; the surgeon is in the lounge talking with the medical examiner, the others grabbing a cup of coffee before the cleanup begins; your anesthesiologist wishes they hadn't left the door open.

You arrive at the door to your operating room.

The Operating Room

As you roll into the operating room, a tangle of equipment seems to surround the dominant central item: the OR table. It is narrow with black plastic cushions that feel cold and firm on your back and buttocks when you are instructed to scoot over from your parallel-parked stretcher. Overhead, scooped-out lights glare down at you.

Operating Room Sights

The operating room contains the following equipment:

- *Double doors* for patient entry on a stretcher.
- *Side door* with small window for personnel entry; your surgeon backs into the door and enters the OR with arms in the air to avoid touching anything unsterile.
- *Windows* over a scrub sink permit a view of the operating room. May be covered if the patient is a VIP.
- *The operating room table* with a large base, a narrow surface with black plastic cushions, and an electronic or manual control system to position the feet or head.
- *Special brackets* on the ceiling for huge articulating arms and attached platforms holding TV screens and other laparoscopic equipment; can be swung near OR table during "lap" cases or left against the wall for open surgery.
- The ceiling may have *hollow metal columns as conduits* for hoses for oxygen and anesthetic gases, and banks of electrical outlets for equipment.
- The walls have *built-in cabinets* with glass doors for supplies; bandages, sutures, instruments, tape, thermometers, etc.
- A wall will have an *erase board* (white) with a holder for felt-tipped color pens and an erasure brush; used for the sponge, needle and instrument counts, notes, patient and doctor's phone numbers and reminders.
- A wall will have double-panel *X-ray viewing boxes* for examining mammograms, orthopedic films, chest X rays, CT scans, skull X rays, etc.
- An *intercom* connected to the front desk and pathology.
- A *sharps receptacle* (mounted plastic box) with a one-way fliptop for all needles, syringes, scalpel blades, etc.
- *Stainless steel tables*, covered by sterile sheets, on which the instruments and equipment are placed during surgery.
- *Case cart* with instruments and equipment is rolled into room, un-

loaded and rolled out in hall to be used to return soiled materials to the central sterilization area.

- *Storage bins* on wheels with extra or specialty instruments and equipment for a particular case.
- *Stainless steel desk* with a computer, phone and radio; a place where the circulating nurse can write in chart, document the case, etc.
- *Chair* on wheels for desk.
- *Stools on wheels* for scrub tech and surgeons to sit during delays.
- *Pyxis medication station*; requires code access to withdraw drugs.
- *Cautery unit*, often blue with setting for *cutting* and *cautery* or a blend chosen by the surgeon; wire attaches to unit from sterile field.
- *Suction apparatus* consisting of hoses from wall or ceiling to a wheel-based unit with four plastic disposable receptacles (buckets) to hold blood or other body fluids removed from the surgical field.
  (**NOTE:** *Any connecting devices* such as wires for cautery, laparoscopic cords, catheters, suction tubing, etc., that must go from the sterile field to an unsterile machine in the room *always* are sterilized and included in the surgical kit; the scrub tech hands off the connectors to the circulator, who plugs them in to the appropriate equipment.)
- *Electrical outlets*—often a bank of several in a wall or overhead metal column from the ceiling that delivers suction, anesthetic gases, etc.
- *Compression boots*—actually disposable plastic inflatable wraps that encircle the patient's calves and expand at regular intervals to milk blood from the leg veins to avoid phlebitis (deep vein clotting); they are connected by hoses to a machine (often mounted with the cautery machine) that intermittently pumps air into the boots.
- *IV poles* on wheels.
- A *Mayo stand*—a small tray that slips under the OR table with a tray at foot of bed; covered with sterile drapes and holds only selected instruments used repeatedly during a case; avoids scrub having to constantly turn his back on the surgeon to find an instrument.
- *Laundry hamper and hazardous wastes hampers* with special red plastic bags.
- *Anesthesia machine* with monitors and screens, dials and columns for inhalation agents (gases), drawers with equipment—and lots of bells and whistles.

- *Anesthesia cart* with more equipment, stacks of bags of IV fluid, syringes, emesis basins, gauze, endotracheal tubes, special video laryngoscope for difficult intubations, etc.
- *Metal frames holding large metal basins* used by surgeons to wash their gloves or deposit large surgical specimens when first removed from the body—instead of handing the specimen to the scrub tech.

Operating Room Odors

Standing in the operating room, the staff smell nothing unless a terrible case with dead tissue is underway. In that instance, knowing they are dealing with black, necrotic intestine or a dead leg, the OR folks unconsciously begin to mouth-breathe, thus bypassing their delicate nasal olfactory end-organs!

However, a visitor might be aware of any of the following *operating room odors:*

- Various antiseptic agents that constitute the *hospital smell*, including alcohol, formalin, iodofor and detergents and floor cleaning products.
- The adhesive *benzoin*, which possesses a pungent, not unpleasant odor of cleanliness.
- *Blood*, which gives the odor of a meat factory if spilled over the drapes and onto the floor in large quantities.
- *Urine*, which has its own characteristic smell.
- *Dead bowel*, particularly if perforated ("burst"), challenges the most seasoned OR staff; fecal stench floods the room, and the circulator attempts to help by opening an air freshener; at times, the anesthesiologist and anyone else not scrubbed in just leave the room.
- Pus is formed by tissue debris, bacteria and white blood cells and issues various odors, the worst of which is feculent in character.
- Unwashed body odor from any staff who are either lazy or come from cultures less obsessive than Americans about body cleanliness and showering.
- A hint of perfume or deodorant may reassure everyone that all is well in their operating room world.

Operating Room Touch

The idea of touch in the operating room is basically to learn what *not* to touch. The sterile field is defined by sterile drapes and a zone around the OR table that has no clearcut boundaries. But everyone knows how to avoid contamination by not touching anything near the field.

Operating Room Sounds

What is heard in the OR depends to a very large degree on just how well the case is going. As described previously, the operating room is a place of many moods—most of them established by the operating surgeon. The mood in the OR is thus reflected in what people say and how they say it. There are other sounds in the operating room as well.

The following *sounds* may be heard individually or all at once in a cacophony of seeming confusion:

• *Discussions of the anesthesiologist* with nurse anesthetist or resident; may become mildly frantic if the case becomes difficult.

• *Voice of the surgical team* asking for instruments; may be single requests or a mumble of several requests delivered all at once; may be social exchanges, golf scores or Wall Street jabber; may cut suddenly to demands for more or special instruments if the case goes awry.

• *Patients talking* if under sedation and local anesthetic; may get verbose and bold, call the surgeon by his first name, etc.

• Scrub tech and circulator *voices* at the beginning and the end of the case counting instruments, needles and sponges and asking questions if the counts aren't correct.

• *Suction* sounds occur throughout a big case, intermittently drowning out voices.

• *Laser* zapping sounds and "off–on" commands punctuate laser surgery.

• *Cautery* makes a buzzing sound as it is turned off and on by a button mounted on the probe; cutting and cautery have slightly different sounds.

• A *dermatome* (used to take skin grafts) makes a loud high-pitched whine from a rapidly oscillating blade.

• *Monitors* beep incessantly, and occasionally an *alarm* will sound from the anesthesia machine.

• *Metallic clinks of instruments* striking each other as a scrub tech removes them from the metal carrier on the back table.

• *Radio* or *CDs* with anything from country to classical music and everything in between; may be soft and contemplative or loud and boisterous.

The Scrub Sink Alcove

Usually set between operating rooms, the scrub sinks are against the wall containing a window to the OR, which permits the surgeon to view the room setup as she scrubs. But no place in the hospital is free of equipment debris, and other surgical materiel finds its way into this space. Some of the equipment is placed here by design, including:

- a large autoclave for sterilizing instruments between cases; not the main sterilization area
- a stainless steel "warmer" to heat saline solutions that will be used in surgery; must be warm, not hot
- scrub sinks with faucets that have either automatic, panel or kickarm "off–on" control
- boxes of masks, scrub brushes, a soiled linen hamper, a mirror, mops and buckets used to clean the floor between cases and gallons of detergent
- a *Steris system* for sterilization for delicate scopes, etc.
- metal storage shelves for various equipment such as suction canisters, glove boxes, mask boxes, sheets and towels
- a rack for lead aprons to be used to protect techs, the circulator and surgeons when fluoroscopy is used during surgery
- a rack holding oxygen tanks

From the operating room the patient next is wheeled, in a state of profound residual sedation from anesthesia, to the PACU—the postanesthesia care unit. The PACU and its staff have one task: to look for acute life-threatening events and treat them before they cause harm.

Thus, in the PACU as in the pre-op holding area, there are stations or cubicles created by curtains for large numbers of patients, all of whom are being monitored with zeal. The *PACU setup* includes:

- walls with sets of monitors recording the patient's EKG, blood pressure, pulse and oxygen saturation; shelves with emergency equipment
- suction equipment for each slot
- a nearby crash cart for a CODE BLUE
- central desk for telephones, computer, radio, etc.
- a Pyxis medication station—code access
- additional desks with computers and phones for doctors and nurses

- one or two isolation rooms for critically ill post-op patients or anyone with a serious infection requiring isolation
- storage bins on wheels with IV bags, IV tubing, catheters, syringes, Foley catheters, etc.
- storage bins for sheets, towels, soap, etc.
- sinks and a refrigerator

The typical postoperative patient will have the same appearance regardless of the operation. Vital functions are monitored in a similar fashion for all surgery patients. When the patient arrives in the PACU, the following steps are followed:

- The anesthesiologist rolls the patient into a slot indicated by the PACU nurse.
- The EKG leads are attached to the PACU monitor.
- If extubated, a face mask with oxygen is placed.
- Any nasogastric tubes are placed on suction.
- Foley catheters are checked for function and a recording of IV fluid *intake*, and NG tube, Foley catheter and any other drain or tube *output* are calculated and recorded (this will be continued throughout the post-op recovery period on the surgical floor).
- Surgical bandages are checked for security of tape and drainage.
- The patient's level of consciousness is checked frequently.
- The patient's pain level is carefully checked, and additional medication is administered as needed.
- When the patient is deemed alert and stable, he is transferred to a regular surgical floor, an intermediate care area (more monitoring than a regular floor but less than the ICU) or to the intensive care unit.
- Some critically ill surgical patients bypass the PACU and are taken directly to the ICU and usually intubated on a ventilator.

SPD—The Sterile Processing Department

Case carts are returned to SPD after each case where they are emptied and the instruments are hand-cleaned if needed and resterilized. Workers wearing special glasses, gloves and gowns clean hundreds of surgical instruments and load them into autoclaves, where they are sterilized. Following this process they are repackaged in sterile (interior sterile towels and exterior unsterile wraps) kits that are loaded onto case carts according to the surgeon's *preference card.*

Every surgeon has a card (now a computer sheet) that describes all instruments needed for a specific type of surgery. The following issues summarize how case carts are assembled:

- Basic instruments make up each kit for a given procedure.
- A surgeon may wish to substitute a particular type of forceps or hemostat for the standard instrument in the kit.
- The surgeon may wish to have added numbers of certain instruments.
- The surgeon may request other equipment or medications to be added to his kits.
- The surgeon may have an extra or accessory kit with special instruments, which is either opened routinely for a case or kept in the room to be used as needed.
- The surgeon may request additional instruments, such as large vascular clamps in anticipation of possible massive bleeding, for a particularly difficult case.
- For some emergency operations the circulating nurse and scrub tech may have to ask the surgeon just what kind of kit she needs, as the booking and list on the big board may not make the exact nature of the operation clear.

The OR Locker Room

Professional athletes can't hold a candle to the sloppiness seen in the OR locker room. Surgeons and other OR staff toss scrubs, masks, shoe covers and caps all over the floor and walk away, whether they won or lost the case. There's a real atmosphere of entitlement in the OR locker room. Any of the following aspects of the locker room may be observed on a given day:

- rows of double lockers, too small for street clothes in many cases
- benches or stools
- an autovalet for card access to scrubs (pants and tops of various sizes)
- a second return machine next to the autovalet for soiled scrubs— card access; if not returned, the cardholder is told by the machine he is out of credit
- in locker rooms with scrubs stacked on shelves, dirty scrubs tend to

accumulate on the floor along with discarded masks, shoe covers and caps
- shelves at the exit door with caps, masks and shoe covers
- large X-ray envelopes may be found leaning against a wall or on a stool
- reprints of scientific articles may lie on benches or stools
- a toilet facility with showers; toilets and sinks also collect masks and caps and towels
- an (understandably) grumpy housekeeping person cleaning up after the teams

Finally, the patient might *feel* most of the following sensations as she lies on the operating room table:
- fear of the unknown, seeing the hardware of the OR
- the cold impersonal cushion beneath one's body
- the narrow table edges and restraining band across one's thighs
- arms outstretched on arm boards with an IV in one and an oxygen saturation monitor on a finger or thumb
- blood pressure cuff automatically inflating impersonally
- oxygen mask over face, smothering
- perhaps legs in stirrups, personal anatomy exposed
- after a spinal, legs up or spread with no sensation, loss of control and apprehension about possible permanent paralysis

There's a difference in the operating room environment and mood between smaller elective cases and larger emergency operations. In the emergency situation you would see:
- the surgeon and anesthesiologist moving more quickly, a sense of urgency in their actions
- more commands for things rather than requests
- more personnel in the room for both teams
- more IVs running, blood hanging and running into patient
- more machines such as the "cell saver"; the open-heart bypass machine if needed
- more tubes in the patient, including Foley, CVP, Swan-Ganz heart catheter and arterial line, as well as endotracheal and nasogastric

tubes (It is said you are truly sick if the number of tubes inserted exceeds the number of your natural orifices.)

Specialty Operating Rooms

Each surgical specialty has slightly different needs.

For example, urologists use a lot of water to irrigate the bladder, and visualize the inside of the bladder with fiberoptic cystoscopes. Urologic surgeons wear rubber aprons in an attempt to remain dry during surgery. They also need immediate access to fluoroscopy to take X rays, and thus have a fixed fluoroscopy unit set up with the operating room table. And they often operate sitting down.

Orthopedic surgeons who perform total joint replacement procedures wear huge helmets and special gowns to eliminate any chance of infection. If a joint becomes infected, the hardware must be removed and the procedure must be repeated at a later date. Air exchange occurs on average fifteen times an hour in most operating rooms, but occurs more often in the orthopedic rooms.

Ophthalmologic surgeons and some other specialists use the laser and need well-trained nurses and special equipment to perform their operations. In fact, the laser has only a few applications in surgery. Cryosurgery is also used in cancer surgery, and these special units must be wheeled into the OR for each case. Harmonic scalpels require a special unit, and all laparoscopic surgery necessitates cameras, TV screens, insufflation equipment and extra personnel to hold the camera for the surgeons.

Neurosurgeons use an operating microscope, which is bulky and again requires special personnel and attention to detail during delicate operations. Some oncology surgeons will employ intraoperative radiation treatments, and the equipment must be rolled into an operating room large enough to accommodate it, or be set up with a permanent fixture.

Finally, minimally invasive surgery has transformed abdominal surgery by making access less traumatic, with tiny incisions for trocars through which are placed instruments and a telescope with a camera. Visualization of organs thus is a matter of indirectly viewing them on a TV screen. TV screens mounted on brackets or on rollaway carts fill the OR room even further. Chest and vascular surgery also may be done employing minimally invasive techniques.

> ## *Levels of Urgency in Booking Surgery*
> **ELECTIVE SURGERY** booked days or weeks in advance
> **ADD-ON CASES** to be done within twenty-four hours
> **EMERGENCIES** to be done within two to four hours if possible
> **EMERGENCIES** to be done when *next available OR room* opens
> **DIRE EMERGENCIES** to be done as soon as the patient arrives in the OR

Surgical Bookings

Before anyone is rolled to the operating room, the case must be booked ahead of time. This is done in a number of ways depending on the acuteness of the case.

ELECTIVE CASES require the surgeon's secretary to book the case—and many others like it—days or weeks before surgery. The hospital's booking agent and the surgeon's secretary scan their books while they talk on the phone and set up a complete operating schedule for a given day weeks in advance.

Between now and then the secretary may have to arrange for an assistant (another surgeon with his own schedule and booking problems), cancel the case because the patient needs a formal cardiac, pulmonary or renal clearance, or rearrange the whole day so the biggest case is first or last. Or fit in a professional hockey player's hernia repair before the Stanley Cup playoffs.

Hell *is* the details of an OR schedule.

ADD-ON CASES are next in urgency—surgery that must be done that day, or the next day at the very latest. These cases may be fractures that must be set and casted or pinned, lacerations of the face or hands involving tendons, and laparoscopic gallbladder surgery for someone whose pain recurs and won't go away—or wait until the booked time. These cases are typically fit into the daily surgery schedule when the surgery in a room is done or if cases are canceled at the last moment.

EMERGENCY cases vary with the degree of urgency and thus the time it takes to get to the operating room. Acute appendicitis—without perforation, shock or wildly out-of-control infection (sepsis)—must be done within about two to four hours, if possible. A perforated ulcer goes to the next available room. A ruptured aortic aneurysm or severe trauma such as a stab wound to the heart—if not operated on in the Emergency Center—

often arrives in the OR following a curt phone call during which the surgeon announces, "We're coming down with a _____!"

In extreme cases time is not negotiable.

Bumping Booked Surgical Cases

You have a case of acute appendicitis booked. They say you'll go at about six P.M. I call the OR with a perforated intestine. In shock. Got to go now! What happens when the hysterectomy in Room Four closes?

I *bump* you.

It means my patient is sicker than yours and is in danger of becoming even more unstable. The procedure is for the nurse at the desk to inform you you're being bumped. "You can't bump me!" you scream. And you make up some malarkey about how your patient is becoming septic—things have changed since you booked the case. No, you certainly cannot be bumped. Not tonight.

After all, you've got executive box tickets to a basketball game that starts at 7:30. The Knicks are playing the Celtics. But you get bumped anyway.

More gray area? You bet. And at this point the anesthesiologist assigned to run the OR schedule for the day steps in and referees. He asks questions and defines whose patient is really in trouble. And, of course, a patient in the ER in shock with a perforated viscus goes first. You miss dinner and the first period of Boston versus New York.

BUMPING Getting the sickest patient under the knife the quickest. Personalities flare and eventually simmer. Most of the time the order of surgery is the correct one. Occasionally lying takes over, as sad it is to admit. Surgeons know how to bend, mold, squash, elongate, taper, flatten and cudgel the truth.

Most surgeons accept the reality of the bumping process and realize it will all balance out over the course of twenty-five or thirty years. You watch the second half of the game on the TV in the surgeon's lounge.

The Rituals of Surgery

The operating room is a magical place where no one works unless they have paid their dues. And their dues include mastering a lot of rituals, many of which make sense. Once a member of the clan, OR people cher-

> ## *Instrument, Sponge and Needle Counts in the OR*
> - Three counts are done—before the operation begins, before the body cavity is closed and after the major layer (fascia) of the cavity is closed.
> - A fourth count is performed for surgery done on a "cavity within a cavity"; e.g., opening the urinary bladder.
> - For smaller cases, sponge counts are not required.
> - Counts are for prep sponges, operative sponges, sharps (needles, blades, etc.) and instruments.

ish their uniqueness, as well they should. They are in a position to help a lot of sick people through a difficult treatment: surgery. To get to this professional position they have no doubt suffered many fools, some of whom would be more effective employed in the laundry.

Each separate surgical ritual must be learned and followed precisely be-cause—it's impossible to argue this reality—repeating the same drill over and over and making certain everyone does it the same way results in the best outcomes. Even so, some of the people following these rules are unable to function outside of the checklist "box." Recently, the following remark-able scenario occurred to one of the authors (DWP) and will challenge your sense of credulity: After an abdominal operation, a clip applicator (a large scissors-like instrument about eight inches long) was missing when the in-strument count was performed, even though *it was never used* on the case and never (theoretically) left the scrub tech's table—or wasn't there in the first place. Policy mandated that an abdominal X ray be taken while the patient was still on the OR table to search for this nonexistent instrument.

An equally absurd request for a post-op X ray occurs when three of a particular instrument are counted at the end of a case, when there were only *two* at the time the case started. Where did the third instrument come from? The X ray was ordered to look for a fourth instrument. Why? Do they always come in sets of two? Were we again seeking an instrument that never existed?

Are these rituals ridiculous? Not at all.

To provide the most good for the largest number of people, certain rules and procedures must be followed to avoid repetitive errors. How-ever, a situation often arises when the checkup procedures seem absurd and someone with common sense must intervene.

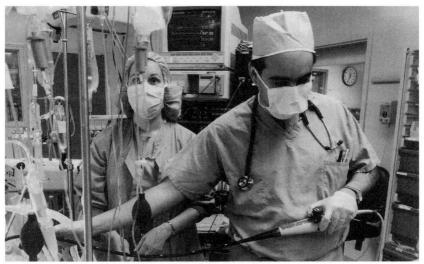

Anesthesiologists attend to dozens of IV lines and pumps during surgery. The cardiac telemetry monitor is shown at the top center of the photograph.

Important rituals direct the operating room team's behavior, and we'll examine more of them now.

First, let's trace the steps of the individual members of the surgical team as they move through a typical case. Procedures and unwritten rules of conduct will be mentioned from various points of view. Each person experiences the operating room from a different vantage point and from a specific position of authority (or lack of it).

The surgeon isn't the only important member of the operating room team.

The Anesthesiologist

Presumably because surgery evolved over many years without the need—or should we say availability—of proper anesthesia, surgeons have always labored under the delusion that they were in charge of the operating room. And, in fact, for many years surgeons administered anesthesia as well as performed operations. But once the doctor (anesthesiologist) at the head of the table commanded better anesthetic agents and improved monitoring equipment, the surgeon was left with no reasonable choice but to cooperate. After all, the anesthesiologist is a superb clinical pharmacologist.

Not all surgeons saw it that way.

To this day, ego-encumbered surgeons still don't get it, and miss the point that the anesthesiologist has total control of the patient—and to a very large degree determines the success of the operation. No doubt many anesthesiologists nod their agreement rather than speaking when the surgeon glances up at the EKG monitor and says something incredibly stupid such as, "Is she getting enough oxygen?" This to a physician who knows more about oxygen transport than the surgeon understands about tying square knots.

Of course, most surgeons work in harmony with their anesthesia brethren, and the patient benefits from this synergy. Still, there are times when things go badly and everyone lashes out at someone else. In surgery, there is *always* someone to blame. For example, it is not unheard of to observe a surgeon whose gown is dripping crimson who insists, "No, we're not losing much blood down here. What's the problem up there?"

"Up there" behind the screen of sterile sheets which separates the surgeon from the anesthesiologist, the anesthesiologist is counting sponges with the circulator and noting the amount of bloody suction fluid. Indeed, the patient has lost significant blood—despite the surgeon's denials.

The anesthesiologist's day often begins even earlier than that of the surgeon. In his assigned OR room, he checks out the drugs he will use, the anesthesia machine with its intricate piping, valves, dials and monitors, the prehung IV lines and bags of fluid. He prepares his intubation instruments and his other supplies, and then goes to the holding area and meets his patient.

In the pre-anesthesia holding area the anesthesiologist reads the patient's history and asks about the upcoming surgery to test the patient's understanding of what is to occur. He may order a sedative for the patient at this point (and wish he could slip one to the surgeon). When the surgeon has talked with his patient—assuming the surgeon does this; they're all different—the anesthesiologist wheels the stretcher to the room and, with the help of the circulating nurse and an orderly (now often called an *OR assistant*), transfers the patient onto the OR table.

As the anesthesiologist places a mask on the patient's face and administers oxygen and more sedative, the scrub tech arranges instruments on her back table. Earlier, she stood at the scrub sink, tore open a prepack-

---

The Operating Room Assistant's Job
- help to set up cases with regard to cleaning the room, getting equipment, etc.
- help bring the patient in the room and transfer onto the OR table
- hold the patient for a spinal or epidural
- shave the surgical area or hold arms or legs for surgical preps while an assistant washes and paints extremity with antiseptic solution
- serve as a runner for emergency supplies for surgeon and anesthesiologist
- clean and restock anesthesia machine (often a designated individual)
- scrub and hold camera for laparoscopic cases
- at the end of the case, transport patient to PACU, making sure safety strap, side rails and blankets are in place
- mop floor and wash walls for next case

---

aged scrub brush and peered through the OR window, wondering what sort of mood the surgeon would be in today.

An OR assistant may be required to hold the patient for a spinal anesthetic. This means the assistant stands beside the OR table, holding the patient and helping to keep the patient curled up in a ball in order to open the intervertebral space the anesthesiologist is seeking with a needle from the opposite side of the patient.

The Scrub Technician

Beginning with her fingers, the scrub tech swirls soap up her knuckles, wrist and forearm, stopping at her elbow. The brush has a sponge side filled with antiseptic soap and a brush side for scrubbing the skin. She works her way up the other arm, shifting the brush to the opposite hand, circling down to her hand again and rinsing—and then scrubbing some more. This ritual lasts at least five minutes and is repeated for each subsequent case.

The old scrub sinks—and no doubt those still in operation in small community hospitals—use arm bars on the faucets or a knee bar or automatic kickpad below the sink, all of which are designed to turn on the water. "No hands, Ma. Got to keep' em sterile." In a modern operating room the water switches on as soon as an electronic eye senses the scrub tech's, or surgeon's, hands under the faucet.

Consider: The water used by the operating team comes from the city water supply and isn't sterile . . . and the surgeon uses an antiseptic . . . when does the scrubbed skin *become* sterile? It doesn't. It's just *really* clean. It's one of many dilemmas with what we call *sterile technique*.

Dripping soap and water, the scrub tech enters the operating room through a side door, fanny first and hands held up, and crosses the OR to her tables and removes a sterile towel waiting there for her. The circulating nurse helped her set it up beforehand. With her hands dry, the tech picks up her folded gown, shakes it loose and dons it, followed by her gloves. The tech knows how to pick up, open and don sticky gloves without help, an impressive little ritual.

Before and after surgery, the scrub tech has a number of duties:
- arrive ahead of the surgeon and check his preference card (often a computer printout sheet) for any special requests for instruments or sutures
- with the case cart in the room, check all components (sterile bundles) to make certain all required instruments and other equipment are present
- get additional instruments, sutures or other special requests from the central supply area or have them brought to the room
- scrub, glove and gown; open the sterile kit (bundles) containing the instruments and count them, making certain all instruments are, in fact, there
- identify any instruments in need of repair, mark them and hand them off to the circulator
- glove and gown the surgeon and assistant
- complete the case (see list of intraoperative duties below)
- after patient leaves the OR room, place all soiled drapes in laundry hamper and place instruments on case cart and return it to the central sterile processing area
- prepare for the next case

From the beginning to the end of the case the scrub tech's job during surgery includes:
- handing instruments to the surgeon and the assistant, who are looking into body cavity, not at her, and with open hands expect the

right instrument at the right time—even if they only mumble something that approximates the instrument's name

- asking the circulating nurse for suture material, devices to be used, additional instruments, more sponges, saline, etc., before the surgeon realizes he wants or needs it
- retract for the surgeon when an extra hand is needed, as well as still loading handles with scalpel blades, mounting sutures on needle holders, passing the surgeons sponges—doing it all with one hand
- accepting tissue specimens for pathology, placing them in proper containers or handing them off to the circulator—while still retracting
- working in close with the surgeon without protective equipment
- standing tall when things go badly and the surgeon is finished abusing the anesthesiologist and his assistant

When the case is over, the scrub tech removes soiled sheets, suction tubing and cautery wires from the patient and places them in the trash or in a hamper in the corner while the wornout surgical team stretches and checks the bandages. Moments earlier, she joined the circulating nurse and completed the last instrument, sponge and needle count. The surgeons depart to relieve themselves and enjoy a cup of coffee, but the circulating nurse and scrub tech continue to clean up, joined now by the OR assistants.

When the surgeon exits to talk to the family, the scrub tech, circulating nurse, anesthesiologist and OR assistants begin the ritual of preparing the room for the next case. The doors are closed now and, as the odor of disinfectant fills the air, they talk about the case and the surgeon.

Some surgeons hire a private scrub tech. The reasons are obvious. Because the interaction between the tech and the surgeon is crucial to the success of the case, some surgeons prefer to solidify this part of their day. Others are lucky enough to have a tech who scrubs with them on a regular basis, a tech who knows the surgeon's every move and requests even before the surgeon asks for something!

The Circulating Nurse
The circulating nurse coordinates the flow of instruments, equipment and personnel in the OR. A registered nurse, who no doubt belongs

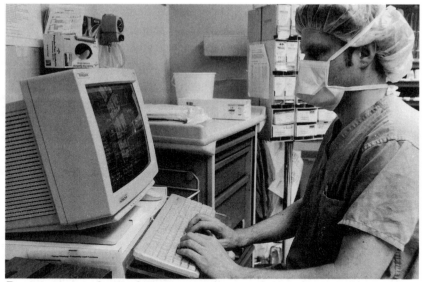

During surgery, the circulating nurse will get needed supplies such as sutures or drains from the supply area. They can also obtain drugs from the computerized Pyxis machine which dispenses drugs.

to the Association of Operating Room Nurses, she is the ambulatory equivalent of the scrub tech. Anything that must be done in the room or retrieved from elsewhere in the OR falls to the circulator. She must understand sutures, instruments, asepsis, procedures, techniques, terminology and the fine art of juggling egos.

The circulating nurse may have to keep three or four inflated egos in the air at any one moment. At the same time she must observe literally *everything* that goes on, including watching for potential breaks in sterile technique, retrieving fallen instruments (which must be re-sterilized) and noting the need for more IV fluid, blood, drugs and anything else the anesthesiologist may demand. At her very best, the circulating nurse may be seen getting things for *both* the surgeon and the anesthesiologist while juggling a conversation with PACU, the phone cord stretcher and the receiver tucked into her neck.

When all of these duties are completed—actually between running for equipment and counting sponges and changing the setting on the cautery and changing the suction canister and adjusting the laser setting and other chores—the circulating nurse must record all of this information in the patient's chart. In many cases this occurs casually while surgery is performed in relative quiet; in big cases these duties overlap and intersect, creating a matrix of havoc.

The circulator wears gloves, mask, gown and protective eye gear and handles bloody sponges, towels, dead legs, smelly colon specimens and containers of all manner of body fluids—and also must occasionally mop up excessive floor puddles before the end of the case (before the orderlies arrive).

In a real sense the circulating nurse—in tandem with her scrub tech associate—engineers the success of the day in the operating room.

Rules of Conduct in the Operating Room

Many written and unwritten rules govern behavior in the operating room. Procedural issues, which are carefully spelled out, include how to scrub, how to handle body fluids and parts, all aspects of antisepsis (reducing bacteria and other infectious agents) and asepsis (eliminating bacteria, etc.). With the advent of the era of frequent HIV and hepatitis infections in the patient population being served, *universal precautions* have been instituted and serve as absolute dogma. No one breaks these rules and remains employed.

What are some of the unwritten understandings that grease the wheels of respect, interaction and efficiency—or lack of them—in the operating room? Perhaps this is the softest and most contentious information in this chapter—and for that reason the most interesting. These suggestions about how people are supposed to behave and how they sometimes do interact should give you considerable insight into the OR culture.

And while ritual rules the operating room environment, behavior is less predictable. Understand our intent in discussing surgeon demeanor in the OR: While most surgeons are proper in their interactions with the staff, a significant number of them behave poorly at regular intervals.

Some operating room rituals are amusing. They don't have to make sense. However, the dictates of professional conduct have to be followed without question in order to keep the OR team functioning smoothly—unless you're the surgeon. And the more junior you are (e.g., a medical student), the more accountable you will be held. The ironclad manifesto, "Because that's how we do it . . ." was no doubt birthed in the operating

The Circulating Nurse's Job

- Admit the patient in pre-op holding.
- Review the chart, the proposed surgery, the side and the expected anesthetic, and obtain permission for the surgery and anesthesia (making certain the signed permits are on the chart).
- Make sure the history, physical exam, labs, EKG, etc., are on the chart.
- Assist in transporting the patient to the OR room, transfer to OR table, arrange sheets, preserve the patient's privacy and assist the anesthesiologist in intubating the patient.
- Expose area of concern, often insert Foley catheter into bladder, prep the skin, place cautery pad on patient's thigh, place compression boots (full-leg sleeves to intermittently squeeze stagnant blood from legs to central circulation) and attach to machine, make certain suction is working and attach cautery wires and suction tubing to appropriate machines after accepting sterile ends from scrub tech.
- Snap back of surgeon and assistant's gowns.
- Check for hair coverage with caps and appropriate masks, help with attaching sterile drapes to IV poles at head of table, adjust cautery setting to surgeon's preference and review scrub tech's back table.
- Start getting last-minute instruments, sutures and new scalpel blades; adjust radio and insert surgeon's favorite CD.
- Record time of starting case, later end of case and all pertinent data; e.g., names of surgeons, assistants, students, name of procedure; handle specimen when removed; and meet all needs of the anesthesiologist for drugs, tubing, etc.
- Replace scrub tech if time or circumstances necessitate tech leaving the case.
- Know all potential disaster drills such as a cardiac arrest, malignant hyperthermia (MH) treatment and location of special crash cart for MH; call for special vascular clamps in cases of unexpected hemorrhage and handle frozen section specimens for immediate pathological evaluation during case.
- At end of case remove soiled drapes with tech, move patient onto stretcher and transport patient to Post-Anesthesia Recovery Unit (PACU).
- During the case handle all communications coming into and leaving the room.
- Return to pre-op holding and introduce herself to the next patient with a smile, no matter how the previous case went.

room. It confirms the unspoken reality in medicine in general that, "Stuff flows downhill."

A surgeon who accidentally touches something unsterile and doesn't recognize his error might not be noticed, but let a medical student bring her hand to within six inches of her face and the scrub tech will scream, "You contaminated yourself! Go out and rescrub!"

The real substance of unwritten OR guidelines involves a lack of substantial challenge of the surgeon's conduct. While the activities of the operating room are coordinated by the anesthesiologist, the actual operation is the surgeon's sole focus. Once skin is cut, the show is on. And what a show it can be!

What confronts a surgeon each time he walks into the operating room? Why is the confrontational nature of this performance so stressful? Why doesn't extensive experience eliminate worry about how the case will proceed *today*? Consider the following aspects of the surgeon's world.

No two operations are the same because . . .

- Every patient's anatomy varies slightly from the previous case.
- The pathological process is never exactly the same.
- These two features combine to produce uncertainty.
- The surgeon must attempt to exclude all distractions from the day, including angst from his personal life.
- Other emergencies may arise during the course of the operation, necessitating the surgeon to provide a plan of treatment while continuing the operation at hand.
- Unexpected bleeding or unexpected additional pathology may require the operation to be prolonged.
- The surgeon has commitments which immediately follow the case; e.g., a full office that was supposed to start thirty minutes ago.
- The surgeon may be ill (a mere cold or sprained ankle won't slow down a surgeon who survived five or more years of hellish training).
- The surgeon may have a personality conflict with the assistant (often assigned to him without choice, if it's a resident).
- The scrub tech and the surgeon may have a history of not getting along, and every instrument may be delivered a fraction of a second too slowly.

A small but persistent segment of the surgical population have earned their reputations as prima donnas because of the arrogance that is often expressed during the good times—at the end of operations that went well. Pleased the stress is over, standing proudly as the conqueror of all of the sundry threats confronting him that day, the surgeon's treatment of the personnel surrounding him implies he did it all himself. Failing to thank the team, he strides out of the OR without detecting that everyone in the room was ever so slightly nauseous.

Still, when things go well, everyone sighs a maskful of relief. And when the self-indulgent surgeon leaves the OR to speak to the family, as the anesthesiologist—who made the surgeon's display of magnificence possible—wakes up the patient, the radio goes back on or the station is changed to rock. Now alone, the tech and nurse really say what they're thinking in the closed room, and the orderlies come in and join the cacophony of pent-up annoyance.

The good guys are more tuned into the people who make their professional lives pleasurable. At the end of a successful case, the scrub tech and circulator may bubble happily because the surgeon was in a good mood and treated them well. Most surgeons are good people. Most operations go smoothly.

Operating room conversations are usually politically correct. At the very least, they are civil. But not always. If you doubt the angst suffered by scrub techs and circulating nurses, you may be interested to know the *very first* thing they do each day is check the big board to discover which surgeon they'll be working with for the next eight to twelve hours. A lot of begging for room changes goes on at 7 A.M.

Surgeons Under Stress

What happens when a surgeon becomes abusive?

The issue of abusive surgeons is a Great Plains of gray. A huge behavioral no-man's land spans the extremes between a cordial demeanor and clearly unacceptable behavior. Even unacceptable behavior is difficult to define. Who is qualified to judge a person fighting for another's life? Especially when something goes abruptly wrong?

Here are a few comments from one of the authors (DWP), who has performed well and badly over twenty-five years of surgical practice. Personal experience with a multitude of difficult cases and observations of one's own mistakes and eventual growth inform this delicate discussion.

Seasoned scrub techs and circulating nurses have seen it all. They know what can happen in a big case where tissue unexpectedly falls apart and won't hold sutures, or when contamination from spilled feces occurs or blood pours out of a huge hole in an artery or vein and the patient's blood pressure suddenly plunges. Or, after a nine-hour vascular bypass graft operation, when the drapes are removed, the patient's foot is cold and pulseless, and the surgeons go out to rescrub and start all over again—and the rest of the OR team scrambles for instruments as the anesthesiologist puts the patient back to sleep.

When a competent surgeon is performing an elective (things are supposed to go well) or in an emergency operation (a high level of stress already exists because the patient is sick to begin with), when something isn't right, even the "good guy" surgeon may become a little unhinged. The people in the room adjust. Everyone tries to do their job just a little faster, a little better.

Even the good guys get rattled at times. It's interesting that the circulator and scrub tech protect this surgeon, even though for those hairy moments he yelled and trampled them a little. At that stressful moment he didn't notice. But at the end of the case he realizes what he's done, what he put the team through, and he apologizes.

The team understands what's involved in those frozen, terrible moments when the surgeon loses control. They forgive him. There is no idle talk about the case. This is the conduct of professionals at their best.

Then there's the insensitive, self-indulgent surgeon with poor impulse control when things go badly. Along comes bad luck, and his case turns into a disaster.

The verbal abuse explodes, over and over, a one-way diatribe of uninterrupted bile. Everyone else keeps quiet. The patient comes first and these unsung heroes—the thousands of scrub techs and circulating nurses in hospitals everywhere—keep this unwritten principle alive.

Until the case is solved. But the surgeon in this instance continues to make unreasonable demands of the OR personnel, yelling and criticizing them even though the danger is over.

After he leaves the OR there is no levity. Only silence and perhaps the soft sound of weeping. This may be followed by a parade to the supervisor's office to fill out incident reports on the surgeon's behavior. And he will do it again.

And he'll get away with it again.

Were those instruments supposed to be on his kit or at least in the room? Did the circulator forget to have them available? Why wasn't he assigned a higher level surgical resident with more experience? Didn't the circulator know where his special sutures are kept? Can you blame him for becoming just a little upset?

How do you separate the slippery elements of this complex interaction when the endpoint may be removing the surgeon's operating privileges? In general most hospitals don't get very far when they tamper with a doctor's privileges.

On the other hand, there is a truly gray area in all of this.

Some surgeons make *every* case a difficult operation, no matter how smoothly it may go. In other words, the surgeon develops a method of absolute control by always being in a state of fury, and that keeps the room unsettled and off balance. The surgeon then calls the shots, as if catastrophe is just around the corner.

With other surgeons the setup for a miserable day in the operating room comes in the form of always finding something wrong. These surgeons aren't as miserable as those insecure souls who sulk and sour the operating room atmosphere with terror. The surgeon who *always* finds something wrong—a fogged laparoscopic camera, the wrong-size needle handed to him, a dull scalpel or a shredded sponge—is more annoying than abrasive.

These surgeons fit Eric Hoffer's adage: Rudeness is the weak man's imitation of strength. This behavior approaches whining.

The operating room may be a crucible for heating up personalities and challenging proper conduct. Anything can happen in the compressed time of major surgery. The imperative to repeatedly perform flawlessly under the stress in this restricted, but public, place highlights the demands imposed on a surgeon.

Distractions During Surgery

The telephone may become a source of annoyance for the surgeon who doesn't establish ground rules about calling into his room. The front desk can't make judgment decisions about which calls are important and which can be logged and ignored. Some surgeons let anyone call in.

Communication Interruptions During Surgery

BEEPERS Some surgeons keep their beepers on, and when they scream (the beeper), the circulator must fish around under the surgeon's gown at belt level to turn it off . . . right! Often residents are required to leave their beepers at the front desk.

TELEPHONE Calls into the room are handled according to the surgeon's wishes; some accept all calls, some are selective.

OVERHEAD PAGING SYSTEM Although not actually in the room, the speakers in the hall outside may carry into the room; not part of the system, although the paging operator will put nurses' and doctors' calls directly through.

INTERCOM Connected to the front desk and to pathology; permits communication between the desk and the surgeon about bookings for the day, emergencies and cancellations, as well as direct communication between surgeon and pathologist regarding frozen (immediate-diagnosis) sections.

Imagine the surgeon and his assistant up to their elbows in intestine when the wall phone rings. The circulator answers it. "Sir, it's your wife . . . your dog is having puppies. She would like to know what to do."

Or: "Doctor, there's a patient in the Emergency Center asking for you."

Or: "Doctor, this is East Six. Your gallbladder from yesterday just spiked to one-oh-three . . ."

Or: "Doctor, your office wants to know how late you're going to be today?"

It is up to the individual physician to determine what sort of interruptions he will tolerate. Some accept only true emergencies. Others actually talk with their stockbrokers during complex surgery.

Different people may wander into the room during surgery.

Another nurse may be looking for an instrument for the surgeon next door. Or she may want to ask the circulator about lunch. A surgeon may waltz in to see what's going on, especially if he's somehow involved in the case. Maybe he's just interested. Most folks in the OR survey the big board next to the main desk, where all of the day's operations are listed.

Everyone who works in the operating room knows what's going on when the mayor's wife is having her hysterectomy and when the Chair-

> ### *The Main Operating Room Case Board*
> - room number
> - surgeon's name
> - assistant's name
> - type of operation
> - type of anesthesia
> - anesthesiologist's name (plus resident's name or CRNA)
> - a code indicating the readiness of the case; e.g., next to the name on the board, red dot for "in the room" and yellow dot for "in pre-op holding"

man of Psychiatry's daughter is undergoing a breast augmentation. These rooms will have their windows covered by sheets taped to the inside wall by the circulating nurse to provide privacy.

Still, someone's bound to peek in the room.

What happens to specimens when they leave the operating room? How are they wrapped, transported and handled? What are the common types of specimens? Here's a list of tissues and other samples which are harvested during surgery and sent for further evaluation and processing.

- blood samples drawn by anesthesia for the usual labs (e.g., cross and type for blood transfusion, chemistries, etc.) placed in standard (color-coded caps) glass vials
- cultures of body fluids or pathological collections, such as pus, transported in sterile test tubes labeled with date, source and patient's name
- tissue specimens for frozen section sent "fresh" (without preservatives) in sealed plastic cups for immediate analysis; usually looking for cancer
- entire surgical specimens such as a resected colon, kidney, uterus, tubes, ovaries, etc., sent in formalin for analysis; these specimens are the result of complete cancer operations and must be assessed for clear margins (around the cancer), number of lymph nodes containing cancer, blood vessel or lymphatic invasion, etc.; sent in large, sealed plastic containers
- amputated legs, arms, jaws, genitals, etc., placed in large sealed plastic containers as with surgical specimens, or in special red plastic

---

"See One, Do One, Teach One"

One of the romantic, yet flawed, ideas about learning procedural medicine, how to perform interventions requiring motor skills, is summarized in the oft-quoted expression, "See one, do one, teach one." Implied is a narrow window of opportunity that presumably underlies medical education. Also, this quote denies the reality of the need for repeated performance of a motor skill in order to get it right.

---

bags used to identify biological specimens as compared to routine OR trash; sent to surgical pathology
- hardware from orthopedic cases (e.g., rods, screws, plates, etc.) or material such as body fluids containing illicit drugs, bullets, knives and other impalement objects that may have forensic importance bagged and sent to the pathology lab

Teaching the Skills of Surgery

All of the rituals we have discussed in this chapter must be learned by the surgical resident during five arduous years of training. How to scrub, gown and prep the patient precede the learning of how to tie knots, handle instruments as an assistant, sponge at the appropriate time and suction without getting in the way. Some of these skills are learned as a medical student.

For the most part these important maneuvers are not complicated. Still, they must be mastered in order to progress to the stage of actually learning how to perform surgery. But how do you let someone operate for the first time?

Each year of training has set goals and objectives, recognizing that not all residents progress at the same rates. Some second-year residents are able to perform a major part of an operation with good assistance from the Attending, while others have difficulty tying a secure knot. The dilemma for the teaching surgeon is how to permit a resident to progress in the mastery of surgical skills; the answer is to provide *graduated responsibility*. How this is done varies from institution to institution as well as among Attendings.

There is a marked difference in most surgical training programs between the private surgical services and the so-called "resident" services,

The Elements of Teaching Surgical Technique

- The resident must first learn how to assist, to hold retractors and instruments in the proper position without moving and to move smoothly with the surgeon as directed. Part of assisting is tying knots, a difficult skill where every potential bleeder grasped by a hemostat must be secured with a well-tied knot.
- The resident must learn to make a clean incision and continue the dissection as directed by the surgeon; to use each instrument safely, including dissecting scissors (Metzenbaums), scalpel, hemostat, probes, etc., to identify and outline normal anatomy and the specific pathology. This is begun on simple cases at first; the resident then learns how to suture, including layered closure of body cavities.
- The resident progresses to more complex dissection in areas with more detailed and crucial anatomy and must follow directions explicitly. Also, the use of more complicated suturing techniques on the bowel, blood vessels and other organs is learned. The use of sophisticated stapling devices and other high-tech instruments, including laparoscopic instrumentation, and the demands of non-tactile dissection are added in later years.
- Finally, the resident learns to operate independently, with supervision but as the surgeon, making her own decisions, performing the procedure with junior residents and completing the case without direct Attending input, unless needed.
- The progression of responsibility given the training surgeon should follow the dictates of providing *graduated responsibility*, sequential addition of more complex cases as the resident demonstrates a growing competency.
- After five years of basic surgical training the surgeon may practice or go on to a fellowship in a special area such as trauma or oncologic surgery; specialties require varying number of years in general surgery before acceptance to their programs in pediatrics, orthopedics, plastic urologic surgery, etc.

because the latter only treat unreferred patients who do not have a private doctor. Board-certified surgeons are ultimately responsible for the patients on both services. But the residents on the private service are supervised more closely than on the "unreferred" service. Whereas the residents who run their own service are allowed more liberty to conduct it, private patients are more closely monitored by the Attendings.

Of course, residents rotate on both the private and the so-called "resident's" service several times during their training, so they are exposed to both types of training. With time and repeated opportunities to evaluate, diagnosis and operate on patients, to perform the same operation over and over under careful supervision, residents become proficient. At the end of five years the chief resident is *board-eligible* when he graduates from the medical center's program. By then, the resident will have performed hundreds of operative cases and evaluated and treated, as well as followed up in clinic for postoperative care, a large number of surgical cases.

The growth of a young surgical resident from an intern to a competent chief resident requires countless hours of hard work by the resident, including thousands of pages of reading. Also, Attendings dedicated to teaching surgical residents invest energy and time, as well as accepting the responsibility of permitting residents to operate on their patients under strict supervision. The principle followed by the private surgeons is that their patient gets the operation they would have done themselves if alone, but some or all of the procedure is performed by the resident.

No free-lancing is permitted on the private service. On the resident's service the Attendings permit for freedom, as it is here that the young surgeons must demonstrate their organizational skills, judgment on individual cases and maturity in dealing with patients and families.

To complete the discussion of what happens in the operating room, we will present a number of unrelated but important topics.

Blood Loss in the Operating Room

No surgery is completed without the team experiencing real or threatened exposure to blood products. For this reason the circulating nurse and anyone else who may come in contact with the patient's body fluids must wear

- an impervious gown
- (nonsterile) gloves
- eye protection (goggles or special glasses)
- a mask

To measure blood loss during surgery, the following maneuvers are carried out:

- measuring the volume of bloody fluid in a suction canister minus the irrigant volume

- counting the soaked, bloody sponges (weighing sponges on pediatric surgical cases for small differences)
- grossly assessing blood in stainless steel bowls, which contain huge blood clots in certain cases (e.g., an upper GI bleed where clots are scooped out of the stomach)
- grossly assessing blood on drapes and the floor, if indicated

Some cases involve major hemorrhage. These operations may be identified ahead of time so that certain techniques may be employed to avoid excessive transfusions. Also, some patients such as Jehovah Witnesses refuse blood products. In any case, requiring conservation of blood, the following techniques may be considered:
- having the patient pre-donate blood days before surgery to be administered on the day of the operation if needed
- removing some of the patient's blood at the beginning of the case and replacing it with intravenous salt solutions, and then transfusing the blood back as needed at the end of the case—this is known as *hemodilution*
- retrieving the shed blood as it is lost during the case with a special device known as a "cell saver"—this is a suction device with a special filter that conserves the patient's own blood

A Cardiac Arrest in the Operating Room

For patients who are intubated under general anesthesia—which represents most cases where an anticipated or completely unexpected cardiac arrest occurs—control of breathing is already accomplished. The patient's intubated and on a ventilator, on the anesthesia machine with oxygen and on an EKG. Left to complete the resuscitative process is cardiac massage.

The surgeon often begins with a chest thump (we're considering a common abdominal operation where the lower chest is draped and part of the field). If this doesn't reverse the arrythymia, external chest compressions are begun. Rarely, in extremely difficult situations, it is necessary for the surgeon to open the chest. If done, a scalpel is used to swiftly divide the tissue between the ribs on the left lateral chest (thoracotomy), after which the surgeon inserts his hand and massages the heart.

If the patient is in a different position it may be necessary to turn the body into the supine (face up) position and institute cardiac massage. In any instance, the anesthesiologist also has at hand the numerous drugs used to convert cardiac rhythm problems and to boost cardiac function.

If the "code" is brief, the patient may do well. If prolonged in a patient with multiple medical problems, a cardiac arrest on the table is a harbinger of bad things.

Often these latter patients don't survive the arrest.

Death in the Operating Room

When a patient dies on the operating table, the case becomes a *medical examiner's case* until the body is released. It is the surgeon's duty to contact the Medical Examiner (ME)—or *Coroner*, depending on state laws—and describe the case and why the patient died. If there is no questionable reason why the patient expired—the victim was in shock from bleeding or sepsis and the chances of surviving surgery were slim to begin with—the ME will release the body. That means the ME has no further interest in the case.

Now the surgeon is free to contact the family and request an autopsy (this is seldom done, as the surgeon has in effect just performed one) or release the body to a funeral home.

Before the ME releases the body, no tubes or other hardware are touched. If the ME decides she wants to autopsy the body, all incisions, tubes and other drains, etc., are left in the body when it is transported to the morgue. Sutures are used to close the abdomen while the body is still in the OR in order to keep the abdominal contents inside the body cavity as the body is moved. The surgeon or her assistant will notify the family, followed by the hostess desk, the telephone operator and the nursing supervisor for that shift. The death certificate must be filled out by the surgeon or his assistant, and all personal belongings are returned in a plastic bag to the Admitting Office, where the family may retrieve them.

If the deceased's religion requires last rites, the face sheet of the hospital record should have noted if this has occurred. If it has not happened, a priest is notified.

The body is transferred from the OR table to a special morgue stretcher that conceals the body. In the morgue the body is placed on a

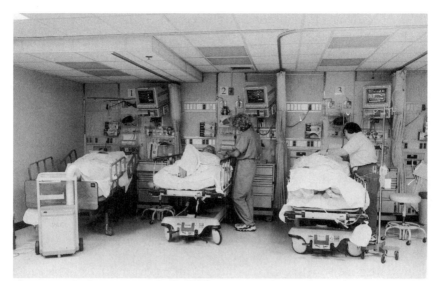

A post anesthesia recovery unit (PACU) team attends to patients who are recovering from their recent anesthesia. Above each bed is a cardiac telemetry monitor, and each recovery bay has its own suction, oxygen and emergency equipment.

refrigerator stretcher with the head propped up on a wooden block. The body is placed in a body bag and picked up by the funeral home requested by the family.

The Post-Anesthesia Recovery Room (PACU)

Successful surgery is celebrated in the PACU, where the awakening patient is greeted by specially trained nurses and plugged into the careful routine of this monitoring area. Immediately after the anesthesiologist extubates the patient and replaces the breathing (endotracheal) tube with a face mask (and oxygen) is the most dangerous time for the patient. Connected to an EKG monitor, oxygen saturation is checked with a pulse oximeter, and blood pressure, pulse rate, respiratory rate and level of consciousness are noted and recorded.

In addition to these routine vital sign checks, the patient is evaluated for stability of the surgical area. For example, a patient who underwent reconstruction of a leg artery (femoral-popliteal bypass graft) would have pulses frequently examined with the help of a Doppler instrument (which gives an audible signal) in the PACU, as the first few hours are the most likely time when the graft might clot off. Patients who have undergone tissue flap rotations from plastic reconstruction will have the color of the flap assessed frequently, as failure due to inadequate blood supply once again will occur early—in the PACU. All bandages are checked at regular intervals in the PACU for bleeding, as are surgical drains for volume of output.

If a chest tube, for example, keeps producing a couple of hundred cc's of blood per hour in the PACU after a thoracotomy for a lung resection, the PACU nurse would call the thoracic surgeon, who almost certainly would take his patient back to the operating room and search for the uncontrolled bleeding. If a patient underwent a craniotomy (exploration of the brain) for tumor, aneurysm, etc., and developed a dilated pupil on one side after surgery, the neurosurgeon would be notified and would assume excessive intracranial pressure from swelling or bleeding was the culprit. If medication (steroids) didn't solve the problem, the patient would return to the OR for a re-exploration.

For the more fortunate—who travel the route from surgery to the hospital's surgical floor much more frequently—the next step (after PACU) is the surgical floor, or a *stepdown unit*, also known as an *intermediate care* area. On the floor the patient is seen by a nurse and her assistants a few times a day as all activities of daily living are resumed. In intermediate care, monitoring of many of the same vital functions followed in the PACU (EKG, oxygen saturation, BP, pulse, respiratory rate) is continued until the patient is deemed stable enough to be sent to a regular floor, or to an unmonitored bed on the same floor.

The next step is home.

Over twenty million surgical procedures are performed in the United States each year. A majority of well-trained surgeons carry out this workload efficiently and in cooperation with the other members of the operating room team. Prima donnas will always punctuate the ranks of surgical specialties, favoring cardiac, thoracic and neurosurgery. Perhaps it is the greater demands of these anatomic areas that necessitate a stronger-willed operator.

Surgeons rank high among professionals who must perform before their public every day without failing. The culture of the operating room is unique because it is not an exaggeration that death rides the shoulders of the participants and complications remain an insoluble problem. Besides, nobody is perfect.

But unlike their professional sports alter egos, surgeons don't have next year to correct their mishaps. Everything counts, and the score can't be taken off the scoreboard.

CHAPTER FIVE

The Medical Staff and Personnel

With the recent shift of uncomplicated medical care away from the hospital and into the home, clinic or other facility, we find what's left to treat is complicated, confusing and expensive. Many doctors no longer have privileges to admit patients to the hospital; others do nothing but "in-house" care. Some hospital-based physicians work in a single location; for example, the intensive-care unit or the ER. Others serve as overseeing administrators of specialty departments.

To the doors of the modern hospital come the broken bodies culled from our highways, our inner-city streets and our homes. What we call *accidents* seem more like predictable acts of violence against each other. Equally destructive are diseases that result from slovenly living, the by-product of civilized existence. Too many calories, too little movement. Heart disease, cancer, diabetes and obesity all emanate from who we are and what we eat. All of the pathologic fallout from "having it so good" eventually wends its way to the hospital. And yet some illness is just bad luck.

No one is exempt.

Expertise may be found at all levels of care in the modern hospital. While there tends to be a disparate level of competence between green-horn interns and white-haired clinicians, each person in the academic scheme possesses a well-defined body of knowledge. Each clinician has cultivated unique skills, and in the larger teaching institutions this exper-tise is passed along to trainees. Some skills involve diagnosis; others in-volve delicate treatment procedures. The common ground for large medical centers and small hospitals alike is the assumption of competence: The public assumes their doctors know what they're doing.

Problems arise when physicians attempt to work beyond the margins of their training. Again, it can happen to an intern or an established physician when the need to rule the academic roost outstrips common sense. And no matter the size of the hospital, the issue of competence underpins most discussions of how best to provide medical care. Of equal concern are two issues: When does a young doctor have enough experience to practice independently? When should a senior physician or surgeon stop performing procedures or surgery?

Always in the treatment equation is the wary patient.

Conflict begins and ends in the modern hospital with the concept of *expectation*. Confusion between what is actually offered in the form of treatment with what the patient *thinks* is going to be provided often results in unhappiness, resentment and litigation. Media blasts of heroic medical care and frequent emphasis on medical care gone wrong push the bar of expectation into the ionosphere.

Americans have refined the art of creating unreasonable expectations. If we can put a man on the moon, goes the rationale, why can't doctors perform surgery without complications? Aren't complications really mistakes? Immense expectation baggage arrives at the hospital with the sick and injured.

Physicians have traditionally perched at the top of the medical pecking order, leaders in clinical practice, unchallenged as authority figures—at least not until the last three decades of the twentieth century. Today we hear the expression *health care professionals*, which includes doctors, nurses and other allied paramedical personnel whose training varies considerably and whose experience may be quite disparate. Whether intended or not, the concept of *the practice of medicine*, with its unambiguous physician authority, has become anemic; respect has hemorrhaged from the doctor's role.

The physician's diluted authority goes hand in hand with an unfounded implication that there is equality of knowledge and experience with other less well trained health care personnel. Medical jargon and buzz words create a superficial sense of comprehension among paramedical neophytes. Among allied health care workers who are not competent to diagnose and treat patients, the machine-gun spray of "medspeak" often gives the illusion of certification, of unwarranted validation.

Beyond specific specialty considerations—the above assessment of physician's status notwithstanding—even doctors who work in the hospital setting do so with variable amounts of experience and training. Because medical education is heavily hospital-oriented, and especially because residency training relies on the hospital environment, in-house patients frequently become exposed to doctors in training. These young physicians occupy niches in all levels of competence, just like their elders. A source of conflict often exists, for example, between a July intern in the intensive care unit managing a very sick patient and a seasoned ICU nurse. The above discussion notwithstanding, the neophyte doctor will do well to heed the admonitions of the nurse, whose expertise *at that moment* exceeds that of the young physician.

Physician credentialing serves as a quality-of-care assurance barrier for the public, a speed bump in the doctor's movement into private practice. The credentialing process is carried out by individual hospitals. Records of one's medical degree, resident training and certificates of board certification, as well as state licensing documents and letters of recommendation, are all part of the package. Stories arise with surprising regularity describing how someone faked a medical degree and completed a residency training program without being suspected of not having attended medical school. An occasional impostor practices for years before being caught. Always a good plot idea.

Medical education inserts itself into hospitals of all sizes in one form or another, and different issues arise because of the presence of students and residents. Least intrusive in physician training is the small hospital, where the learning doctor's prior training as well as current ability would become an issue only if the resident is not properly supervised. Students and residents may rotate to small peripheral hospitals to gain experience with a particular physician who has expressed an interest in teaching. Medical education is most obvious at academic teaching hospitals, where hoards of white coats flock to the various specialty floors in search of learning, all the while providing much needed (and often unappreciated) medical care. And if the major concern with practicing physicians is credentialing—making certain a doctor has the expertise and experience she claims she has—the most important issue in medical education centers on the issue of *supervision.*

You will recall the Libby Zion case, in which a young woman was treated by house staff in a New York hospital and, for unclear reasons, subsequently died. Excessive resident working hours and inadequate supervision purportedly explained away the perceived poor quality of care. Ignoring the various interpretations of the facts, the real issue for a writer when probing the envelope of doctor training is the conflict that so often arises in a teaching hospital. Of course, the mirror-image conundrum is seldom broached—that of inadequate care in small hospitals where physicians must perform all of the scutwork themselves and where the doctor may not arrive in time to treat a critically ill patient. In these smaller hospitals the respiratory therapists and other nonphysician personnel perform emergency procedures such as resuscitation (CODE BLUE). How much of it is poorly done? How tired and inefficient do our community medical troops become when taking call week in and week out? Are they less visible to the competency hounds who smell out a training doctor like a wounded fox?

How Are Doctors Trained?

It is useful to consider medical education the backbone of our discussion of the professional medical staff in a hospital. Once you recognize the intermediate steps between premedical student and board-certified clinician, regardless of his specialty, you will understand the interrelationships between these individuals in our discussions of hospital organization and patient care. Somewhere along this arduous path from layperson to seasoned clinician a dramatic change overcomes the neophyte, and from the nurturing cocoon (the hospital) emerges a creature of immense potential and beauty. Not all of this training occurs in major medical centers; smaller community hospitals play a significant role in doctor education, and thus we see trainees amid the busy white coats outside of mainstream academia as well.

Some will become butterflies. Others will remain moths.

Medical education is facing several important challenges that will carry into the next millennium. Choices are being forced upon academic centers, and these include:

- the need to reduce the total number of students accepted into medical school

- the need to reduce the number of medical schools (currently 120) by 20 percent
- the need to reduce the number of residency programs, especially specialty training programs, and make primary care slots more available
- the need to deny entrance of foreign medical graduates to residency programs
- the need to continue medical research with significantly less funding

Premedical Students

There was a time when you didn't set foot inside an American medical school without a bachelor's degree in science. Hard science. It helped to have graduated from college cum laude (with high honors) or even better, summa cum laude (with highest honors). Only one out of three (or more) applicants to medical school in the 1960s were accepted—the cream of the crop: valedictorians and private school students, many from medical families. Some of the best schools received almost thirty applications for every student accepted. Severe competition marked premedical education in American colleges.

Over the last twenty years, as managed care insinuated itself into the business of health care, doctors have become disillusioned with their shrinking role in health care and have restrained themselves, pushing their children less and less toward the medical profession. Not only are fewer children of professionals attending medical school today, but the standards for acceptance have changed. Most folks who have been patients would agree the acceptance of more women into the profession (over 50 percent in some schools, including a recent Harvard freshman class) has enhanced the profession. The acceptance of students with less remarkable qualifications—often from minority cultural groups in order to enhance available medical care in those communities—has been received with mixed reviews. Today, more and more medical students are women or from minority groups previously not adequately represented in the profession. The medical profession as a consequence is more culturally diverse and balanced. But the old conundrum of elitism still haunts the admissions process.

The standard protocol for admission to an American medical school has changed little in the last thirty years. Dr. Harold Morowitz of the Yale University School of Medicine perhaps best states the case. He writes, ". . . show me a student who has a 3.95 GPA and MCATS in the upper few percentiles and does not exhibit overt sociopathic or pathologic behavior, and I will show you someone who is going to be admitted to medical school regardless of subtle personality factors such as a sense of empathy." Morowitz also makes the point that in the undergraduate setting the premed students are somewhat alienated from others students because of their fierce competitiveness.

Which premed students are selected to become America's doctors?

The Issue of Empathy

Is there a place in the human psyche for extreme competitiveness *and* compassion? Does an emotional veil descend across one's empathy, segregating survival in academia from affection for a suffering soul? Maybe. The point is it seems few if any members of medical school admissions committees are committed to specifically seeking out empathetic premed students. Besides, how does one judge *genuine* empathy from merely acting concerned about one's fellow man? Should there be a summer camp for premedical students to assess their humanity over two or three weeks?

We should not be surprised to discover in some studies first-year medical students are better than third years in taking a medical history, more perceptive in discovering what is really bothering the patient. First-year students—unencumbered with a critical mass of medical knowledge—listen more carefully: They hear the *story* of illness. They have no preconceived ideas, what we call *education*. Third-year students with their exposure to medical instruction seem to lose their empathetic edge and would rather seek out disease—pathology, the good stuff of thick textbooks—than listen to patients tell their tale.

How much compassion do premedical students begin with? Where does it go? Can it be brought back? Resuscitated? Can it be nurtured?

The story of a premedical student who loaned his skis to a classmate in order to outstudy and thus outperform the second premed student highlights the dispassionate and competitive nature of the young people who will become our doctors. Will this ski-lending student become the doctor who will not let go, who will refuse to permit an elderly patient to die with dignity? Will he insist every drug and piece of hardware be thrown into the battle against insurmountable pathology because his ego is glued to the patient's survival and his own statistics? If this doctor's patient succumbs to cancer or stroke, will he view his efforts as futile, leaving his ego horribly skewed toward failure?

Where does the cold, calculating mind come from?

Are American medical schools selecting the brightest without attempting to identify and cull out those without a shred of compassion? In a 1990 article in *The Journal of Medical Humanities*, Robert H. Coombs, Ph.D. and Morris J. Paulson, Ph.D., ask the question, "Does the system of premedical education lead to a lack of physician concern for patients, interpersonal warmth and humanitarian care?" Their answer: "In all likelihood it does. As the first stage of a lengthy and elaborate socialization process, it sets the direction and scope for a pervasive scientism—an overvaluing of numerical empiricism and technology, and a devaluing of less easily measurable, but no less important, phenomena." These authors conclude that premedical education sets the stage for the ongoing neglect of experiences that could expand the young doctor's emotional repertoire. Other authors agree that the competitive impulse requisite for medical students to complete their daunting studies must be directed—expanded from its encroaching focus. Still others challenge the notion that studying the basic sciences blunts one's humanity and that, alternatively, education in the humanities *fosters* compassion.

What is clear from data from the American Association of Medical Colleges is that applicants to medical school with majors in biology, chemistry, mathematics and the natural sciences have a higher acceptance rate than those with a background in the social sciences or humanities. At Harvard Medical School, 80 percent of applicants, as well as those accepted, are science majors. Finally, in a 1978 article in *The New England Journal of Medicine*, "How to Fix the Premedical Curriculum," Dr. L. Thomas states, "There is still some talk in medical deans' offices about the need for general culture, but nobody really means it, and certainly the premedical students don't believe it." What's the point of being compassionate?

In other studies, medical students were described as highly motivated and self-disciplined, with significantly higher than average ability in math and science. They were also seen as possessing lower than average skills in writing and speaking ability, creativity and leadership capability. Still other studies describe medical students as less mature, less humane and less honest. Coombs and Paulson quote Rosenberg's unpublished remark, "The joy of learning, even the joy of life, seems to be greatly diminished in these very gifted young people at a critical time in their lives."

Despite the intellectual chatter by admissions committees and medical school deans, medical students are still chosen primarily for their GPA and MCAT scores, with empathy perhaps dragged along unintentionally. Faced with the rigors of the medical school curriculum, these aggressive students plunge ahead, disregarding the potential threat this level of stress may cause them. Imagine the shock when these intellectually gifted individuals smack headlong into a patient suffering grievously. Is it any wonder they divert their entire attention to the biochemical, anatomic, physiological, pharmacological and interventional aspects of management? Is it possible to care?

Medical Students

American medical schools are organized to provide two science-oriented pre-clinical years and two patient-oriented clinical years. Although the precise methods of teaching clinical skills and basic science courses have changed in some schools, the principle is to require basic sciences for two years, which includes clinical anatomy, embryology, physiology, biochemistry and genetics, along with an introduction to patient interviewing in the first year. The second year adds pathology, pharmacology, physical examination, etc., and serves as a bridge to the third year, which is spent in the hospital. By the end of the second year the student is well versed in basic science as well as the elements of performing a history and a physical examination.

All major clinical areas are covered during the third year of medical school, including surgery, medicine, pediatrics, obstetrics and gynecology as well as subspecialty areas such as nephrology (kidney diseases), pulmonary medicine, cardiology, radiology, emergency medicine and, of course, rotations on primary care (internal medicine) services. In the fourth year the student devotes herself to more clinical rotations and slants the year toward a specific specialty or toward more components of primary care, such as dermatology, rheumatology or neurology. It is at this juncture in the medical student's education that a decision must be made regarding postgraduate training. Many students complete their third year without a clear idea of what they want to do. Excellent mentors and interesting clinical rotations complicate the decision-making process for motivated students, who find *everything* interesting.

Many students select primary care. This choice allows future doctors to continue to learn about all aspects of medicine while in medical school without narrowing their focus, as is seen in students who wish to become specialists.

On major rotations such as medicine and surgery, fourth-year students serve as "subinterns," becoming part of the flock of white coats seen in hospital corridors during morning or evening rounds. The fourth-year student functions much like an intern. Of course, the "sub-i," as they are known, without the intern's experience or knowledge, remains a stutter-step behind the "tern," and thus becomes the lowest lifeform in the modern teaching hospital's high-pressure academic food chain. In the last year of medical school the student learns how to perform lesser interventions such as inserting various catheters and performing minor surgery. The fourth-year student also becomes a more accomplished diagnostician and assumes more responsibility for his clinical activities, but without the burden of having to make the final treatment decision.

Learning and Listening

Before moving to a discussion of postgraduate training, we will complete our consideration of medical students by analyzing a novel perspective on the evolution of the American doctor. As alluded to above, the medical student shifts his method of problem-solving as he progresses through medical school. As stated by Dr. Stanley Reiser, "The disparate behavior of first- and third-year medical students was the result of education. First-year students listened to the story of illness. Third-year students strove to write a story of disease. For them the disease was the thing: Classification, or merging the patient with preceding patients, was their objective." It seems as students learn more, they listen less. Does medical education enhance the dissonance between academic accomplishment and compassion?

This trend toward cultivating an "internal" ear, learning to hear the patient selectively while mustering up huge chunks of data from one's memory banks, surely distances the future physician from the patient. Somewhere in the distant past there appeared an editorial in *The New England Journal of Medicine* entitled, "I Can't Hear You While I'm Listening." It made the point: a doctor would rather employ his stethoscope and search for signs of disease than listen to the patient tell him *how he feels*. Someone once said if you listen to your patient long enough he will tell you the diagnosis. How often do doctors peer at exquisite X rays and body scans, puzzling over shadows and asking each other questions about the patient's history?

In evolutionary theory there exists a cumbersome and quite possibly outdated concept referred to as "phylogeny reflecting ontogeny." Simply stated, the idea is that the stages in an organism's embryological development—going from a ball of cells through various degrees of organ development; for example, limbs that at first look like fins and then develop into arms and legs—reflect evolution. Thus, as a human develops it goes through stages which look suspiciously like, in order of appearance, amphibians, reptiles and, only in the end, mammals. What's this got to do with medical education?

In the seventeenth century doctors knew little of body function, and the study of human anatomy was still in its infancy as a requirement for doctors. What early physicians did well was to listen to their patients. What else could they do? Then, in the early nineteenth century the stethoscope was developed, and one of the first enduring inanimate objects was thrust between the doctor and his patient. Now the doctor could access the noises of illness. He could look for something other than verbal clues to determine what was wrong with the patient. Technology had forced itself into the practice of medicine, wedged between the tactile skin of the examining hand and the febrile integument of the wretched patient.

The trend seen today, where doctors take a cursory—as opposed to a careful and complete—history and move on to a brief physical examination before ordering a complex X ray or other test, expands with each generation of physicians. Doctors chide each other about asking their patients what's bothering them and then ordering a CT scan of the offending body cavity. As usual, it's not always easy to take sides in medical arguments. A recent study from Massachusetts General Hospital proved that in that institution the CT scan was more reliable in diagnosing acute appendicitis than a board-certified surgeon. A CT scan better than a good history and physician examination? Is traditional medicine dead? Is educational phylogeny now reflected completely in individual medical student ontogeny? Have we lost the ability to listen to our patients, instead sending them sliding through an electronic hoop for the diagnostic answer?

Will our students evolve from good history-takers (first year) through pathology-seekers (third year) to clerks (interns and residents) ordering high-tech tests? Are physicians *devolving*? Are doctors' clinical skills becoming less proficient in dealing with sick patients?

It would seem the answer is mixed. The MGH study demonstrated that as our scans improve, becoming more capable of defining gross disease, the diagnostic skills of the clinician become less important. Unless, of course, you live in the boondocks where there are no expensive diagnostic machines. For some illnesses the CT scan will forevermore set the standard for diagnosis and, in some cases, treatment. For many diseases only the physician's intellectual power and observational acumen will permit the proper diagnosis to be made.

A significant aspect of physician development is the acquisition of confidence. So much of what a doctor does in practice revolves around making difficult decisions or performing complex motor skills on living tissue—real patients. Yet, in every medical school there exist professors— those icons of academic superiority and dedication to teaching—who verbally humiliate and abuse students. This is hardly a benign interaction.

According to Michael K. Schuchert, reporting on the relationship between verbal abuse and medical student confidence in *Academic Medicine* (August 1998), "Students experiencing verbal abuse during medical school was significantly associated with their having less confidence in their clinical abilities at graduation." From his data Schuchert feels highly motivated students suffer the fallout from public humiliation as much as the poorer students who may have entered medical school with a marginal confidence level.

Inherent in the teaching relationship is a need for respect on both sides, not merely student adulation for the professor. Grades and deans' letters (aimed at residency program directors) have the potential to be used in a similar and possibly more subtle way as professorial verbal recrimination to demoralize students.

Medical education, perhaps much more than other learning arenas, is awash with intellect, motivation, ego and oddball personalities.

Postgraduate Medical Education

Before looking into the work of residents at each level of training, we will study some of the basic principles applied to postgraduate learning. No longer in classrooms, sitting in lectures and writing tedious notes, not even participating in small-group problem-based learning sessions, the intern and resident are launched onto the wards and into clinics where their real education begins. Before the era of the modern teaching hospital, Americans acted as though their physicians came through the mail, prepackaged, ready to solve any diagnostic dilemma. Few nineteenth-century patients wanted to be "practiced on," and few were exposed to students because the doctors back then didn't have any clinical training worth commenting on. Not so in the modern era.

Many folks still feel slightly put upon when a medical student or resident enters their hospital or clinic life. "Where's the real doctor?" sits between the intern and the patient. "Maybe I'll permit this green intern to examine me, as long as someone else sees me as well." And, as certainly as Orion adorns the New England sky in the fall, the Attending clinician working with the intern assesses the patient and renders an opinion.

"Who's gonna do the surgery?" asks the worried woman.

"I'm your surgeon," responds the Attending. "This resident will assist me. She may perform certain parts of the operation under my guidance."

"Yeah? I dunno . . ."

In the old days doctors presumably learned on charity cases, people who couldn't afford a private doctor. Everyone benefited. When the doctor became good enough, he could then turn his newly honed skills to the care of private patients. Was it a matter of a two-tiered system? Probably. Doctors have always worked pro bono, and at welfare reimbursement rates today they still pretty much work for peanuts. In an imperfect system most folks are cared for, and many indigents—as well as those who can't or have elected not to obtain health insurance—receive excellent care. It's an interesting side issue that doctors' office buildings overflow with upscale cars, many driven by people who claim they can't afford health insurance coverage.

At any rate, in the end, everyone is part of the medical education system.

Patients' attitudes partly determine how well the medical educational system works. At the end of the twentieth century our attention is being shifted from issues of reliable medical care to consumer protection from a capitalistic, uncaring managed-care environment. Training doctors are caught up in this imbroglio. With constraints placed on medical practitioners, who will decide what to tell the residents about their ethical obligations? Does this patient need to be seen in the ER? Could she be treated at home? Is it a *medical* decision or is the Attending being pressured from the HMO or managed-care plan? Is there conflict between the resident and the Attending on what are really ethical grounds rather than disagreement as to what represents reasonable treatment options? To burden the decision-making process even further, everyone knows it costs more to take care of a specific illness in the teaching hospital than it does in nonteaching facilities.

The buzzword for the immediate future is *continuous quality improvement*. In the day-to-day care of patients this refers to the quality of what happens to each individual patient, as compared to those medical educators who seem distracted by the *one-on-one*, population-based concept of patient care. Certainly there's an element of wisdom in eyeing the big picture of available resources and facing the issue of rationing every time a doctor treats an individual. But for now we must track our individual successes and look at outcomes—and teach residents to do the same. What are your results? Not: What can you quote from ancient research that comments on *someone else's* results with a particular clinical problem? This is referred to as *evidence-based medicine*. "Show me the money!" at its best.

As we examine the learning environment, it is vital to recognize the overriding constraints placed on learners and teachers alike as well, as on those private practitioners who may be exposed to residents. Foremost are the financial manacles ensnaring residents and Attendings, restraints not aimed at the often-touted quality care issue but at the Wall Street-driven, unethical managed-cost paradigm designed for profit that is in need of replacement. And when this paradigm is eradicated like the plague it represents, it must be replaced by an ethically motivated system that places the patient-doctor relationship back in the center of medical care.

Important to the teaching environment is the energy brought to the learning experience by the professors. For example, Dr. Janice C. Probst and her associates conclude that, in a Family Medicine Training Program, the faculty's satisfaction with their jobs as well as the inherent organizational strengths of the program determine how the residents and other staff members view the learning environment. In programs with high faculty satisfaction, the teaching program was felt to be superior. In fact, other studies have shown a correlation between faculty job satisfaction and students' performance on standardized tests. And the degree of autonomy among faculty and their ability to complete tasks without interference were rated as of critical importance. Probst et al. summarize the following issues, indicating their importance in Family Medicine programs (and almost certainly in any residency):

- organizational climate
- job satisfaction
- job-related stress
- employee autonomy
- goal attainment

The Internship Year
(PGY 1; Postgraduate Year One)

As the training doctor progresses up the residency ladder, certain tasks must be addressed and conquered. Not all of these areas are equally represented in each year. Clinical work on the wards reigns supreme for the more junior resident, whereas the senior resident is burdened with administrative and scholarly chores.

Nothing characterizes an intern's life quite as much as the smothering presence of sleep deprivation. Armed with a fresh, untested M.D. degree, the new house officer discovers she has just slipped from the "top dog" position in the medical school hierarchy to the bottom of the postgraduate learning scale. In the course of taking care of sick hospitalized patients, house staff (interns and residents) perform a variety of tasks. And they perform these task at all hours of the day. Sick people flood the emergency room at night, become admitted for evaluation and treatment and spill onto medical, surgical and pediatric wards. Each patient needs a history taken, a physical examination performed and tests ordered. Blood must be drawn, IVs started and tubes placed. Someone has to do it.

Four Major Categories of the Resident's Workload:

- **Learn the components of one's area of concern**; e.g., primary care, surgery or OB. This is the area of knowledge in which the resident will become expert.
- **Complete clinical work involving patient care.** This is the "scut" portion of the job, which also has immeasurable educational value.
- **Perform the needed administrative duties for the service the resident is on.** These tasks befall the more senior or chief resident on the service, including on-call schedules, patient bookings and lecture and visiting professor schedules.
- **Complete a body of research.** This scholarly work is performed in one's area of interest with the intent to publish in a scientific journal.

First in line is the intern, the quintessential scut puppy.

If the senior physician's professional life is dense with cerebration and void of physical activity, the intern's existence runs to constant motion, with minimal opportunities for genuine reasoning. An animal of burden—after all those years in school! Does it take a GPA of 4.0 to start an IV? How much reasoning does it take to order an enema? Yet all of this plays out in a rigidly guarded postgraduate educational system characterized by a strict professional hierarchy. And of course the intern participates in some of the intellectual sparring on rounds.

The intern begins the working day at about 5 A.M. Before the whole team makes rounds at 6:30 A.M. (that's for surgeons; most internists start later), the "tern" must dig up X rays, check updated lab values in the computer and personally examine the most ill patients on the service. She'll be quizzed by the chief resident when the team makes work rounds. The team consists of one or more interns, two, three or more residents of various levels of training, the chief resident and, at some point in the day, the Attending physician. And throw in a nervous third- or fourth-year medical student for good measure.

Somewhere in the chaos of the day the intern is expected to read about the cases he's managing as well as prepare periodic oral presentations of various diseases that must be researched through the hospital library's computer search machines. Instead of lunch. Or going to the john.

Rounds

PATIENT ROUNDS

Whenever a doctor or group of doctors goes from room to room to check up on their patients, it is called *making rounds*. Usually the patient's chart is taken along to review, the patient is asked how he is doing and examined briefly, and then decisions are made regarding treatment and tests.

TEACHING ROUNDS

Teaching rounds are performed in a teaching hospital for the purpose of instruction. An attending staff will take medical students, interns and residents on rounds to see interesting patients. During the brief examination of the patients, students are questioned about their findings, about the disease process and about their thoughts on treatment.

CHART ROUNDS

Chart rounds is a means of reviewing charts on all the patients on a particular service. This is both for teaching and practical purposes. Usually an attending staff or instructor will sit at a table along with medical students, interns and residents. Each patient's chart is reviewed, results of tests are discussed, students are quizzed and new tests or treatments are decided.

GRAND ROUNDS

Grand rounds is a formal hour-long teaching conference, usually attended by a large number of doctors, both attending and students, from all specialties. Usually one patient's case with an unusual or difficult diagnosis is presented and discussed. This is a teaching conference only, and is to discuss a particular disease rather than a specific patient.

REPORT

When nurses change shifts, the nurses going off duty give a report to those coming on duty. They sit together and have each patient's chart for review. They will discuss how each patient is doing, those with new problems, and any difficulties that have occurred during their shift. Those going off duty give a report, those arriving take a report.

Junior and Senior Residents (PGY 2–5)

Whether participating in the treatment of a case of pneumonia or removing a gangrenous gallbladder, the training doctor must follow the dictate of accepting *graduated responsibility*. Interns don't perform brain surgery. And not all surgical residents know how to open a chest or belly in an

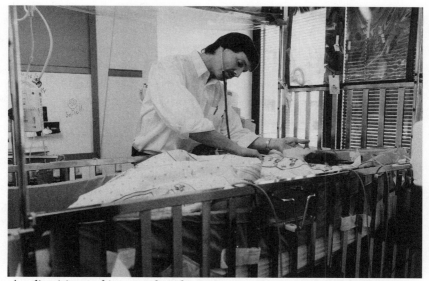

A pediatrician making rounds on his patients examines a young child. Following this, he will write progress notes in the chart, describing the current problems and possible tests to be ordered.

emergency. But they learn quickly and, contrary to the average citizen's understanding of training doctors, these hard-working residents save a lot of lives.

The learning process centers on allowing a resident more involvement in patient care activities with each additional year of experience, permitting more complex procedures and surgical operations to be performed. The design and completion of medical treatment programs, following established guidelines, allows a gradual increase in responsibility for the resident and is a complex process. Incremental learning with increasing responsibility sits at the heart of physician training.

Every time a resident scrubs in on a surgical case, the delivery of a baby or a complex radiological intervention, she is expected to first assist the physician or surgeon and learn how the procedure is performed. With time the Attending lets the house officer close the skin after an operation or advance a catheter under X-ray guidance to get the feel of the unseen tissues. On other cases the resident will do part of the case—presumably an uncomplicated maneuver where the consequences of a mistake are minimal. Yes, such parts of many operations do exist. By the time the resident reaches the last two years of training she is capable of performing major operations and diagnostic and therapeutic interventions.

This teaching process is (usually) done with careful supervision.

Or at least it should be. More story conflict. Studies demonstrate that even delicate procedures such as removing the parathyroid glands in the neck, structures the size of half a pea, may be performed by surgical residents under careful supervision with the same results as if the Attending surgeon had done the entire case himself.

Not all residents learn at the same rate. Actually, some surgical residents will put in an extra year in order to correct academic or motor-skills deficiencies. A certain amount of flexibility is built into many programs to accommodate varying learning abilities. It is a staggering truth that residents aren't specifically tested to determine how well they learn motor skills before being accepted into a residency program—including future surgeons!

How does one evaluate compassion? Who is a professional? Is a training program responsible for instilling honesty, integrity and respect? (At least one prominent surgical educator doesn't think so). Who's supposed to assess the future doctor's empathy? If not the medical educators, then who? Finally, a return to the question posed earlier: Is it possible for an objective, calculating doctor who is able to make hard decisions to also harbor the seeds of compassion?

Complex characters may be forged from such polar personality traits.

Eliminated from surgical training programs are the so-called "pyramids," or progressive diminution in the number of available slots for residents as they complete each subsequent year. It used to be training programs would start with ten or so first-year slots, but only graduate two chief residents. This former universally cutthroat system fostered intense competition and intellectual industriousness. But it wasn't *fair*. The system of graduating one or two chief residents from a huge pool of juniors encouraged favoritism and unkind behavior among house staff in competition with each other. Those released from a specific teaching hospital were left to apply to less desirable programs or were forced to give up their goal of becoming a surgeon or other specialist. Many entered general practice.

On the other hand, residency programs today by virtue of their quadrangular ascent structure ensure graduation for most competent candidates. As one might anticipate, these programs remain at some risk for encouraging laziness and academic mediocrity. Some medical educators also feel residents don't work hard enough. Laws prohibiting excessive working hours require the resident to restrict in-hospital and on-call time to humane levels. That bothers some medical educators. Perpetuating abuses in the residency system does no one any good. The job of ensuring high-quality residents who will become excellent candidates to graduate and take the various specialty board examinations falls on each residency Program Director.

Finally, for medical students and residents alike there are inherent risks in their jobs; exposure to abusive patients, some of whom are violent, as well as to other people's body fluids. Exposure to blood-borne pathogens, the most worrisome being the HIV and hepatitis viruses, may cause permanent disability or death. It is not always possible to know who may be infected. Also, life-saving interventions, in the ER particularly, may involve people infected with HIV and may include performing invasive procedures where blood is spilled and often contacted by the house staff despite gloves, gowns and special glasses.

Forty-eight percent of graduating medical students recall being exposed to potentially infectious body fluids during the last two (clinical) years of medical school. A majority of these encounters involved skin punctures or muco-cutaneous contact with patients' body fluids. The actual number of students or residents infected isn't known, but health care workers in general have contracted AIDS in three of every one thousand contaminated needle sticks. The likelihood of contracting AIDS is higher if the patient dies within sixty days of the body fluid contact—a little like waiting to see if the dog who bit you is rabid.

The Association of American Medical Colleges requires for accreditation that medical schools make disability insurance to cover such possibilities available to students. And although Workman's Compensation laws prohibit other health care employees from suing the hospital, medical schools are at risk of being caught in civil litigation arising from body fluid exposure.

All residents learn in the hospital as well as in the clinic and in the private doctor's office. Graduated responsibilities and a progressive knowledge base are thrust upon the learning physician. The rigorous training schedule demands dedication, hard work and the consumption of dull textbook material when sleep seems to be a more rational choice. Then, when other students close their texts and drift off to sleep, the resident closes his eyes only to hear the screech of his beeper, forcing him to rise, dress and return to the floor, the operating room or the ER. This grueling schedule lasts four or five years. Each year becomes more difficult, more challenging and more responsible.

Until, in the end, the doctor is privileged to take the various licensing examinations, board-certification written and oral examinations and then join a practice, wherein he again is subjected to other people's body fluids, lawsuits and a wonderful sense of accomplishment.

Danger and Controversy of Long Work Hours

Residents are working ridiculously long hours, killing themselves and endangering patients in the process. The time-honored tradition of re-quiring residents to work painfully long hours during their training has grown out of control.

Last year the state health department in New York fined twelve New York hospitals for violating a law that limits resident work hours to 80 per week. Residents in surgery and obstetrics were found to be working in excess of 100 hours per week. On-call residents were working more than 110 hours a week!

Patient care is suffering because residents are sleep deprived.

Funding cutbacks in nurses and ancillary staff due to managed care have contributed to longer work weeks. A combination of sicker patients and fewer support staff to move patients, draw blood or transport them to the laboratory or radiology has lengthened the residents' days and added more stress. Patients are sicker (because appropriate care early in the illness has been denied), and patients are discharged earlier, giving residents more paperwork to do in less time.

Long work hours affect residents' mental capabilities and ultimately the quality of patient care. Several hundred residents in a public forum told stories of fatigue that nearly led to disasters in patient care.

According to an article in *American Medical News* (March 1999), residents become so tired at times they sleep while standing in halls during rounds or while talking with patients. In one instance a resident fell asleep while he was holding a patient's liver during surgery.

A third-year resident died in a one-car crash after falling asleep at the wheel after he finished working an overnight shift in the cardiac care unit.

But many hospitals find it difficult to (or refuse to) comply with state laws regulating residents' work hours. As hospitals feel the financial crunch, they look to the residents to do more.

The Attending Physicians

The practicing physician represents someone who has graduated from a qualified residency program and has completed one or more certification examinations, as well as having been assessed by one or more state boards of registration in medicine and most probably a specialty organization. The practicing doctor has been extensively screened. And now not only is this information available to the hospital where the doctor applies for privileges, it is also available to the public from the National Practitioner's Data Bank. This training forms the basis for public trust. It is the answer to the patient's expectation of quality care.

Nonetheless, there is a qualitative—if not easily identifiable—difference in the quality of the care provided by physicians in the same specialty or in the arena of primary care. Although it's easy to recognize the absurdity in the old adage that half of all doctors graduated in the bottom half of their class, it is less appealing to realize that a small but significant number of physicians are marginal. Some docs just don't get it. A high IQ and a 4.0 GPA do not confer common sense.

Practicing doctors range from remote, dedicated small-town physicians who work diligently as America's unrewarded heroes to the university professors whose expertise and research with (usually) a single disease may confer international notoriety. Between these extremes are the bulk of doctors practicing and caring for large numbers of patients. A steady stream of physicians flows from American teaching programs into practice, replacing those who die or retire. And now many overseers believe there are too many doctors in the United States. Only time will prove what the appropriate level of physician numbers is for America, as well as the distribution of specialists, generalists and researchers.

At the top of the academic food chain, board-certified physicians, surgeons, pediatricians and obstetricians and their associated subspecialty splinter groups live lives of predictable uncertainty. Emergencies crowd out booked patients for office visits, tests and procedures. Alive with

> ### *The Responsibilities of Attending Physicians*
> - to practice compassionate, safe medicine
> - to keep updated on new developments in the field
> - to participate in the quality assessment process to ensure other practitioners are competent to participate in the education of medical students
> - to participate in the education of residents and fellows
> - to participate in community programs designed to educate patients
> - to participate in regional and national medical organizations and share expertise
> - to keep oneself healthy and drug free, setting a meaningful role model

"strokes" received from grateful patients, medical leaders who teach also reap accolades from an army of respectful residents.

Summary of Medical Education Requirements
Premed Student
- takes courses in college to prepare for medical school (anatomy, biology, organic chemistry, embryology)
- taking a premed curriculum in college does not guarantee acceptance to a medical school
- only a fraction of premed students are actually admitted (usually at the end of junior year or beginning of senior year of college)
- must complete four years of college and graduate with either Bachelor of Science or Bachelor or Arts degree

Medical Student
- first two years are classroom/laboratory courses in anatomy, pharmacology, histology, embryology, pathology, microbiology, physiology
- last two years are clinical, spent with patients, attendings and residents in the hospital
- must take and pass the National Boards or Flex exam prior to graduation
- graduates with M.D. (doctor of medicine) degree

- must take the state medical board examination to be licensed to practice in that state

Internship

- an intern has earned an M.D. degree and is licensed by the state (after passing state board exams)
- an internship is a one-year hospital clinical rotation under the direction of residents and attending staff
- intern has far more responsibility than medical students, can write prescriptions and write orders on in-patients (without requiring co-signature)

Residency

- this is a three- or four-year hospital clinical rotation with advanced teaching and instruction in a specialized area
- these include Pediatrics, Radiology, Internal Medicine, General Surgery, OB-GYN, Orthopedics, Family Practice, Anesthesia, Pathology, Radiation Oncology, Psychiatry
- during residency, there are lectures, review of journals and teaching of medical students
- the resident is given responsibility for much of the patient's care under supervision of attending staff
- after completing residency, the resident takes board examinations to become board certified in that specialty

Fellowship (Post-Residency)

- this is an additional one to two years of subspecialized training in a narrow specialized field of medicine
- e.g., after internal medicine residency, one can subspecialize as a fellow in cardiology, neurology, gastroenterology, pulmonology, endrocinology, etc.
- a surgery resident might subspecialize in pediatric surgery, thoracic, cardiovascular, neurosurgery, plastic surgery or opthamology (There are many more sub-specialty fellowships than are listed here.)
- a fellow has already completed a residency and has responsibility nearly equal to that of attending staff

- after completing a fellowship, the fellow must pass subspecialty boards to be board certified

Summary of Medical Education Training

pre-med	4 years of college with B.S. or B.A. degree
medical student	4 years of medical school, graduate with M.D. degree
intern	1 year of clinical rotation
residency	3 or 4 years of specialty training; board exams given
fellowship	1 or 2 years of sub-specialty training
TOTAL TIME:	12 to 15 years of education beyond high school

As can be seen from the outline above, a medical education is a grueling, demanding, expensive undertaking, requiring twelve years or more of education. Moving from an undergraduate pre-med student to becoming a board-certified sub-specialist is a vast undertaking, requiring a significant portion of one's life, rigorous training, and a huge expense which takes years to repay. Many people do not have the fortitude or dedication to complete this arduous task.

But there are no shortcuts for training qualified physicians.

The Visiting Professor

Many internationally known professors travel the lecture circuit dispensing their expertise in other teaching programs. Dealing with visiting professors becomes a way of life for residents. During the course of the academic year—from July 1 to June 31—every residency program has as part of its educational activities a visiting professor schedule (referred to as "visiting firemen" by students and residents). Heads of departments and their talented underlings head off around the country to give slide shows about basic science topics, research results or occasionally presentations that are less data intense (and therefore less interesting to those academicians imbued with their own importance) on topics such as ethics and medical economics. Many times the professor is *the* leading expert on the topic in the country or the world. Residents and students are given a unique opportunity to hear vital information from the scientist who performed the original research.

In addition to providing lectures, some visiting professors spend two or three days in one institution, making rounds with the residents as well as scrubbing in on selected cases in the operating room or assisting with special procedures and interventions. If the professor is known for having designed a new surgical procedure, for example, the operating room may be flooded with local surgeons as well as residents. Often this is the best method of teaching a novel technique and spreading new technology and skills.

During the course of a visiting professor's stay, cases are often presented in the form of a complex problem that may not be resolved. The professor's opinion may be informal, or he may examine the patient and make specific treatment recommendations. Other case presentations may take the form of "stump the expert." In a large auditorium the resident unfolds the patient's story by presenting the medical history, gives pertinent physical findings and eventually, at the professor's request, presents special X rays such as CT scans, arteriograms and other tests. As the X rays are evaluated, the visiting honcho may ask further questions and then formulate an opinion.

Before the patient's actual dilemma is revealed by the resident, the professor declares his diagnosis and spells out what he would do with the patient. The resident then tells the audience what actually was done, as well as the outcome. If there is a significant disparity between the way the local doctor handled the case and the recommendations of the visiting dignitary, fur often flies. Training doctors are privileged to see different ways to manage complex clinical problems, as well as how to deal with the reality of less than adequate treatment.

Promotion in Medical Education

For the most part, resident doctors are respectful, curious and energetic. Some are sloppy; some are lazy. The teaching Attending must determine who deserves to progress in the program and who should be converted into a electric meter reader. A Promotions Committee consists of full-time academic physicians, surgeons, OB-GYN doctors or pediatricians, as well as community representatives of the appropriate specialty who practice in the hospital and work with the residents, all forming a group given the awesome responsibility of determining who will be permitted to complete the specific program. Promotion is determined by melding

together several sources of information, including:
- the results of in-service multiple-choice examinations
- monthly evaluations by the attending physicians and surgeons on whose services the resident rotated
- any adverse reports from attendings, nurses or patients and their families regarding resident performance on specific cases
- evaluations by senior residents
- reports on the resident's individual research
- medical students' evaluations of the resident as a teacher

Attending physician evaluations are extremely important. The only reliable information regarding the resident's core of knowledge, his ability to diagnose disease, manage a complex caseload and perform delicate procedures and surgical operations comes from the clinicians who work closely with the training doctor. Deficiencies documented early in the resident's training must be corrected, and this improvement must be documented and agreed upon by a majority of the Promotions Committee members. Not infrequently, faculty personalities and individual prejudices get in the way, as inevitably the various members of the committee favor certain residents. This arena of personal opinion may weaken the selection process if not arbitrated appropriately by all members of the Promotions Committee.

The characteristics that the committee seeks in a resident include:
- teachability
- talent
- motivation/energy
- response to constructive criticism
- preparedness for cases; e.g., well read, reviewed literature
- empathy
- curiosity, sense of humor
- trustworthiness

Mistakes
Throughout their academic lives, medical school leaders and hospital administrators know that at some juncture someone is going to make a mistake. It may occur to one of their own patients, or it may happen to another doctor's patient on the same service. The adverse event may be

the result of the action of an intern, a resident or a seasoned Attending. Perhaps it could have been anticipated or avoided. Maybe it was inevitable. A serious complication may result or the patient may die.

When mistakes occur all hell bubbles to the surface.

For a moment let's examine how doctors deal with their mistakes. Because some of the most egregious errors involve surgical patients, we'll use surgery as an example of what might happen to a patient and the treating resident and attending team on a specialty service. Young or old. Male or female. Mistakes happen. This discussion implies that the application of this type of conflict resolution should occur in the larger picture of physicians as *interventionists*. Mistakes—large or small—occur periodically to all doctors.

What can go wrong with a procedure?

Regardless of specialty, more and more doctors are performing special procedures, invading the body with catheters and tubes and fiberoptically lighted hoses. It's all in the name of diagnosis and treatment. And as critical as one may become about excessive things being done to too many patients, it is this intense diagnostic and therapeutic activity (for example, in the form of cancer surveillance and aggressive early treatment) that has improved the survival rates for many diseases. For each new technique there is a learning curve or performance pattern where more mistakes and complications occur early in the physician's experience.

Two kinds of errors are recognized by physicians: *technical* and *moral*. In his seminal book *Forgive and Remember: Managing Medical Failure*, Charles L. Bosk reviewed how surgeons handle mistakes, how they identify them and how they correct them. Bosk's overall conclusion is that technical errors may be corrected and are uniformly forgiven. Moral errors, however, are seldom forgiven and are held to be more severe and worthy of dismissal. This is important in an era of increasingly sophisticated medical technology.

Bosk makes clear his premise that error is an "essentially contested" concept. He states, "We need to see under what circumstances, by what criteria, with what consequences, for which audiences an act is or is not considered an error." For example, surgeons perform in public, executing specific tasks, removing tissue and reorienting structures to solve an identified problem, a diagnosed disease. As Bosk concludes, there is a tighter link between what the surgeon does and the outcome, how the patient fares and the cure or complication of illness. Surgeons can't hide from their mistakes. On the other hand, Bosk adds, "In many branches of internal medicine the physician's interventions are relatively nonspecific. This fact allows internists to attribute failure to the inevitable pathophysiology of the disease process rather than to the nature of treatment itself."

Internists may be able to delude themselves. But surgeons work in a stadium where all seats are on the fifty-yard line, their performance scrutinized suture by suture, a crucible heated with real-time expectation.

Malpractice

When litigation results from a perceived wrongful act by a surgeon, the deficient clinical activity is easily attacked, pronounced inadequate with little ambiguity. U.S. courts rumble along arbitrating the residue of presumed surgical misadventure—what appears to be the flawed performance of a skilled actor whose every matinee carries personal risk as well as the potential to harm the patient. Certainly surgeons make mistakes. Most immediately explain the problem to the patient and the patient's family and then present their difficulties to their colleagues at a weekly complications conference, where a heated discussion often occurs. For the most part the public isn't aware of this intense scrutiny the profession requires of itself.

Consider the following generic reasons why surgeons are sued:
- The surgery performed was unnecessary.
- The diagnosis—usually of cancer—was delayed or missed.
- The procedure was performed negligently and incompetently.
- The complication was avoidable.
- The surgeon was compromised.

As you read this list, it will strike you as self-evident that not one of these issues is objective—provable beyond doubt. Remember also that the surgeon is the most visible of practitioners, the doctor whose hands display their skills and deficiencies, and whose results cannot be disguised or hidden from view. What is *unnecessary* surgery? How early can breast cancer be diagnosed if a mammogram is timely and negative? Who is to judge a surgeon's skill? What complications are truly avoidable? Perhaps even the issue of a compromised surgeon may be difficult to approach without confusion.

By comparison, consider the internist who orders cardiac medicine or an antibiotic, intervenes in the patient's care and follows established treatment guidelines—and yet the patient dies. Was the dose correct? Was it administered on time? By the correct route? Were other drugs more suitable?

It requires little imagination to understand the plight of the treating physician or surgeon whose actions are based on experience, knowledge and intuition. Doctors don't follow precise equations. Perhaps most startling is the observation of a malpractice case in which the doctor, who is the defendant, listens to a lawyer describe what putatively occurred—and the doctor does not agree. What does even a well-schooled lawyer know of the intricacies of cardiac anatomy or the functioning of the colon? Does anyone other than a surgeon know the agony of tissue collapsing as it is sutured, refusing to hold stitches, falling apart in defiance of excellent surgical technique? Does anyone know what it feels like to sit in court and be told after such an experience with unsalvageable protoplasm that the patient failed and died because it was *your* fault, Doctor?

How does a young, impressionable medical resident feel after leaving a patient's room after a failed cardiac resuscitation, a room crammed with silent nurses and other hospital personnel, resuscitation equipment, discarded syringes, gauze pads, blood-spattered sheets adorned with various spent tubes and catheters and an immobile, very recently dead body? How does it feel? The resident tried everything in the book, but the old man's heart muscle lay dejected against all flogging, medications, chest thumping and electrical jolts. It was, it seems, the old man's time to die.

Months later, just before graduating, anticipating his role in one of the best medical practices in the Northeast, which has chosen him as their new associate, he discovers—before accepting his diploma signifying his advanced training—a letter in his mail from a lawyer. And his life changes. He experiences anger and depression where only elation and expectation existed a mere day earlier.

This young internist—the brightest and the best—has been sued for medical malpractice. Why? Because an old man died.

Let's return to what is actually done in training programs to deal with errors when they occur. And they will continue to occur as long as medicine is the performing art it is, and as long as new doctors are trained to replace those leaving the field. It's a natural flux of experience and enthusiasm. The majority of medical malpractice suits have nothing to do with malfeasance and little to do with error on the part of the treating doctor. Most arise from unhappy patients, or their families, who sense a huge gap between what they expected and what actually occurred. Most medical legal fights, as reflected in the court records of all fifty states, are about a bad result.

It is the Attending physician or surgeon who must ultimately identify errors and institute remedial tasks for the trainee. Often mistakes are picked up by the residents themselves. They are expected to survey their own activities and document their difficulties, and then discuss them with their Attending. Some mistakes are only noted by the Attending, perhaps a lesser issue which the resident doesn't view as particularly egregious. It is the Attending who sets the high standard of care that will be followed. Because if the Attending and resident participated equally in the care of a patient who subsequently develops a complication, it is the Attending's responsibility to assume blame.

As will be discussed, a weekly morbidity and mortality conference permits a detailed public presentation of cases that must stand the scrutiny of the remainder of the hospital staff. It is here where truth-telling is critical and, at times, tarnished. Unfortunately, unlike surgeons, not all departments hold no-holds-barred complications conferences.

Technical Errors

Earlier we defined two types of clinical errors: technical and moral. So far we have been discussing the consequences of an adverse performance, something not done well. So first let's look at examples of technical errors in more detail.

It is difficult to define how many technical errors are permissible, as a range exists for most procedures. Should a surgeon performing colon surgery have a 5 percent or a 10 percent incidence of wound infection? How many of his anastamoses, the reconnecting of the bowel ends with sutures or staples, can be expected to fall apart, necessitating a second and third operation, before the surgeon is considered technically incompetent? Who's keeping score? Or was the complication because of the well-known patient-specific factors such as poor nutrition, smoking or failure to ambulate after surgery?

Is there an allowable number of misadventures for each operation or intervention performed by doctors that may stack up before someone blows the whistle? Is this the irreducible number of complications doctors describe when they provide informed consent and have patients sign a permit acknowledging this possibility? It is correctly said that the surgeon who insists he has no complications is either retired or a liar.

For example, placement of a central line—the insertion of a plastic catheter mounted on a needle *blindly* into the skin beneath the collar bone, through tough connective tissue and beyond into the subclavian vein—is fraught with potential complications. These include lung collapse, puncture of the subclavian artery and injury to the large nerves of the arm. All of these structures are within *millimeters*, not inches, from the subclavian vein, the needle's target. All house staff must learn this technique. In the beginning the learning curve is steep: More complications occur in the first twenty central lines a doctor places than in subsequent procedures.

Complications occur in the hands of the seasoned clinician as well as in the shaking grasp of the neophyte. Supervision is crucial when such procedures are performed.

Nonetheless, not all interventions go well, and yet when these cases are presented at the weekly Morbidity and Mortality Conference, discussion centers on how the problem might have been avoided. Did you do this? Did you consider trying that? Options. And in the end everyone knows there will be more complications next week. And the week after.

It's called the practice of medicine. No one ever gets it right all of the time. Each case is different, and on-the-spot decisions must be made over and over. In the end, the doctor's colleagues who listen to and comment on the misadventure realize that next week it may well be them up there at the podium attempting to explain why things went sour. Because of the multitude of factors that determine the success of an operation, most surgeons are willing to discuss bad results but stop short of attacking the performance. Unless, of course, there is a moral breach involved in the technical error, such as public drunkenness.

Ethical Errors
Ethical issues are an entirely different matter.

Charles Bosk finally concludes, regarding the resident's moral performance, "Deficiencies in moral performance say more about an individual's ability to improve and become a reliable colleague than do deficiencies in technical performance, which may speak to momentary and easily correctable shortcomings." And just as judgments about technical errors are minimal or suspended, so is the Attending's judgment of a subordinate's moral code swift and severe. The offending house officer may find himself ignored or chastised in public—harsh criticism may flow up to and beyond public humiliation. This is in contrast to the forgiveness witnessed during the performance of a procedure or in a conference where the resident states his self-criticism, expanding on what he might do differently the next time and accepting his role in the error.

Attendings are vigilant in searching for growth in their charges. Teaching physicians look for the resident's work ethic, his willingness to learn and make changes in conduct and engage enthusiastically in the work of that particular hospital service. When a Junior Attending is chosen from the ranks of available chief residents, issues such as work ethic, moral fiber and affability supersede considerations of who is a technical superstar. Most practitioners understand they can help their junior associates become more proficient in performing specific interventions, refining their motor skills, but they cannot mold a distorted ego or mend a morally flawed personality.

Resolving Disputes
The American Medical Association's Council on Ethical and Judicial Affairs in 1994 identified two areas of concern regarding the interaction of trainees and their supervisors. They are
- improving existing dispute-resolution mechanisms
- providing strategies for immediate dispute resolution

Grievances may be a chronic problem or they may arise acutely and involve potential risk or harm to patients. The first problem may be resolved electively through due process. Acute problems involving errors in moral judgment or even an impaired doctor must be identified, reported and resolved before patient care is compromised.

In studies designed to identify abuse and mistreatment of medical students by residents or other staff, a significant number of trainees indicated a problem. A ten-school study of fourth-year students revealed over 85 percent of these students felt they had been humiliated and verbally abused. Over 25 percent said they had been threatened with physical harm!

Other complaints by medical students included:
- being assigned tasks purely for punishment
- being threatened with unfair grades
- someone else taking credit for the student's work
- being placed at unnecessary medical risk without adequate protection
- sexual harassment
- gender discrimination
- racial harassment

Studies of residents and interns confirm significant problems in these areas for these members of the house staff as well. Also, both groups describe excessive conflict—more than one might expect from reasonable disagreement or discussions of options—with their supervisors and attendings over patient care decisions. When taken to the extreme, the assessment of who is right and who is wrong erupts into an angry declaration by the Attending that the resident or student is incompetent.

Now what happens?

Disagreements between trainees and their supervisors are most easily handled by direct negotiation and open, frank discussion. But at times the hurt is too deep or the criticisms are serious enough to raise the issue of the resident dismissal. Formal grievance procedures must then be followed. According to the AMA's Council on Ethical and Judicial Affairs, "Impaired colleagues should be reported to an in-house or external impaired-physician program; [to] appropriate supervisors such as chief resident, chief of staff or chief of the appropriate clinical service; or, if necessary, to the state licensing board." Also, if laws are violated, the appropriate law enforcement authorities must be notified.

What if there is a risk of imminent harm to a patient? What if the doctor is, in fact, impaired or makes an unethical decision? Does the resident refuse to give the drug? Does she walk out of the operating room and leave the compromised surgeon to his own devices? The answer is no. The resident must honor her obligations to assist in the care of the patient until such time as dispute resolution can be addressed. If the house staff refuse to complete the intervention in question, the patient may be done more harm.

Finally, the resident or student must be protected against retaliation by the supervisor or attending physician if conflict results from the senior doctor being identified as having been compromised in some manner while caring for a patient. The rules of engagement, so to speak, must be understood by everyone in the teaching program so that disputes may be handled in a sensitive and timely fashion.

The modern hospital carries on the historical tradition of caring for the sick while training physicians, nurses and other allied health personnel. The public should be as responsible in this alliance as the treating doctors, because those patients who refuse to deal with students and residents place the next generation—their own children and grandchildren—in jeopardy. This peril will only be vanquished when patients and doctors both view the hospital as a vehicle for benefit as well as a focus of recognizable risk.

Hospital Organization

All organizations are inherently hierarchical, with levels of authority determined by the individual's expertise based on education, experience and innate talent. The relationships among the administrative branches of the hospital and medical, nursing and nonphysician professionals is as complex as it is conflicted. Alliances are forged in committee, in the hospital's corridors and in the country club, melded together as a by-product of professional necessity.

No one is completely in charge in the modern hospital.

The hospital of the twenty-first century is an unwieldy physical behemoth harboring expensive hardware managed by intelligent business people, with talented, yet distrustful, specialists forming its elite core. The modern hospital serves as the physical arena for the provision of intricate medical care. Each year in the United States over 30 million patients are admitted to the hospital; another 300 million outpatient visits occur in various clinical settings, from hospital clinics to private doctor's offices. The approximately 5,200 U.S. community hospitals hold about 920,000 beds.

Someone has to run the show.

In chapter six we will assess the role of the physician in detail as their extensive training, core of knowledge and skill underlie a remarkable healing capacity. Yet, much overlap exists today between the medical and nursing professionals and what is termed the *nonphysician clinicians (NPC)*. Additional training permits the NPC to provide a variety of services formerly completed by doctors. It is still only possible to become a competent diagnostician and interventionist—a physician—by attending to the rigors of extended undergraduate, medical school and postgraduate residency training. But the complex health care environment has changed dramatically, and the paradigm of the future will emphasize individual care within the context of a clearly defined social context. Nurses, physicians and hospital administrators form the team that keeps the hospital viable, while nonphysician clinicians contribute to patient care both within and outside of the hospital. The doctor's focus is the individual patient; the hospital administrator's task is to distribute fewer resources than are available to meet the demand established by our current ethical dictates. That is, we can't give everyone everything they want.

In the following sections we will examine the training and job descriptions of nurses, hospital administrators and nonphysician clinicians in detail, and also review and list the multitude of other health care workers who contribute to hospital care. The conflict between the principle of individual demands by patients and the issue of distributive justice— assuring adequate but not complete care—for all citizens underlies the problems between doctors and the hospital's bean-counters. As in fiction, the argument accelerates to a holy war because the choice is between two "rights" with no "wrongs," a choice between two morally compelling and competing absolutes. As yet, Americans have not decided what they want. Thus, physicians and administrators struggle to provide the best medical care they can within a shrinking budget.

The Hospital Administrator

Hospital administrators suffered the derision of the medical profession in the 1970s and early 1980s, as a transition was occurring in hospital size and complexity and reimbursement shifted from simple fee-for-service to the near-meltdown of prospective payment schemes. No longer was it possible for doctors to practice medicine *and* run a hospital. Professional hospital administrators with strong business backgrounds moved in and guided the multifaceted, technology-dominant hospitals into the present. Doctors didn't like it.

Today, all physician groups of any size employ part-time or full-time business administrators to handle complex contract negotiations, personnel issues and the numbing details of the balance sheet and all of its implications. Thus, just as doctors remain the only competent health professionals capable of dealing with complex medical issues, so do these business professionals, in private practices as well as in hospitals, serve the tasks of hospital administration.

Complex and painful professional relationships evolved over the last two or three decades as medical care became more intricate, time-consuming and data-intensive. Doctors no longer had the time or the expertise to run a hospital, and certainly were incapable of administrative leadership in a modern high-tech facility. The authoritarian, autonomous (usually Caucasian male) physician of the recent past could not function alone in today's hospital. The doctor's power base has been eroded, his authority challenged. Buffeted by health care business professionals who equate their knowledge and managerial capabilities with the doctor's clinical skills, the old-time doctor would decompensate when advised—or instructed—to adhere to a clinical pathway rather than his own pet, but possibly less efficient, method of treatment.

Medical authority has become decentralized. In the process, some aspects of care have improved, and others risk serving avarice rather than cure. This is particularly true today because new pharmaceutical agents and expensive hardware continue to flood the medical marketplace. Antibiotics typify an area of intense debate about drug choice in everyday practice. Does a mother want her child on the new drug she just heard about or read about on the Internet, rather than penicillin or one of its less expensive derivatives? Is the expensive harmonic scalpel any better than sharp, cold steel?

Who will get what? Richard D. Lamm of the Center for Public Policy and Contemporary Issues, University of Denver, suggests, "Physicians understandably have difficulty looking at the social context of disease." He emphasizes that the medical culture and ethical demands under which doctors function as patient advocates insist on the provision of health care that the public advocate cannot consider paying for. He continues, "No government can fund *any* public 'need' to the level that medical ethics now demand of physicians." Parenthetically, it is interesting to observe that doctors are being asked to deliver a level of care demanded by their patients, *not* supported by public policy, which—if not provided to meet the individual's demands—leaves the physician at risk of being sued without any federally mandated protection!

Three sources of power exist in the hospital:

- the medical staff
- the board of trustees
- the CEO

Before we look at the Chief Executive Officer, let's review the basics of how a hospital may be organized. Long before physicians took it to heart, it was known that specialization led to improved efficiency. This is true of large organizations as well. The following principles form the groundwork for most hospital bureaucracies (I. Donald Snook, Jr., "Hospital Organization and Management" in *Health Care Administration—Principles, Practices, Structures and Delivery* by Lawrence F. Wolper):

- **DIVISION OF LABOR** written job descriptions and task lists of specific technical jobs with some crossover capability
- **PYRAMID ORGANIZATION** hierarchical organization with department heads at top and assistants and workers at lower levels; authority flows from the top down
- **A SYSTEM OF RULES** limits set on acceptable behavior and job boundaries, described in the personnel handbook; important in defining areas of expertise
- **UNITY OF COMMAND** each employee answers to one boss, and the violation of this principle results in disciplinary action
- **SPAN OF CONTROL** each leader or supervisor may direct a relatively small number of workers—the higher up the hierarchy, the fewer the number; the complexity of the subordinates' jobs determines how many report to a specific supervisor
- **DELEGATION** assignment of decisions to the lowest appropriate level of function and talent consistent with the decision; some supervisors fail to "release" power to their subordinates

- **LINE AND STAFF FUNCTIONS** *line authority* refers to direct supervision of workers, while *staff authority* is more indirect, more advisory; line authority involves "Do this, now." Staff authority conducts meetings to discuss options and suggest guidelines to underlings.
- **COORDINATION** between departments, both clinical and non-clinical; requires good communication among all middle managers and staff

The Chief Executive Officer (CEO)

The first university business course for hospital administrators was offered in the mid-1930s at a time when hospitals were run by older members of the nursing staff, clergy or a retired physician. Growing up in the system is no longer possible because of the complex nature of the CEO's job. Usually a master's degree in business administration or public administration, public health, is required. In the 1930s the hospital administrator dealt primarily with internal affairs, while the CEO of the 1970s and today has become overrun with governmental policies, labor party concerns and innumerable third-party-payer issues. As we will see, in the waning years of this century the job got tougher.

Today the CEO must coordinate a delicate balancing act between limited resources and the hospital's mission, trim personnel and services and keep the medical staff supplied with the proper tools with which to carry out their patient-care programs. Not all doctors understand that they can't have every gimmick on their wish list. Not all hospitals have the same goals. The CEO must understand the hospital's blend of service, education and research. External issues constantly compete and impinge upon these internal components of the hospital's mission.

The CEO must ensure high-quality patient care. The internal issues include ensuring a solid physical plant with appropriate technology and equipment, a chore more daunting today, with every department insisting the latest hardware must be purchased in order to remain competitive (doctors have learned a lot about business as well). Also, the supervision of hospital operations and employees is the CEO's responsibility through a complex extension of assistant administrators to whom the CEO delegates specific tasks. The CEO must keep the trustees and doctors informed of any strategic planning decisions. Most important is the CEO's relationship with the hospital's physicians, keeping the established staff happy while at the same time attracting new doctors.

Board meetings serve as the platform for communicating information about established hospital policies and anticipated changes, and to discuss future directions. With his staff, the CEO prepares annual budgets and submits them to the board of trustees, who must approve the fiscal plans. The chief administrator acts as the board's representative in the day-to-day functioning of the hospital. The third power source in the hospital—the medical staff—must be dealt with in a partnership atmosphere to enhance communication.

Even though the medical staff is ultimately answerable to the board of trustees, physicians and other health professionals follow the dictates of their own medical staff by-laws. These two leadership groups, doctors and hospital administrators, often rub against each other for the reasons mentioned previously, and conflict may arise. It is a natural by-product of the lofty, but divergent, traditional roles of physicians and the hospital's business leadership. Good communication usually solves most conflict—unless your story requires disagreement.

And, of course, on top of all of this is the CEO's need to keep the rest of the family happy. This includes the nurses and all of the ancillary personnel in sundry departments. Finally, the CEO is responsible for patients receiving appropriate care in a safe environment with adequate confidentiality.

Then there are numerous external issues that have mushroomed in the last two decades. These *external activities* of the CEO include:

- relating to the local community and keeping the public updated on hospital care and new programs
- educating the public about what is available as well as about wellness issues
- projecting a favorable image in the media
- negotiating with third-party payers and cultivating the best deal for the institution
- dealing with governmental reimbursement agencies and keeping updated on all new changes as they affect the hospital's bottom line
- negotiating with multiple vendors in order to obtain the best deals for the hospital without compromising principles or showing favoritism in dealing with local merchants and businesspeople

In order to accomplish all of this, the CEO usually has an assistant or vice president in charge of each major department or area of the hospital. Reporting directly to the CEO, these assistants ensure that each hospital unit is covered and incorporated under the overall administrative umbrella. Some physicians are becoming involved with hospital administration, particularly at a time when early retirement leaves this pool of talented doctors in search of new horizons. No doubt in the future hospitals will rely on an evermore intimate interaction among seasoned doctors and administrators to make the difficult decisions regarding what represents effective care and what is truly marginal medicine. In other words, these two sources of hospital authority will jointly decide what costs can be cut out of the budget.

The Medical Staff and Hospital Administration

Every hospital has a medical staff that consists of physicians—both allopathic and osteopathic—dentists, podiatrists and other allied health care personnel. The medical staff deals directly with the evaluation and treatment of patients. All other personnel are supportive in varying degrees. Not only do staff doctors possess the requisite authorization of the board of trustees to practice in the hospital, but they are also the only group that possesses the moral authority to do so. And no matter how powerful the hospital administrator, that individual has no moral investment in direct patient care. For this reason a physician's demands may be challenged and denied, but they cannot be ignored.

Appointed by the board of trustees, the medical staff then forms its own governing body and practices by its own by-laws. The profession holds its members to high standards and must police its members, some of whom are single-minded, disgruntled and, at times, obtuse. The Joint Commission on Accreditation of Healthcare Organizations has outlined the procedure for accepting a new physician to a medical staff position. Spelled out in each hospital's by-laws, the following steps in the appointment process are completed by the doctor applying for privileges:

• The physician completes a full application form, which is sent to the CEO.

• The application is reviewed for necessary data and sent to the specific department under whose leadership the doctor will practice; e.g., pediatrics or surgery.

- The application is then sent to the credentials committee of the medical staff; they review qualifications as well as any past professional activities; this committee may ask to meet the candidate.
- The medical staff executive committee reviews the application and, if acceptable, forwards it to the board of trustees.
- The board, through its entire complement or a committee, will accept or reject the application; more information may be required, and the application may be deferred to a joint conference committee.
- If acceptable, the CEO notifies the candidate of the successful completion of his application for staff privileges.
- The doctor must apply for and limit her practice to specific interventions, treatments and/or procedures as spelled out in the *delineation of privileges*; a surgeon thus may not perform just any operation, but only those identified in his privileges.

Through the function of specific committees, the medical staff is responsible for hiring well-trained doctors, ensuring they have appropriate qualifications, continuing medical education and appropriate monitoring of their clinical activities. If necessary the medical staff must discipline their members and censure doctors whose behavior is inappropriate and inconsistent with the standards set by the medical staff in its by-laws. Medical staffs may be *open* or *closed*. Any qualified doctor may apply for privileges on an open hospital medical staff. But in those institutions, for reasons of need, skill or availability of patients, the hospital restricts physician numbers on staff—not all doctors are accepted. Restraint of trade and other legal issues may be raised by excluded doctors, but the hospital is on solid ground if these decisions are made for economic and resource reasons.

Who are the other health professionals?

If the care of the severely ill patient requires the physician's energy to be directed at diagnosis, workup and complex interventions, who carries out the basic treatment plan? As the house staff are constantly reminded by their Attending consciences, nothing ever got done by writing an order. Someone has to administer the IV antibiotic, inject the medication, book the physical therapy appointment, remove sutures and change dressings. And when the patient is discharged, someone has to play a lot of fancy phone tag to complete plans for transfer to another facility or home with assistance.

The nurse does all of that. And much more.

The Nurse

It is curious, in retrospect, to recognize the dominant role of nurses in the origin and administration of early American hospitals. Doctors held little hope for, and participated only marginally in, the *almshouse*, as the early hospital was called, and its putrescence and its poor, uneducated denizens. Affluent patients were treated at home. The adverse conditions of the early hospitals in Europe and the New World have already been discussed. Thus, the fundamental issues of public health and the provision of care—perhaps the subtext in this latter discussion point is the first instance of *caring*—were addressed by the emerging nursing profession long before doctors regularly set foot inside the hospital.

The twenty-first century will present enormous challenges to the nursing profession. As physicians struggle to solve the dilemmas of the elderly, the intricacies of transplantation medicine, the special physiology of the critically ill with multi-organ failure and the riddles of the AIDS virus and its devastation to the human immune system, so will nurses need to manage the victims of these complex diseases. New skills and additional knowledge will be required to care for patients with co-morbid conditions. New operative procedures requiring special postop care, mysterious and previously unwitnessed infections treated by new antibiotics, novel nutritional support requirements served by complex carbohydrate, fat, protein, mineral and vitamin solutions, to mention but a few issues, will tax the nurses' armamentarium of clinical talents. The addition of computers and intricate technology has already changed the face of hospital care provided by nurses.

Modern nursing theory captures the essence of the evaluation and management of ill patients, the nurse's fundamental goal since the beginning of compassionate care. In the current era much scientific material has percolated down from the medical profession to the nursing profession, which has become evidence-based and outcomes-oriented, much like the physician's goals. A resource which underpins this discussion is the *Illustrated Manual of Nursing Practice*, edited by Beth S. Buxbaum, Elizabeth Mauro and Crystal G. Norris (Springhouse Corporation, 1994).

The American Nurses' Association defines its focus: "Nursing is the diagnosis and treatment of human responses to actual and potential health problems." Although the origins of nursing are embedded in a militaristic tradition of obedience, it was Florence Nightingale who started nursing schools, which were independent of hospitals and where she encouraged critical thinking and patients' rights. The first American nursing school opened in 1873, and in time most realigned themselves with hospitals for financial reasons. From basic (and very much needed) sanitation issues and public health concerns, nursing changed in the fifth and sixth decades of the twentieth century as medical care became more sophisticated.

Specialization fit into the nurses needs just as it did for doctors. By midcentury opportunities for women's education had improved, opening the door for the nursing profession to move ahead, independent from physician domination.

Nurses have been referred to as the doctor's handmaiden, angels of mercy and sex objects. Their real role seems closer to a mother, a giver of unconditional care. It seems the media has anchored the nursing profession in a gender stereotype, although TV programs such as *ER* and recent movies portraying women as leaders in health care as both nurses and physicians should erase the misperception of women in "follower" roles. Part of the problem is undoubtedly the broad landscape nurses cover in their training and education.

Types of Nurses

The American Nurses' Association recognizes two categories of nursing practice:

- professional
- associate

The minimum requirement is a baccalaureate degree in nursing, the BSN degree, acquired at a four-year college or university. The associate's degree in nursing, the ADN degree, may be obtained from a junior or community college in two years. In addition to these two degrees, a nurse may train at a hospital-affiliated diploma program, or acquire a master's degree or a doctorate. All of these degrees allow the candidate to sit for the RN licensing examination. Not to be confused with these nursing degrees is the LPN, the licensed practical nurse, whose education involves only one year in a vocational, technical or trade school, a hospital or a community college. LPNs are also called *LVNs* (licensed vocational nurses). LPNs always work under the supervision of a registered nurse, and are not allowed to pass medications out to patients unless they have obtained a special medication certificate.

Certified nursing assistants take a six-month course, are tested and receive a state certificate as nursing assistants. They are not allowed to give medications, but they are allowed to do IM (intramuscular) injections such as immunizations.

Nurses' aides usually receive on-the-job training at the hospital where they are employed and help on the floor with making beds, bathing patients, providing bedside water, and helping patients to the bathroom or into wheelchairs.

Duties and Opportunities

The *Illustrated Manual of Nursing Practice* describes the following opportunities for nurses in the new century:

- **ENTREPRENEURSHIP** nurses have started businesses associated with health care, including ownership of agencies
- **PUBLIC POLICY** assuming roles in local, state and federal government, nurses have impacted health care policy
- **PRIMARY CARE NURSING** delivering well-baby, screening and educational programs to communities; also provide site-friendly care to individuals
- **HOSPITAL CARE** provide high-tech care to complex patients with multiple problems in intensive care units, stepdown units and regular medical, pedi, OB/GYN and surgical floors—all more complicated today; this reduces the nurse's traditional role as intimate one-on-one caregiver; may become clinical nurse specialist with special knowledge and skills
- **CASE MANAGEMENT** a single nurse may provide uninterrupted comprehensive care to a particular patient to obviate fragmentation; nurse may orchestrate all aspects of workup and followup, and manage the patient during subsequent hospitalizations
- **TELEMATICS** the storage and retrieval of medical information and the associated issue of confidentiality involve nurses and doctors

alike; nurses are beginning to become involved in this aspect of communication, including the daily use of floor computer systems

- **ANCILLARY PERSONNEL** as fewer dollars flow into the hospital from payers, more and more help for the ill will come from families and trained assistants who will perform tasks formerly assigned to the nursing staff; this raises the issue of the competence of lesser trained personnel
- **LONG-TERM CARE FACILITIES** young and old with short-term and long-term disabilities require special care with chores daily; nurses may elect to dedicate themselves to the special needs of this population; includes spinal cord and head injury victims, orthopedic surgery and those recovering from life-threatening medical diseases
- **GERIATRIC NURSING** America is aging swiftly, and large numbers of the elderly need special care as they grow feeble; this patient population also requires special care when they fall prey to the illnesses of old age such as arthritis, heart failure, cancer and stroke
- **COMMUNITY NURSING** home care will continue to be an important aspect of the health care package offered to most Americans; high-tech equipment, the hardware of surgical and other interventional treatments, now often goes home with the patient; nursing care in the home requires familiarity with the drains, tubes, etc., of hospital treatment
- **OFFICE NURSING** although many variously trained personnel work in doctor's offices, nurses are especially needed to assist in performing office procedures and chaperoning where assistance may be needed with special equipment and the handling of specimens

Perhaps the best way to appreciate what a nurse does is to examine Maslow's hierarchy of needs as listed in the *Manual*. It is insightful for all health care providers to consider the needs of human beings across the biologic spectrum, as the ranking of these essential issues often occurs unconsciously in the setting of complex care. Maslow provides a hierarchy of needs, a fundamental list of physiologic forces that drive us all to our sundry behaviors. It would no doubt be useful for physicians to think of their patients in these terms as well.

Since the beginning of time, humankind has struggled up the ladder of Maslow needs, becoming more sophisticated as the species developed increasingly abstract thoughts. Still, at the most concrete level are survival issues. Thus, the Maslow hierarchy lists human needs as follows:

- **BASIC PHYSIOLOGIC NEEDS** shelter from the elements, temperature control, protection of the body and the satisfaction of the instincts involving sex, fighting, feeding and dominance
- **SAFETY AND SECURITY** need for security from assault and psychological threat and stability in one's life situation
- **LOVE AND BELONGING** need for love and alignment with a family and/or group to provide affection and reassurance
- **SELF-ESTEEM** need for a sense of self-worth, dignity and independence
- **SELF-ACTUALIZATION** growth of self as independent thinker, autonomy and realization of one's own potential

A patient who arrives in the ER following a major motor vehicle accident with chest trauma and a fractured extremity doesn't need to discuss his life's work with the ER triage nurse. He needs a chest X ray, a splint, a leg X ray and possibly a stat chest tube—to mention only a brief assessment. This victim is wallowing at the base of Maslow's needs hierarchy, his life endangered by trauma, his "higher" thoughts placed on hold. Survival is the patient's primary goal. Alternatively, after morning rounds by a surgical team during which time her prognosis was discussed, a patient with liver metastasis from colon cancer is left depressed and despondent. This patient needs a nurse who is sensitive to her emotional state. The patient requires support; she needs to be listened to by her nurse. No physical treatment will render her disease free.

The Nursing Process
Every nurse is taught the same *nursing process*. While this approach is similar to what physicians do to assess their patients, the nursing evaluation process focuses more on the total needs of the patient. The following steps are followed by all nurses caring for a patient:

- assessment
- nursing diagnosis
- planning
- intervention
- evaluation

The medical record documents the doctor's pathophysiologic diagnosis, the determination of what's gone wrong with the body machinery. The nursing diagnosis refers to the patient's response to that illness. In the case of the terminal cancer patient just mentioned, the nurse understands the dismal prognosis. Thus, the nurse's assessment is of a depressed patient who is malnourished and stressed from anesthesia and surgery. While the physician's treatment plan may include postop chemotherapy, the nurse focuses on emotional support, colostomy care, dietary needs and comfort issues, including pain management. Nursing interventions evolve from these concerns. Then the nurse determines whether the things she is doing are working. Certainly in the example of a terminal cancer patient, comfort care will succeed where chemotherapy is doomed to fail.

As with practicing physicians, nurses are encouraged to follow *practice guidelines*, predetermined protocols that spell out the best care plan for a given situation. And as with medical guidelines, these nursing guidelines are not always met, or at least not in their entirety. According to the *Illustrated Manual of Nursing Practice* a nursing intervention includes the following steps and obligations:

- to clearly state the action to be taken
- to tailor the interventions to fit the patient's needs and ability
- to ensure the patient's safety
- to follow the rules and standards of your facility
- to consider the patient's other health care needs and activities
- to include available resources

Documentation is just as important for nurses as it is for physicians. The course of action taken by the nurse should parallel that pursued by the doctor of record, and there should be concordance on goals and expected outcomes. If a substantial difference exists between the nurse's notes and the doctor's progress notes, the medical record is weakened. This becomes a real issue in cases of medical malpractice, from which nurses are not immune.

Thus, as physicians set into motion the intricate technologic treatment capabilities of the modern hospital, the nurses provide their own caring and direction for these patients, guiding patients through their hospital course and aiding them in planning their after-hospital convalescence.

During hospitalization as well as after discharge, other health care professionals enter the therapeutic picture as well.

Nonphysician Clinicians

As the number of medical school graduates is reduced and the number of residency slots are cut, doctors will be less available to perform the tasks traditionally assigned to them. This despite an excess of American physicians by some calculations. To fill in and complete the care patients expect is a group collectively known as *nonphysician clinicians (NPC)* or *physician extenders*. The number of NPCs in ten categories doubled between 1992 and 1997.

Physicians have traditionally used state and federal regulations, licensure and exclusive third-party-payment agreements to control the delivery of medical services in the United States. Added to this mix was the increased production of doctors in the 1970s, 1980s and 1990s in all specialties. Only at the turn of the decade, with health care costs continuing to soar, have alternative ideas about patient care become viable. These nonphysician clinicians now perform many of the lower skill level tasks previously handled by doctors.

The following chart lists the basic personnel who assist doctors in various settings as NPCs. Richard Cooper et al. describe three reasons why doctors are being displaced from some of their traditional roles. These are:

- changes in state laws and regulations favoring NPCs
- the marketplace is providing new opportunities for NPCs in clinical practice
- the number of NPCs is growing

Between 1992 and 1997 the number of training programs for certified nurse midwives doubled, and the increase in training programs for physician assistants rose by 50 percent. Although the number of chiropractic schools has remained unchanged in the last ten years, the total number of graduates has doubled since 1965. Acupuncture schools reached thirty-three in number by 1997, and four naturopathy schools graduated 170 naturopaths in that same year. By contrast, specialty training in optometry and podiatry have remained constant since 1990.

Categories of Nonphysician Clinicians

TRADITIONAL DISCIPLINES
- nurse practitioners (NP)
- physician assistants (PA)
- certified nurse midwife (CNM)

ALTERNATIVE DISCIPLINES
- chiropractors
- naturopaths
- acupuncture and herbal medicine practitioners

SPECIALTY DISCIPLINES
- optometrists
- podiatrists
- certified registered nurse anesthetist (CRNA)
- clinical nurse specialist (CNS)

Critical to an understanding of the nonphysician clinician's role in the health care system is the evolution of ever-new regulations that determine the NPC's autonomy and level of authority. Specific types of uncomplicated primary and specialty care have been identified, which adds another level of care to an already complex medical system. According to Richard Cooper et al., in a study designed to evaluate the practice prerogatives of nonphysician clinicians, five trends have emerged as legislative directives emerge for NPCs.

- There is substantial variation in the range of prerogatives granted to NPCs in different states.

- In those states that have granted the most extensive prerogatives, the NPCs in fact have significant authority and autonomy.

- Overall, NPCs' activities overlap with some services provided by doctors in the realm of what is called "simple licensed general care" and "routine licensed specialty care."

- The nonphysician clinicians' participation is increasing as these clinical tasks become well-defined and as the market influences how medical care is provided.

- The parallel growth of NPC prerogatives is occurring at a time when more practitioners are being trained to perform these very same NPC disciplines.

It becomes clear that, as these members of an ever-increasing pluralistic health care workforce participate in the performance of what were once physician's duties, that additional regulations and supervision will be required. Already turf battles are developing between NPCs and doctors regarding reimbursement. What is of most concern to traditional physicians is the potential for abuse in such a multidimensional system. The essence of the role of NPCs becomes: Will a nonphysician clinician miss a lethal disease because of a lack of training or a failure to appropriately refer a patient to a doctor?

NPC Training and Authority

To grasp who these health care workers are, let's look at their basic training and what their roles in medical care are supposed to be. Again, Cooper et al. state, "The goal of chiropractic education, which spans four years, is to prepare chiropractors to be primary care providers who can serve as the portal of entry to the health care system, performing wellness care, general primary care and musculoskeletal care." The quandary is that only 15 percent of a chiropractor's education is devoted to an understanding of organ systems other than the musculoskeletal system. Practitioners of acupuncture and herbal medicine after a three-year course usually limit their care to the relief of such relatively nonspecific disorders as musculoskeletal complaints, headache, fatigue, menstrual cramps, fibromyalgia, low back pain, asthma, anxiety and depression. Naturopaths receive a baccalaureate followed by four years of postgraduate training in health promotion and disease prevention. Their philosophy of treatment is based on stimulating the body's own defenses against disease and doesn't permit them to prescribe drugs or perform simple procedures.

All fifty states permit the three alternative-discipline practitioners to perform physical examinations and diagnose patients' conditions. This includes ordering and interpreting laboratory tests and X rays. Despite their outpatient-based training and primary care orientation, naturopaths are allowed to suture and to attend uncomplicated deliveries without physician supervision. None of the three disciplines may prescribe controlled substances.

The three *specialty* NPCs have broader authority. *Optometrists* are not designated as "doctor" by state statute, even though the term is used in practice, but they are able to examine the eyes, make a diagnosis and prescribe corrective lenses. Optometrists may also remove foreign bodies, and in some states may treat glaucoma. *Podiatrists* train for four years, just as the optometrists do, and cover a wide variety of topics from anatomy, orthopedics and trauma to anesthesia and sports medicine. They are certified in all states and practice independently. They may perform surgery under local anesthesia, offer medical treatment and prescribe prosthetic devices. Again, the term "doctor" is frequently used in daily practice, but only six states specifically allow the use of the term "podiatric physician" or "podiatric surgeon." *Certified Registered Nurse Anesthetists* receive extensive training in the administration of various anesthetics, as well as in pain management. In only nine states are CRNAs allowed to prescribe controlled substances, while in the other states a physician—it may be an anesthesiologist (usually) or a surgeon—must serve as a supervisor. *Clinical Nurse Specialists* have a master's degree in a specific clinical area. In twenty states they may practice independently, while in twenty-four states a physician's supervision is necessary. In only nine states CNSs prescribe controlled substances.

Thus, many areas of overlapping services exist between doctors and nonphysician clinicians, and the differences in training allow varying levels of expertise. Much of the care provided to patients still remains within the realm of a licensed physician. This care is obviously more complex. However, as Cooper explains, "These prerogatives, which are central to the practice authority of physicians, have been granted to NPCs under at least some circumstances in most states, and in many states they have been granted independent of direct physician involvement." Some NPCs evaluate a broad range of clinical problems; others function within a tight specialty focus.

Four levels of care have been described (Cooper et al., 1998):

- **SIMPLE LICENSED GENERAL CARE** wellness instruction; care of uncomplicated or self-limited illnesses is provided by the traditional and alternative care NPCs
- **COMPLEX LICENSED GENERAL CARE** severe, often multi-organ disease is beyond the scope of the NPC and is handled exclusively by physicians
- **ROUTINE LICENSED SPECIALTY CARE** focused care in specific areas performed by both specialty physicians as well as specialty

NPCs such as podiatrists, optometrists, certified registered nurse anesthetists and clinical nurse specialists

- **COMPLEX LICENSED SPECIALTY CARE** care of complicated cases is restricted to specialty physicians

What will the future hold for nonphysician clinicians? Certainly, the current trend toward more involvement in a pluralistic health care system will continue, with NPCs performing tasks previously assigned only to doctors. NPCs cost the system less. To date no overwhelming number of malpractice cases have arisen as a consequence of NPCs performing simple clinical work. The problem with the current system of ten different groups of nonphysician providers is the lack of a uniform philosophy of care. If each group insists on pursuing its own agenda, the fragmentation of American medicine may become worse.

Also, will there be excessive overlap and redundancy? More costs? Can each program be modified to permit uniformity in health care delivery? How much independent practice by nonphysicians should be allowed, and what degree of supervision is appropriate to avoid missed diagnoses, inappropriate treatment and increased litigation? Finally, are these alternative disciplines legitimate, and do they offer substantial gains over no intervention for most self-limited illnesses?

Thus, we return to the nettled question raised earlier in the chapter: Are NPCs providing as part of their effort what is referred to as *marginal medicine*?

The question of validity has been addressed for chiropractic and leaves even more questions to sort out. In the October 8, 1998, issue of *The New England Journal of Medicine*, Dr. Paul G. Shekelle comments on two studies reviewed in that issue of the *Journal*. He concludes that for nonmusculoskeletal disorders, spinal manipulation is of no benefit based on the study of Balon et al. reported in that issue. A second study by Cherkin et al. reported in the same issue of the *Journal* demonstrated a slight improvement in recovery from low back pain with chiropractic spinal manipulation, a response similar to one also noted in that study following physical therapy. However, neither of these treatments had more than a marginal advantage over simply providing the patient with an informational booklet. Perhaps subsets of low back pain patients will prove to respond better to spinal manipulation. At any rate, the real issue is whether or not in the future third-party payers will agree to reimburse for treatments of questionable value.

Technicians and Technologists

A large portion of the day-to-day work in the hospital is performed by trained technicians and technologists. *Technicians* are usually trained for a specific task. They will receive three to six months' training in a specialized area to perform that task well. These might include lab technicians (drawing blood and collecting blood samples on the floors, collecting urine specimens, preparing or staining tissue, etc.), EKG technicians and technicians in various testing areas to perform certain tasks that they have been trained to do.

Technologists, on the other hand, have far more extensive educational requirements and more important roles in the hospital. Technologists take two to three years of college or vocational courses in their particular field of interest, and then receive additional in-hospital training for a year or more. They have courses in anatomy, physiology and pathology, as well as courses related to their specialty. Following their training, they must pass an examination to become a certified technologist. Many technology subspecialties require additional training and separate examinations to be certified in that field.

Technologists have far more responsibility for patient care than do technicians. Radiology technologists perform a variety of examinations on patients, including X-ray filming, GI barium contrast examinations, IVPs, assisting with biopsies, doing all trauma X rays in the ER and performing various studies in surgery. In addition to general radiology, there are many subspecialties requiring additional training and often separate certification such as MRI (magnetic resonance imaging), CT scanning, ultrasound scanning, mammography, nuclear medicine, stereotactic breast biopsies and interventional angiography.

In most of these areas, the technologist is responsible for the patient from the time she arrives in the department until she leaves at the end of the examination. In MRI, technologists are trained in the physics of MRI scanners and are responsible for positioning the patient and performing the scan, injecting contrast during the study under the supervision of a physician and filming the examination. Ultrasound technologists have extensive knowledge of the physics of ultrasound and of the equipment they use. In all the areas mentioned, the technologist, in addition to being well-trained on sophisticated technical equipment, has a good knowledge of normal anatomy and of pathology and will tailor the examinations to better assess any disease process they see during the study.

Highly trained technologists perform a very important role in the hospital, and doctors rely heavily on them to obtain excellent-quality diagnostic studies. Their part in medical care and diagnosis is critical, and as medicine becomes more technologically advanced, the technologist's role is even greater.

Social Workers
The very nature of the modern hospital necessitates extensive discharge planning. Vital to determining the level of ongoing care required for individual patients is the social worker, who is an expert on what services are available in the local community and elsewhere in the state. Levels of care must be identified, and a rehabilitation or chronic care facility selected, for patients unable to function independently. The social worker interviews the patient and the family, and together they identify the appropriate facility for the patient. For patients who only require home health aide or assisted living personnel, the social worker selects the proper agency to set up the necessary home visits.

Hospital Orderlies and Transporters
Orderlies function in many capacities in the hospital. They "fill in the blanks," so to speak, in the provision of smooth care to patients who must not only be cared for but must also be transported to various venues in the diffuse geography of the medical center. Orderlies lift, transport, clean, cajole and comfort patients. They interact with sick people and participate in their care, often performing tasks that may not be viewed as desirable by the patient.

Ill folks must be lifted in and out of bed, pushed in wheelchairs, lifted onto stretchers, walked around the floor after surgery or procedures and cleaned up when they soil themselves. Nurses and orderlies share the many odious chores that make successful, compassionate care possible. The really good orderlies are cheerful ambassadors as well as dedicated workers. Some are resentful and dour. The latter usually don't last.

Some hospitals have a corps of "transporters" whose sole function is to transport patients within the hospital complex. Some hospitals have developed very elaborate transportation systems, with portable phones for each transporter, who is directed to various areas of the hospital to transport patients when needed. There is a dedicated phone operator-manager who answers pages for transport requests and then directs the transporters to those areas where they are needed.

Hospital Volunteers

"Candy stripers," often young girls, populate modern hospitals as cheerful assistants who carry flowers, candy and mail to recovering patients. Often these youngsters have or cultivate an interest in entering the nursing or medical professions. Dealing with the hospital environment as helpers exposes them to patients in all phases of their care and provides the young volunteers with a unique view of reality not seen outside of the hospital.

Many hospital volunteers are elderly folks with time and insight who wish to give something back to the community. Not infrequently, these helpers have recovered from a serious illness themselves and feel they owe a debt to those who guided them through the hospital experience. Their role includes transporting patients and talking with them, a service not addressed well by the sundry busy professionals.

CHAPTER SIX

Patient Wards and Critical Care Units (ICUs)

H ospitals vary in size and complexity, with physical layout and archi-tectural characteristics defined by each institution's unique evolu-tion (the addition of wings). Hospitals range from twenty-bed, rural com-munity facilities to complex urban medical centers with satellite buildings for medical education, research, nursing and other allied health care ser-vices such as physical therapy and rehabilitation. As a result of the parallel development of modern hospitals and the sequential addition of new wings and satellite buildings, most medical facilities can look a little disjointed.

Traditionally, hospitals were divided into four main patient-care areas: medicine, surgery, pediatrics and obstetrics/gynecology. Those four divi-sions still hold today, but as medicine has become more specialized and complex, those broad divisions now possess their own subdivisions. For instance, internal medicine and surgery have become extensively diversi-fied. Internal medicine now includes cardiology, gastroenterology, ne-phrology, rheumatology, hematology-oncology, endocrinology, neurol-ogy, dermatology, pulmonary and allergy. Surgical subspecialties include trauma, vascular, plastics, endocrine, bariatric, oncology, ENT, ophthal-mologic and even one-disease services such as a breast service.

The hospital's complex with its sundry subspecialty services requires dedicated and specially trained nurses and other personnel as well as a multitude of high-tech equipment. The range of services and cost continue to expand.

Hospital Campus

- Each hospital has a main building and one or more outbuildings; some hospitals are campuses with dozens of buildings.
- Each hospital has parking garages and flat or surface parking.
- Specialty clinics may be in satellite buildings.
- Large medical schools may even have specialty hospitals; e.g., complete buildings for pediatrics.
- There are hospitals for surgical specialties; e.g., hernia clinics, cardiac surgery programs and comprehensive breast programs.
- Walkways and underground tunnels often connect hospital buildings.

Usually these buildings are identified by numbers or letters assigned to them for easy reference. This simple lettering (building A, B or C) or numbering allows for quick directions and response from the hospital staff in case of an emergency.

For instance, if there were a cardiac arrest in one of the subspecialty clinics, the overhead page for the code might be:

"Attention, Memorial Hospital. CODE BLUE, building C, second floor, adult team respond."

Or if there were a fire alarm, the overhead page might be:

"Attention, Memorial Hospital. CODE RED, building A, ground floor."

When the hospital consisted of only one main building, patient areas were identified as being on the "surgical floor" or the "surgical ward." These terms still apply for smaller hospitals, where each floor may represent one of the four main medical divisions. Instead of saying the patient is on the surgical floor, it is more common (and accurate) to say the patient is on 5-North, or on 4-South, East wing, or building D 6-West.

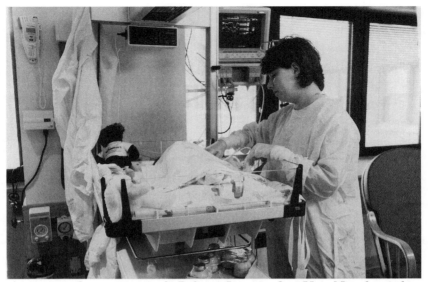

A nurse attends to a patient in the Pediatric Intensive Care Unit. Note the windows in each room, the clocks on the wall and the cardiac telemetry monitors on the wall. In the pediatric unit, there are chairs beside each bed, which allows parents to hold and rock their babies. This parental bonding and human contact is very important for babies.

And since medical and surgical patients are usually located in more than one area of the hospital, the term "surgical ward" no longer applies.

Intensive Care Units (Critical Care Areas)

If the modern hospital's primary task is to provide sophisticated, technology-driven care, then it is the secondary job of the institution to keep patients alive and safe when this care is given. The critical care areas assume their own primary task when used to monitor and treat unstable patients. Whether followup management or initial care is the goal of caring for a patient, the intensive care units in their various forms constitute the core of the modern high-tech hospital.

The intensive care unit has been referred to as the "hospital's hospital." Critical care areas have the highest standards of medical, nursing and institutional support.

The design of an ICU reflects a balance between maximum surveillance and minimum privacy, with open-room and curtained-bed areas.

Intensive Care Units are designed either with glass doors exposing the front of the room to the nurses' desk, or as a large open area, with the nurses' station in the center, where there is constant immediate monitoring of every patient. This ICU with glass fronts to each room affords both privacy as well as clear monitoring from the nurses' desk.

The open-bay area has several advantages, including easier monitoring of the patient and easier access to the patient. However, some ICUs have private rooms with total or partial glass walls and breakaway doors. Sophisticated monitoring devices can be used successfully to supplement visualization of the patient, allowing more patient privacy.

The high risk of cross-infection of an open ICU is often used as justification for solid partitions. But the studies on the relationship between ICU design and nosocomial infection have been inconclusive. Some researchers recommend an open unit; others recommend closed private units. The closed unit (private patient room or area) is more costly to construct than an open ICU. Stepdown beds (in stepdown nursing units) are used for patients who do not need skilled ICU care, but still require continued monitoring.

Stepdown beds require telemetry or portable monitoring. ICU areas have built-in oxygen, suction and monitors, and provide accommodation for infusion pumps, drainage suction and other monitors.

Stress on both patients and nurses is high in the anxiety-filled ICU. Typically, ICU nurses work twelve-hour shifts. And the turnover rate is the highest of any patient area in the hospital. This requires the nurses to constantly learn the history of new patients as they arrive—always in critical condition. Every effort should be made to minimize stress on both the nursing staff and the patients.

Private-room ICU patients suffer less anxiety and less pain (often re-lated to underlying fears). In an open-bay ICU, there is marked stress and anxiety related to watching other acutely ill patients and misinterpreting procedures being done on them. Features of the patient area to help reduce stress should include a large clock, a calendar and a window to the outside to maintain time and day/night orientation. These are very important considerations for any ICU and should not be overlooked.

This is so important that windows are required by code in all ICU patient rooms. ICU depression can be greatly helped with natural light. Rest and sleep are essential components of the recovery process, but both are difficult in the ICU. General lack of privacy, flashing lights, monitor noise, alarms, oxygen bubbling, mechanical respirators, humidifiers and printers all increase patient stress. Walls, curtains or other visual barriers should be used to provide patient-to-patient visual privacy while still allowing nursing staff visual access to patients.

Ways to reduce patient stress in the ICU
- windows for natural light (now required by code for all ICUs)
- patient privacy from other patients
- large visible clock
- calendar
- keep extraneous noise to a minimum

The trend in recent years has been to perform as much diagnostic and therapeutic work as possible in the ICU patient room in order to keep patient transport to an absolute minimum. Procedures would include inserting in-dwelling arterial lines, Swan-Ganz catheters and pace-makers.

Four Goals of the ICU
- direct observation of the patient as part of the monitoring function
- surveillance of physiological monitoring
- provision of routine and emergent therapeutic interventions
- recording of patient information

The vast array of medical experience gained during the Vietnam War was important not only because civilian trauma was on the increase, but also because the picture of the critically ill patient had shifted. Other causes of organ failure began to appear, and in the 1970s hospitals sharply increased their funding for acute care and invested more money for staff and equipment to treat ever-more complex patients. Before ICU care was available, patients with advanced cancer, severe accidents or catastrophic cardiac events were managed on a regular hospital floor.

With better machines came a growing *patient expectation*. Physicians began to understand the common features of acute illness, the similarities and the eventual final common pathway of demise—multi-organ failure.

With growing expertise came new specialists and a higher price tag. The sophisticated care provided by an intensive care unit in the mid-1970s cost approximately $500 a day, a figure felt to be stunning at the time. At the close of the twentieth century the same care costs about $2,000 a day. Of course, there are more critically ill patients admitted to the hospital today, some with illnesses that cannot be cured.

The Role of the ICU
To serve the needs of severely injured and critically ill patients, hospitals began to design special care units in the 1970s, and these early critical care areas have evolved into the well-recognized subspecialty ICUs of a modern medical center. These various units spawned single-disease units such as burn units, neurosurgical units, coronary care units and "shock-trauma" units. A general surgical ICU will treat cases of major trauma and severe sepsis; a medical ICU emphasizes the care of cardiology patients, critical medical problems and patients requiring continuous surveillance.

The United States Office of Technology Assessment in 1984 declared that critical care medicine:

- is a multidisciplinary and multiprofessional medical/nursing field
- provides care for patients who have or may develop life-threatening single- or multiple-organ failure from any disease or injury, necessitating minute-to-minute care and observation
- provides immediate and intensive life-saving therapies

One study (1995) indicated about 46 percent of patients were admitted to the ICU for monitoring rather than active interventions. The number of beds for a given hospital depends on the size of the facility. Also, the number of critical care specialty units is dependent on hospital size: Large medical centers will have neurological units for head injury, postoperative monitoring and stroke patients. Institutions performing large numbers of open-heart and transplant operations will have their own units with specially trained personnel.

Regardless of where they come from, all ICU patients must be discharged from the unit to an appropriate location in the hospital. Strosberg and Teres indicate these units may be of an intermediate nature in terms of the ongoing care of the previously critically ill patient, or the patient may have recovered adequately enough to be transferred to a regular floor.

Critical care treatment areas, also called *intensive care units*, are abbreviated by the hospital staff to "the unit." The Intensive Care Unit (ICU) is a strangely subdued place, often quite quiet and at other times noisy and frantic. What you hear are monitors—the constant beeping and sounding of alarms. Even though the unit is swarming with doctors, nurses, respiratory therapists and medical students, they usually talk in low voices. The background noise of daytime TV that fills most hospital rooms is only present in isolation rooms where patients are recovering and can appreciate the distraction, or in rooms where nurses use the TV for their own purposes (they are also isolated from the hospital world) .

Overhead one sees monitors displaying electronic signals of moving EKG patterns, oxygen saturation data, arterial line wave form and blinking alarm lights. The sounds are of the monitors chirping, a ventilator whooshing and sighing and alarms interrupting one's concentration, especially when the incessant beep-beep-beep suddenly stops.

Units Within the ICU

In small hospitals, there may only be two critical care areas, MICU (medical intensive care unit) and SICU (surgical intensive care unit). Or merely one ICU, four or six beds, which receives any complicated patient regardless of the specialty problem. The intent of the smaller hospital is to stabilize and then transfer critically ill patients, or to treat those problems that are within the hospital's level of expertise. The largest medical centers in the country not only have special care units, but are also usually involved in research; for example, providing patients with the opportunity to participate in protocols for the use of new drugs.

The medical-surgical intensive care unit, the most familiar critical care area, is where the most complicated interventions are used. Subspecialty units will be mentioned at the end of this section but, by comparison, the single-disease units do not engage in the variety of complex treatments seen in the general ICU.

Critically ill patients arrive in the intensive care unit

- directly from the hospital's emergency room
- from the operating room as a planned admission
- from the operating room as a complicated patient who is sicker than anticipated because
  1. surgery was complicated
  2. unexpected findings were encountered, requiring more surgery
  3. the patient deteriorated during surgery or may have experienced an adverse event such as a heart attack under anesthesia
  4. the patient can't be extubated (breathe on one's own)
- from a surgical floor where a patient decompensated after surgery (complication)
- from a medical floor where a patient developed a complication either of the disease for which she was admitted or a new problem
- from an obstetrics or gynecology floor where a postpartum or prepartum complication or new illness developed or a GYN post-op patient developed a complication
- a transfer via ambulance from an outlying hospital; e.g., major trauma or a patient who developed a complication during hospitalization that requires more sophisticated care
- a transfer via helicopter from a distant hospital with a fresh case

(trauma, massive heart attack, etc.) or a patient who deteriorated from any cause at a smaller hospital

- from a specialty unit in the hospital after undergoing an intervention such as radiologic-guided biopsy or drainage procedure, angioplasty or lung biopsy

An easy way to organize critical care interventions as they occur in various special units is to divide the components into three categories:
- basic monitoring
- advanced cardiopulmonary monitoring and treatment
- disease-specific complex interventions

Examples of these interventions for *basic monitoring* would include: EKG (arrhythmia search), pulse, respiration, blood pressure, oxygen saturation, level of consciousness (including recovery from general anesthesia) and wound assessment. A patient who was extubated (breathing tube removed and patient taken off of ventilator) but had a condition felt better monitored in the ICU for a possible recurrence or extension of the disease (more gangrenous bowel after partial removal, or loss of leg pulses after vascular reconstruction, etc.): Any possibility of more extensive disease is often watched overnight in the ICU. These patients are transferred out first thing in the morning or even during the night if there's a bed crunch and a sicker patient needs ICU admission.

Advanced cardiopulmonary monitoring and treatment would apply to the postoperative patient on a ventilator, in shock or requiring medication, blood and fluids to keep him out of shock, or a patient intubated in the ER with a severe stroke, abdominal complaint not requiring (immediate) surgery, septic abortion, overwhelming pneumonia, multiple trauma, etc., whose prognosis is grim and unknown. Special care for the primary medical or surgical problem doesn't alter the fact that, in the interval while further evaluation and workup is being performed, the patient needs life-saving care in the unit.

Complex disease-specific interventions include, for example, dialysis for acute kidney failure regardless of the cause, complicated ventilatory support with unique systems to increase oxygenation, complicated cardiac monitoring with derived (computerized) data and delicate drug interventions. Research

---

The Basic Care of a Critically Ill Patient

- *monitoring* of heart rate, blood pressure, EKG pattern and ar-rhythmia search, respiratory rate, oxygen saturation monitoring and core-temperature monitoring
- *management of cardiovascular system* with intravenous fluid, blood component therapy, cardiac drugs and various levels of advanced cardiac monitoring
- *management of ventilation* with airway control, oxygen supplementation via mask, prongs or endotracheal intubation and mechanical ventilation, assessment of arterial blood gases and indications for intubation/extubation
- *management of renal status* by survey of BUN and creatinine, which assess kidney function, as well as more advanced measurements of renal function and determining indications for dialysis and fluid management, including indications for IV-fluid restriction
- *assessment of fever* in all patients with cultures of body fluids, lines and tubes and with special radiological interventions such as CT-guided aspiration of body cavities
- *provision of nutritional support* by either the enteral (intestinal route via nasogastric tube, feeding tube, G-tube or J-tube) or the parenteral (intravenous) method; the latter may be partial support through a regular IV or complete nutritional support (TPN—total parenteral nutrition) via a central catheter or CVP
- *administration of prophylactic (preventive) measures* such as IV H_2 blockers to reduce the incidence of stress ulcers, prophylactic antibiotics, anticoagulation to avoid DVT or phlebitis, skin care, bowel regimen with enemas as needed, voiding assistance if not catheterized, time-space orientation with a calendar and verbal updates to time, place and person
- *provision of nursing care and total body support* with bathing, wound care, special beds to avoid decubitus ulcers, stoma care, special tubes and lines management and emotional support

---

protocols for a patient with severe sepsis may be used in patients with poor prognoses. These are the "sick sick" patients residents talk about.

What Is Critical Illness?

Intuitively, most people understand the progression of disease, the inexorable march of body deterioration as *something* falls apart, resulting in the patient's demise. The bedside vigil of home care as reflected in great works of art speaks to the helplessness physicians experienced before the era of intensive care for sick patients. That twilight of demise, the family deathwatch, acknowledged the futility of available medical care at the time.

Today, victims of severe illness are admitted to the hospital's intensive care unit. What is not known at that moment of instituting aggressive medical management is whether it will make any difference. Every writer who works in the realm of critical illness must understand why people become so sick and what can be done about it. We will look at what happens to the human body when sudden severe illness strikes, and then review what the different elements of ICU care are for each problem.

The most common reasons for admission to the ICU include (Strosberg and Teres, 1997):

- cardiac arrhythymias (life-threatening abnormal heartbeats)
- heart failure
- ischemic heart disease (acute myocardial infarction or heart attack)
- neurologic dysfunction (coma, stupor, etc.)
- post-trauma (blunt and penetrating; e.g., gunshot, auto accident or severe falls)
- after major (complex) surgery
- acute respiratory failure

Although patients on ventilators made up only 10 percent of the patient population in one study, they consumed 50 percent of the ICU resources. Another author estimated ventilated patients cost twice as much as nonventilated patients and up to eight times as much as a regular hospital patient.

Most patients remain in the ICU for about four or five days, although some will require two weeks of care. Most of the longer admissions are for patients on mechanical ventilation, and thus special respiratory units have been established in many hospitals to accept ventilated patients. Other choices for patients with chronic respiratory failure are rehabilitation facilities and nursing homes.

The above list of reasons for admission to the intensive care unit represents single-organ problems in some cases (heart failure) and multiple-organ involvement in others (trauma). As these patients are treated, some will fail and some will not respond to any of the interventions offered.

Critical Illness

Critical illness is best thought of as a major disruption of vital organ function. Cardiac, lung and kidney function are compromised or lost, and special machines replace the vital organ's capacity to support the body. The ICU staff's task is to utilize life-support machines when needed and to remove them from the patient's care management as soon as possible.

These unfortunate people, regardless of the reason they were admitted to the ICU in the first place, may progress down the path to disintegration of many body organs and tissues.

The terms *multiple-organ failure* and *multiple-systems organ failure* are both used to describe varying degrees of malfunction of more than one body system. The real task of the ICU staff is to look for signs of MOF, and it has been said that multiple-organ failure is defined by the team's efforts to prevent it.

To understand what happens in critical illness, it's necessary to have a basic grasp of normal organ function; without going into detail, the following brief descriptions of vital organ functions precede a discussion of multiple-organ failure. For it is the disintegration of vital organ physiology that characterizes the challenge of ICU care. If you see how each organ works, you'll understand how they fail. Then it's an easy jump to understanding how machines replace lost vital organ function.

Vital Organ Function

Normal vital organ function preserves the rest of the body by providing oxygen and blood and removing wastes. In order of speed of function and failure:

- **THE LUNG** is a double organ that matches blood flow and air exchange in the air sacs (alveoli); the transfer of oxygen into the blood and carbon dioxide out of the blood into the lungs for excretion is finely tuned; to work, the blood flow must match the air exchange and the air sacs must remain dry, which is the function of the membrane between the pulmonary capillary and the alveoli
- **THE HEART** is a four-chambered pump that receives oxygenated blood from the lungs (via pulmonary "veins") and pumps fresh

blood through the aorta to the entire body, with preferential and large amounts going to the brain and kidneys; the cardiovascular system, to work as a whole, must have the proper volume of blood, appropriate tone in the arteries and veins and a vigorous pump; vital organs cannot tolerate diminished blood flow for long, while nonvital organs and tissues (muscles, tendons, ligaments, fat) will survive for some time with decreased blood flow

- **THE KIDNEYS** remove body metabolic wastes, the acids, bases and other molecular debris from all organ function; kidneys work in unison with the lungs to maintain body chemistry and are sensitive to diminished blood flow

Two observations about vital organ function, which tie into the organ failures we will discuss next, are

1. Vital organs possess large reserves.
2. Vital organs respond to infectious and other general stress in a stereotypical manner.

First we will see how these principles apply to *lung dysfunction*. Immediately, you may ask: How does infection in the leg, for example, a long way from the chest, affect the lungs? How does that happen? Do bacteria travel to the lungs?

Rather than the bacteria themselves, the damage to the *pulmonary endothelium*, or the lining of the capillaries, the tiny end blood vessels, occurs because a substance called *complement* attracts neutrophils, a type of white blood cell, which are toxic for the endothelial lining. The capillaries become damaged and "leak," and the air sacs are then flooded with fluid.

Inflammation of the pancreas, an abdominal abscess from any cause, gangrenous leg, severe urinary tract infection and pneumonia—all can affect the lung's functional unit, the air sac-capillary complex. What happens next? Inspired air rich in oxygen never gets to the circulating blood because the air sacs are flooded. Also, there's a mismatch between the air inspired and the blood flowing to the air sacs; doctors call this a *ventilation-perfusion defect*. Not only does the air not match up with the available blood flow to the alveoli, but the flooding of air sacs interferes with oxygen exchange as well.

Causes of Adult Respiratory Distress Syndrome or Acute Respiratory Failure

- sepsis from any cause, including intra-abdominal abscess, gangrenous leg, septic abortion, pelvic infection of tubes and ovaries, perforated intestine or ulcer and urinary tract infection
- fat embolus ("chunks" of fat and bone marrow travel to the lungs after major long-bone fractures)
- amniotic fluid embolism (amniotic fluid enters maternal circulation and travels to lungs)
- cardiopulmonary bypass or open-heart surgery (mechanical pumping of blood)
- the effects of certain drugs
- the effects of blood transfusions
- severe inflammation of the pancreas (acute pancreatitis)
- severe closed (blunt) head injury

The patient's blood oxygen levels plummet (called *hypoxemia*—low blood oxygen levels), and the lungs fill with more and more fluid. On a chest X ray the lung fields look white, not unlike pneumonia (which is no more than infected fluid in the air sacs). Obviously there's support tissue in the lungs, the lace of the lacy air-tissue composition, and this interstitial tissue can also fill with fluid, further impairing gas exchange.

So much for your pathology lesson. The point is that despite great reserve the lung can be wiped out by diffuse leaky membranes, resulting in *A*dult *R*espiratory *D*istress *S*yndrome, or *ARDS*. Shock, trauma and severe infections can all cause ARDS. And other conditions such as blunt or closed head injuries can result in the "wet" lungs of ARDS (this condition goes by the fancy name *neurogenic pulmonary edema*).

Here's the tough part. ARDS, with its clinical presentation of low oxygen levels and chest X ray findings of "wet" lungs, can mimic pneumonia, congestive heart failure, IV-fluid overload and neurogenic pulmonary edema. A lot of ICU patients are potential candidates for more than one of these conditions. If they all look alike, how do you make the correct diagnosis?

We'll return to the answer to that question when we discuss monitoring of the critically ill patient. Because it ties into cardiac and renal (kidney) failure, we need to cover those diseases briefly first.

Cardiac failure also comes in more than one form. The root cause of inadequate forward flow of blood, or the excessive backing up of blood in the lungs—the two edges of the sword of pump function—is not easily sorted out, and in many patients is only identified with sophisticated cardiac monitoring after the identification or elimination of associated lung pathology. Another way to look at heart dysfunction is to pull back the camera and observe the shock states in which the heart, if not a lonely hunter, is at least a major player.

Shock may result in lung, heart and kidney failure, and it seems appropriate to wedge the topic in here between the first two and the final vital organ failure. So intimately are all forms of shock related to heart-lung failure as well as critical illness in general that a review of each major type of shock seems reasonable. The easiest way to keep shock straight is to think of three categories based on the anatomy of the system. (Oh, and seeing your grandmother naked *isn't* shock. It's something, and it may race your pulse or make you cold and clammy, but it isn't shock!)

The *three kinds of shock* seen in critically ill patients are:

- **PUMP FAILURE** the heart can't squirt out enough volume
- **VOLUME LOSS** may be blood loss or body fluid loss from sweating, vomiting, diarrhea, burns, etc.
- **BLOOD VESSEL CAPACITY TOO LARGE** spinal cord injury or anaphylaxis or dilatation or enlargement (a "slackening") of arteries and veins so that there's relatively too little blood for the now-expanded size of the system

Now you know the three types of shock, we'll break the rules and introduce a hybrid shock state that includes all three components and is the baddest actor in the ICU: *septic shock.* You've accepted that distant infection can make the lung capillaries leak and flood the patient, causing ARDS. Septic shock does this and more. It affects capillaries and other tissues throughout the body. A profusion of inflammatory agents wreak havoc all over the body, the worst of which results in lung and kidney failure.

The importance of the septic syndrome is to identify it before multiple-system organ failure occurs. It doesn't matter *why* the patient is infected. What counts is the *extent* to which the infection has progressed. If any infectious process is left untreated for long enough, overwhelming illness results.

What Is Septic Syndrome (Sepsis)?

An inflammatory focus and infection which results in a number of the following features:
- fever or lowered body temperature (hypothermia)
- elevated white blood count (lab)
- rapid pulse rate
- altered mental status, with confusion or coma
- decreased urine output
- lowered blood oxygen levels

Consider a patient with pneumonia—untreated pneumonia. When his infection—it could have been tonsillitis or a boil on his gluteus maximus—advances to the extent that he develops *SIRS—systemic inflammatory reaction syndrome*—he is a goner. Beyond a certain point in any infection, systemic deterioration, reflected in the sequential failure of vital organs, follows in the footsteps of severe bacterial invasion—and the path cannot be retraced.

Renal failure, the third vital organ failure, occurs most often in the ICU because of sepsis or shock. And hemorrhagic or other types of hypovolemic shock results in inadequate blood supply to the kidneys and death of vital cells involved in filtering body wastes. Septic shock and certain drugs have a direct toxic effect on the kidneys, in each case resulting in a high concentration of toxic chemicals in the blood. These substances must be dialyzed off if renal failure is severe.

A patient in renal failure is said to be *uremic*, and the determination of renal failure is made when the blood level of urea and creatinine become elevated. The doctor orders a BUN and creatinine level. Some forms of mild renal failure will not need dialysis; they are self-limiting and resolve spontaneously. This cheerful event is marked by a brisk *diuresis*, or abrupt increase in urine output, because the kidney can't reabsorb the fluid it's filtering at first, as occurs in normal kidney function.

Like chronic renal failure, prolonged acute renal failure requires dialysis, and more than one method of performing this treatment is available. The dialysis machine is brought into the ICU room and connected to the patient; the process may have to be repeated every three days or so. The purpose of chronic renal dialysis is to remove the toxic waste products of metabolism no longer cleared by the kidneys. In acute dialysis in the ICU setting, the additional reason for dialysis is to remove excessive fluid that was needed to resuscitate the patient during the critical phase of the illness. Reducing the volume of fluid also improves lung function and reduces the work of the heart—all three vital organs are intimately intertwined.

Brain Failure

What other organs can fail?

Ask yourself what the heart, lungs and kidneys are vital for? What do they support? The *brain*, of course. The crowning triumph of tissue specialization of our species, the delicate gray tissue and tangle of axons and dendrites with their synaptic connections are the least tolerant of hypoxemia, or low oxygen levels, of all tissues. This intolerance of hypoxia is why CPR is unsuccessful if delayed.

The brain receives about 15 percent of the blood volume pumped every minute by the heart. Of the 200,000 or more victims of cardiac arrest who receive CPR (resuscitation), only 10 percent of the 70,000 survivors (3.5 percent of the total) have normal brain function and can return to their prior lifestyle. The others suffer from brain damage and can no longer carry out a sentient lifestyle or care for themselves.

The reason for the high rate of post-resuscitative brain damage is the dismal amount of blood that reaches the brain during CPR. Attempts to bind the abdomen or to simultaneously inflate the lungs and compress the chest (the "new" CPR) have not resulted in improved cerebral blood flow during resuscitation. The consequences of poor cerebral blood flow during CPR and the post-resuscitation period include the following neurological deficits, in diminishing order of severity:

- **COMA** complete lack of response to any stimuli, with no eye-opening activity or movement
- **THE PERSISTENT VEGETATIVE STATE** characterized by random eye opening, but with no associated recognition of surroundings
- **STUPOR** arousal by vigorous stimulation; deep sleep
- **OBTUNDATION** sleep and apathy state with awareness but lack of focus on surroundings
- **AMNESIA** loss of memory for events before cardiac arrest, and inability to retain new information
- **CORTICAL BLINDNESS** injury to occipital lobes of brain result in

loss of vision despite normal eyes and optic nerves; some patients recover vision

- **SEIZURES** one-third of CPR victims have seizures, and most are not generalized but rather irregular jerky motions (myoclonus), which may be in one limb or generalized

In addition to the brain, the following organs may fail as part of the multiple-system organ failure (MSOF) picture. These organs may demonstrate mild dysfunction or marked impairment.

- **THE LIVER** in mild dysfunction doesn't produce as much of a protein called *albumin*, which can be measured; *bilirubin*, which causes the yellow of jaundice may rise; in severe impairment of the liver, jaundice occurs and the serum ammonia levels rise
- **THE GASTROINTESTINAL SYSTEM** (stomach, small intestine and colon) becomes sluggish in the mild form (called *ileus*), resulting in large nasogastric tube output; in severe impairment, bleeding stress ulcers occur in the stomach
- **THE IMMUNE SYSTEM** may show less responsiveness to skin testing for delayed hypersensitivity, or in the more impaired form results in recurrent ICU-acquired infections
- **WOUND HEALING** may be slowed in the mild form, or result in wounds literally falling apart (*dehiscence*) in severe impairment

Of the organs that fail, acute respiratory failure is the most obvious, because mechanical support with a ventilator is immediately needed. Respiratory failure is usually the first to occur, with cardiac, coagulation problems, kidney, liver and central nervous system failure following in that order. That's when machines start accumulating in the ICU room.

Monitoring the Critically Ill Patient

Physicians who work in the ICU live by numbers. Caring for sick patients in the unit isn't a matter of making discreet observations in the tradition of William Osler, or discovering subtle physical findings or deriving a clever differential diagnosis the way they do on the medical floors. In the unit you need data.

Information comes from many sources in the ICU, and the most reliable data is from a monitor, a lab sheet or an X-ray report. Many reports

The telemetry of several patients can be observed at once from the nurses' station by observing the bank of cardiac monitors in the critical care area.

are verbal. You can't wait for a transcriptionist to deliver a computer printout of a study before acting; you go to X ray and force the radiologist to read it right there. Or call up a report—the so-called "wet" reading (reading X rays right out of the developer vat or machine). Patients about to slip into the swamp of multiple-organ failure can't wait for a lazy radiologist to render his opinion the next day.

Numbers form the basis of clinical decision-making in the unit. Many of these numbers are from monitors. In a broad sense everything done in the unit to evaluate a patient is a "monitoring" activity. Even drawing repeat labs (blood samples) monitors the endless number of chemistries that may become abnormal as a consequence of disease or doctor intervention.

A good way to look at practical medical care in the ICU is to think of the diseases and their treatments as being *too much* or *too little*. Blood electrolytes—sodium, potassium, chloride and bicarbonate—tell the doctor whether there is too much of one of these components or too little; for example, too much sodium or too little accompanying water. Think of two parallel walls representing too much and too little: Clinical medicine is bouncing off one wall until you hit the other.

In the meantime the doctor keeps measuring lab values and adjusting his interventions accordingly. It is no more absolute than that. To get it right the physician needs data. And the best data come from monitors. Here are the monitors the intensivist watches:

- pulse rate, blood pressure, respiratory rate, temperature
- oxygen saturation, urine output, drain output, body weight
- EKG rate and rhythm and abnormalities
- arterial blood gases for oxygen, carbon dioxide levels, blood pH
- central venous pressure, arterial pressure contour, amplitude
- Swan-Ganz cardiac catheter showing cardiac output, heart pressures, derived numbers from the computer about peripheral vascular resistance, mixed venous oxygen concentration and other numbers from a computer printout
- multiple chemistries for liver, pancreas and kidney function, chemistries such as blood sugar, electrolytes, lactate for anaerobic (oxygenless metabolism) and others
- respirator parameters such as volume per breath, breaths per minute, airway pressures; weaning parameters such as inspiratory force, tidal volume, minute ventilation and arterial blood gases
- cultures of body fluids; lines and tubes for bacteria and fungi
- less common tests for nutritional parameters such as pre-albumen, magnesium levels, total lymphocyte count, single nutrients such as iron and vitamin levels

These numbers are listed on several charts and entered into the medical record each day in the progress notes, along with their interpretation and plans for treatment or other tests—some new and some repeats.

The essence of monitoring in the unit is to detect evidence of multiple-system organ failure and other life-threatening events such as cardiac arrhythmias before they cause harm. If nothing else, the units are locations where expectant watchfulness is the cornerstone of daily life. The low nurse-to-patient ratio is designed to permit intensive care and intensive monitoring.

Who Is the Intensivist?

According to Strosberg and Teres, "Critical care medicine specialists, or intensivists, are trained to deal comprehensively with a complex patient suffering from the malfunction of one or more organ systems. In a sense, intensivists are generalists for the critically ill not only because they have to deal with all organ systems but also because many life-threatening physiological disturbances are quite similar in critically ill patients, regardless of the underlying disease." Specialization in the critical care world follows traditional lines of division of labor as reflected in age (pediatric and adult ICUs), organ (respiratory care units, coronary care units, etc.) and also combinations (cardiac surgery ICU). Cutting across specialties the way it does, critical care medicine was not able to form a specialty board, but rather—it took years of wrangling, hubris and attention to reimbursement—developed a standard in 1992 known as the *QCCP*—the *Qualified Critical Care Physician*. The Society for Critical Care Medicine itself was formed in 1972 and has fought ever since for board certification. Its failure probably says more for the shortcomings of self-interested, power-hungry doctors than the complexity of critical care medicine.

At any rate, Strosberg and Teres outline the steps a physician must complete in order to become certified in critical care medicine:

- be board-certified in one of four specialties—surgery, internal medicine, pediatrics or anesthesiology
- complete a fellowship approved by the Accreditation Council for Graduate Medical Education, which may last from one to four years
- pass a certifying examination established by one of the American Boards of the four specialties

Some doctors receive critical care training as part of a subspecialty program such as pulmonary medicine, but they usually aren't certified. In smaller hospitals, these individuals may provide the majority of ICU coverage.

Intensivists may serve in one of three roles:
- primary physician
- concurrent physician
- consultant

There are two models for critical care units, the *open* model and the *closed* model. In the first, the intensivist assists in the care of the patient with the doctor of record; in the second, the intensivist *is* the physician of record, and the patient's own doctor relinquishes control. In 1992, approximately 75 percent of doctors responding to a survey indicated their ICUs followed the open model.

In an article in *Annals of Surgery* (February 1999), Ghorra et al. from Brown University School of Medicine described improved mortality rates, decreased use of certain cardiac medications and fewer complications in a surgical intensive care unit. Their recommendation was to allow specially trained intensivists to conduct the business of critical care after major surgery and trauma. However, in the same journal at least one academic surgeon bemoaned the concept of losing control of the patient.

The reality of managed care is that surgeons, as with other specialists, cannot afford to spend long hours in the ICU providing basically nonreimbursed care. Perhaps academic surgeons whose salaries are paid regardless of their activities will be able to maintain the open model of critical care. But what of the situation in which patient-care responsibilities are shared?

As a concurrent physician, the intensivist discusses patient-management issues with the doctor of record, and together they decide the best interventions. When the primary doctor leaves to care for other patients, the intensivist coordinates the care they've jointly agreed upon. Finally, in the open ICU model, the intensivist serves as a consultant and offers his opinion about treatment issues, which may or may not be followed.

ICU consultants may run into double numbers for the very sick patient. Each individual doctor manages one aspect of the patient's care, and this fragmentation may result in no one having a good handle on the patient and a clear view of the whole picture. For example, the surgeon may recommend nutritional support, while the nephrologist (kidney guy) insists the volume of IV fluid needed to provide nutrients will flood the patient, who is already close to renal failure. Who decides on the proper fluid volume?

The smart call is to allow the intensivist to coordinate the care and find a middle-of-the-road solution favoring both of the patient's needs.

The Intensive Care Nurse

The American Association of Critical Care Nurses (AACN) requires nurses to complete a special examination after at least two years of practical experience in the critical care unit. Hospitals have extensive orientation programs in which the training nurse acquires a knowledge of acute care physiology, pharmacology and the nuances of monitoring. Working with a preceptor, the training nurse slowly assumes patient responsibility until he is able to manage patients independently.

Still, today in most hospitals not all ICU nurses are certified.

Only a fool would enter an intensive care area, observe an ICU nurse casually talking with another nurse and assume the nurse isn't paying attention. The EKG monitor wiring and the circuits responsible for the smooth, regular firing of the ventilator don't end at the machine. These electronic circuits extend into the brains of the ICU nurses, into the marrow of their bones and into the very dark corners of their souls.

The ICU nurse knows her patient intimately, and becomes a friend of the family as well. Some of these relationships last longer than the hospitalization of the critically ill patient. Certainly, the camaraderie among the nurses in the unit is unique.

No other nurse in the modern hospital works as hard or knows as much as an ICU nurse. Interns learn this fact of life early. Newly M.D.'d interns find it difficult at times to ask a (mere) nurse for advice about an arrhythmia or an abdominal wound problem. If they don't overcome this obstacle, they fail.

From formulating her own ideas about patient management based on the data available to the ICU doctor to the mundane chores of cleaning their patients and keeping them medicated and comfortable, the ICU nurse traverses rugged terrain. Watching and assessing, administering drugs and adjusting IVs, checking central lines, Swan-Ganz catheters, arterial lines, lab values, drawing blood, counseling families—the ICU nurses' tasks form an endless string of hours in twelve hours of nonstop care.

The intensity of care in the ICU is reflected in the 1:2 or 1:3 ratio of nurses to patients, as compared to the 1:8, and as high as 1:12, seen on the hospital floors. In addition to monitoring and treating responsibilities, the ICU nurse must educate and support families.

The *ICU nurse manager* is responsible for making certain enough nurses are assigned to the various units to cover the patients' needs adequately. There are two trends creeping into critical care that the nurse manager must deal with: the "stretching," or expanding of coverage for each ICU nurse (moving from a 1:2 ratio to a 1:3) and the substitution of so-called "cross-trained" nursing assistants (the person who mopped the floor yesterday draws your blood today).

If the nurse manager isn't sensitive to the stresses placed on ICU nurses, the attrition rate rises—and further beds may be shut down.

What Does It Mean to Be Dependent on a Machine?

Critically ill patients develop organ failure and require either complete or partial support in order to survive a threatening phase of their illness. Without the mechanical support, the patient would die. Often vital organ support is begun at the time when the illness reaches its zenith, when the body can no longer compensate for the ravages of the disease.

Mechanical support may be instituted in any of the following scenarios:

• The patient in the ER presented with acute illness and the doctors recognize the patient will die if not immediately supported.

• The critically ill patient admitted to the ER may be immediately transferred to the ICU, where she deteriorates and support is started.

• The patient may undergo surgery where intubation and other interventions begin the support process, which cannot be reversed when surgery is done, and the patient is transferred directly to the ICU from the OR.

• The patient is transferred from a medical or surgical floor, or other unit such as radiology, where the patient suffered a cardiac arrest and was resuscitated.

Criteria for placing a patient on a mechanical ventilator include:
• oxygen levels below 60 mmhg in arterial blood gas sample
• carbon dioxide levels greater than 50 or 60 mmhg
• sudden inability to breathe from weakness, drugs, cardiac arrest, etc.

How do doctors know oxygen levels are inadequate? The easiest way is to monitor as many patients as possible—this includes any recovery area, ICU, post-partum, etc., with a *pulse oximeter*. This device fits onto a finger or thumb like a splint and measures oxygen saturation using hemoglobin's different ability to absorb light, thus indicating within 2–3 percent the true blood oxygen saturation. When someone's O_2 "sat" plummets, the nurse places supplemental oxygen on the patient, and the physicians begin the process of working up the cause.

As on floors, the ICU staff have simple methods of ensuring adequate oxygenation. These include nasal prongs with flow rates of one to five liters per minute. If this isn't adequate to maintain O_2 saturation, a mask with flow rates up to ten or fifteen liters a minute is available. The next most effective method of oxygen delivery is a *partial rebreathing system* with a tight mask and vent holes that allow some exhaled gas to escape and some to be rebreathed by the patient. In a *nonrebreathing system* one-way valves are placed on the mask to prevent the inhalation of any exhaled gases and to permit more concentrated oxygen delivery with an undiluted source.

When a "jet" mixing tube is used a venturi mask is created, which allows a predictable, controlled flow of oxygen at a specific concentration. Predictable oxygen concentrations are important in certain forms of chronic respiratory illnesses where excess oxygen may cause the patient to stop breathing. If none of the above methods of oxygenation work, the patient is then a candidate for endotracheal intubation and controlled mechanical ventilation.

Oxygen can be *toxic*. At high concentrations oxygen may injure lung tissue and cause major lung damage. Thus, it is both beneficial and deadly. The ICU staff uses great caution in the seemingly simple administration of oxygen.

Sometimes the patient's lungs are extensively involved with ARDS and the air spaces work poorly; a major mismatch between ventilation and blood perfusion of the lungs results in life-threatening low blood oxygen levels (hypoxemia). A novel intervention called *PEEP* comes to the rescue in these critically ill patients. *P*ositive *E*nd-*E*xpiratory *P*ressure (PEEP) is created with a special valve designed to *not* permit the pressure in the airways return to zero at the end of a mechanical breath. This end pressure keeps air sacs that would otherwise have collapsed open and improves the match between blood flow and air flow. Oxygen levels improve.

Weaning from PEEP becomes another task for the ICU team as they search for signs of improvement and ways to test various organs. In this case, the PEEP—set anywhere from 5 to 20cm of water pressure with a valve in the ventilator circuit to the patient—is dropped 5 centimeters of pressure and arterial blood gases are remeasured. If oxygen levels remain adequate, the patient stays at this level for a while and is then *weaned* down further as tolerated.

Sometimes patients can't be removed from their support systems. Let's return to the unit and its sick guests.

The ICU doctors are rounding on a patient on a ventilator, on cardiac drugs intravenously and requiring periodic dialysis and total nutritional support. The task is to treat the event that resulted in the need for mechanical support in the first place. More than one problem may face the intensivist. Consider their patient.

A sixty-six-year-old man who underwent coronary bypass surgery five days ago develops abdominal pain, and tests show he has perforated ("burst") his colon. Emergency abdominal surgery is performed, and a colostomy is created after removing the diseased colon, and the patient is returned to Cardiac ICU. On a ventilator, multiple antibiotics and IV fluid, his blood pressure begins to drop and two "pressors," or cardiac drugs, are started. Three days later, his pressure drops again, despite the medication, and his ventilator requirements double. Maximum treatment continues for another week. The man doesn't respond to stimuli anymore, and nothing the doctors do seems to help.

The doctors tell the family any further treatment is futile. They do not believe he will survive—no matter what else they do. What to do? We'll revisit this case in a moment.

A more favorable result would be the patient who begins to tolerate less ventilator support. The doctors decrease the amount of breathing performed by the ventilator and set up a circuit to permit the patient to breathe spontaneously. And they will also decrease the amount of PEEP in the circuit, but not at the same time as decreasing the respirator rate. One change at a time. Then the pressors are reduced in dosage and stopped. The patient is placed on a T-piece with supplemental oxygen and, two hours later, the endotracheal tube is removed. The next day the fortunate man is transferred to a regular floor.

In this scenario the patient was weaned from the cardiac drugs and from the ventilator. Weaning from mechanical or drug support is the process of slowly decreasing the number of breaths by the machine or the milligrams of medication delivered IV to the patient. If the drugs are being administered to prevent abnormal heart rhythm problems, the

---

Toxic Shock Syndrome

definition: A clinical problem caused by the exotoxin from *Staphylococcus aureus*, which produces lowered blood pressure, decreased urine flow, fever, rash and confusion, and may result in multiple-organ failure.

CAUSES OF TOXIC SHOCK SYNDROME INCLUDE:
- tampons disrupting vaginal lining
- pelvic infections
- childbirth
- other staph infections such as sinusitis

---

patient may be weaned from them slowly as well. Dialysis patiently may be weaned by reducing the number of treatments per week.

What about the patient who doesn't tolerate weaning?

A patient who requires more and more artificial support is telling the doctors that multiple-system organ failure is beginning. Often it begins with the inability to wean a patient from a treatment, followed by the need for more treatment for new complications. For example, in the scenario involving the sixty-six-year-old coronary bypass patient with MOF, as the patient's family is considering what to do the nurse reports fresh blood from the patient's nasogastric tube. An upper gastrointestinal bleed—another organ is failing.

Should the family agree to upper endoscopy and possible nonsurgical control of the hemorrhage? Should they insist on immediate surgery? Is it time to realize nothing is going to save Dad?

Complication of Intensive Care Unit Treatment

The more things you do to a patient, the more things that can go wrong. Tubes, catheters and other hardware inserted into a patient may cause serious complications. The patient is helpless to signal distress, and all of that hardware flirts with mechanical disruption and infection. Here's a list of the common hardware used in the ICU and the potential associated complications.

- **IV LINES** thrombosis of veins, pain, inflammation and rarely infection; need for rotation of sites every three days or so; runaway IVs with excess fluid administered
- **CENTRAL VENOUS CATHETERS** CVPs may be associated with

The Prognosis With Multiple-System Organ Failure	
Number of Failing Organs	Mortality (Death Rate) in %
0	3
1	30
2	50–60
3	85–100
4	72–100
5	100

complications during insertion such as pneumothorax (lung collapse), injury to nerves, artery or clotting of veins to arm, air embolism and possible death; after a while CVPs may become infected or clotted and cause extensive central vein thrombosis

- **FOLEY CATHETERS** may be associated with urinary tract infections; removal by patient with balloon inflated causes tissue damage and bleeding; may be the site of the wrong administration of feedings or drugs
- **ARTERIAL LINE** causes clotting of artery and hand ischemia, disconnected with massive hemorrhage; malposition, giving misleading hemodynamic information, resulting in the wrong treatment
- **SWAN-GANZ CATHETER** balloon rupture may lead to massive lung hemorrhage, catheter infection, thrombosis of pulmonary artery, loss of part of catheter resulting in foreign material embolism; misposition gives misleading information and major treatment mistakes
- **ENDOTRACHEAL TUBE** inflated cuff may rupture, causing air leak and inadequate ventilation or aspiration of gastric contents; tube may become blocked, stopping ventilation, vocal cord and other laryngeal injury (the most feared complication!), via nose (nasotracheal intubation) may cause nose bleeds, sinus infections or ear infections
- **CHEST TUBES** may become occluded, resulting in a recollapse of a previously expanded lung or hidden accumulation of blood in the chest
- **TRACHEOSTOMY TUBES** may fall out, causing respiratory distress; cause stenosis (narrowing of the larynx); hemorrhage; cuff overexpansion, resulting in airway obstruction; cuff rupture, permitting aspiration of stomach contents and pneumonia

- **VENTILATOR COMPLICATIONS** include barotrauma, or rupture of small airways, resulting in pneumothorax (collapsed lung); this is suggested by subcutaneous emphysema (air in the tissues of the chest wall and neck); barotrauma usually occurs with high-level PEEP (positive-end expiratory pressure)

Tracheostomy is the surgical creation of an airway by placing a plastic tracheostomy tube through an incision in the neck *below* the larynx and vocal cords, and is used for prolonged mechanical ventilation. After two weeks or so the ICU team will begin to make arrangements with a thoracic or general surgeon to have a "trach" performed if the patient will need more than a week or two of continued ventilator support.

Some patients are transferred to a regular floor or to a special respiratory care stepdown unit with their tracheostomy in place. Often it is not removed until several days following extubation. The trach is plugged, making it effectively useless and forcing the patient to breathe through his larynx. When it becomes evident that there is no obstruction or other problem with spontaneous ventilation, the trach tube is removed. Within days the stoma closes over and the patient is left with a depressed, circular scar in the lower neck as a reminder of a past brush with mortality.

Triage in the Intensive Care Unit

The intensivist, nurse manager or both must decide who will obtain entry into the ICU and who will be discharged and when. Multiple claims are placed on the decisionmaker. Issues of severity of illness and bed availability compete with claims of desperately ill patients made by politically connected specialists with overwhelming personalities. Will the cardiac surgeon's patient get a bed—as one report proved was the case—instead of a sicker abdominal surgical patient simply because the open-heart program brings in more money to the institution?

In the study mentioned (Marshall, 1992), as ICU beds became less available it was anticipated the severity of illness would rise. Fewer available beds go to the sickest. The degree of illness actually *dropped* because the influential cardiac surgeons insisted on admitting their less sick post-op patients, squeezing out the usual sick patients. The study concluded that in the particular situation under discussion, ICU decision-making was driven by, ". . . political power, medical provincialism and income 'maximumization.' "

The intensivist must deal with these realities. This discussion serves as background to appreciate the two models for organizational decision-making described by Strosberg and Teres. In the *rational model* all parties agree on the objectives of triage and share some central value that guides their choices. Implicit in this model is an agreement on basic ethical principles of conduct. The *political model* assumes the parties disagree about options and have little insight into alternatives. Conflict is usual, and power and influence are needed to reach a one-sided agreement. The process is disruptive and acrimonious.

In most ICUs a blend of both models is no doubt used, as one cannot completely escape the narrow interests of so many different players in the scene. Also, today patients' rights are of paramount importance and, because so many ICU patients are unable to communicate, surrogate decisionmakers are needed. This may further complicate the process.

At the top of the list of issues facing the admissions-discharge ICU policy is the matter of *goals*. What is all of this treatment aimed at? Are we trying to cure? To comfort? To prolong a life?

Strosberg and Teres suggest the following reasons might be used by an ICU decisionmaker in formulating admission and discharge policy:

- meet the formal requirement of institutional policy
- keep powerful physicians satisfied and contributing (e.g., admitting patients)
- keep nurses from quitting or burning out
- keep the quality assurance review process from being triggered

In reality, it is the decision to *not* resuscitate a patient and death itself that bail out the ICU decisionmaker at times. ICU care is not about having too many used cars on a lot: It's about having too many sick people to care for and too few resources.

The graying of America will make ICU admission and discharge decisions even more difficult in the twenty-first century. More Americans will reach the age of physiological deterioration, and some will require ICU admission if survival is contemplated. The case of Helga Wanglie exemplifies the dilemma. Helga was a ventilator-dependent eighty-five-year-old in a persistent vegetative state whose care cost several thousand dollars before she died. Her physicians appealed to the courts against her husband's wishes—and were summarily denied—the privilege of discontinuing her life support. Before her case could be definitively settled, Helga died.

The future of critical care medicine will remain embedded in the matrix of end-of-life decision making. Unlike the rest of the developed world, Americans are unable to let go at the natural (or unnatural) conclusion of meaningful life. If families and doctors cannot easily work through the letting go steps of an elderly woman with no brain function, we are unlikely to solve our medical needs in the future.

For a profound lack of insight, Americans must be prepared to pay unimaginable sums of money on futile medical care in the ICU setting.

What Happens When There Is a Bed Crunch?
Most people don't think about gatekeeping and the rationing of resources as it applies to the intensive care unit. After all, this is America, the land of unending resources. We treat everyone with a critical illness for as long as we can with all of the resources available.

The glimmering light of reason is becoming a faint glow on the horizon of resource allocation. We are beginning to see rationing as unavoidable.

Still, if a loved one is admitted to the ICU, it is next to impossible to have them triaged out to a floor. Triage out of the ICU means either you're cured or you're condemned to die without further aggressive therapy. It's not too difficult to figure out which one applies to any given patient.

Pediatric ICU
These small patients have their own problems. What is not unique to the care of sick kids is the same final common pathway seen in adults. Regardless of the initial illness, the critically ill pediatric patient suffers from multiple-organ failure if sepsis from any cause or trauma and shock are sufficiently severe.

Neonatal ICU
Premature infants with immature lungs and marginal vital organ failure populate the NICU. Endotracheal tubes the size of straws taped to undefined faces with wrinkled bodies only a few pounds into existence create

similar problems for the pediatric ICU nurse, whose watchfulness is, if anything, more intense than that of her adult sister.

A host of infectious and congenital illnesses bring newborns to the PICU for aggressive care. Not infrequently, poor or absent brain development or multiple congenital malformations, or birth defects, result in conflict between parents and staff, among parents and other family members or between the parents themselves. Survival is no more certain than in the adult ICU, but the hope for life reigns mightily in the NICU, and giving up is even more obscene.

Patient Floors and Rooms

Patient floors have traditionally consisted of several rooms along a hallway, with a nurses' station located midway between the rooms. For most hospitals, patient rooms are one of three types: a private room with only one patient bed, a semiprivate room with two patients, or a larger room called a ward, containing four or more beds.

The word *ward* is an all-purpose word in the hospital, and can refer to an area of the hospital, a floor or a large multibed room. There are also "executive" rooms or suites for those who can afford them in some hospitals, but these frills are rapidly being exchanged for basic room accommodation.

Patient rooms on a floor are not as sophisticated as those in the critical care areas. The room has a bed, a screen or curtains attached overhead that can be pulled around the patient for privacy, a bedside table, a chair for visitors, a closet for personal belongings, a TV, a storage bin for towels, sheets and toilet articles, and a bathroom. Many rooms have chairs that fold out into a bed to allow family members to spend the night. Most hospitals have suction equipment and an oxygen source with tubing and mask on the wall.

Rooms are equipped with an intercom connection to the nurses' station. Some rooms may be equipped with telemetry, which monitors the heart rate and rhythm (EKG) and oxygen saturation, and are known as *stepdown beds* or the *intermediate care area*. Some are near the ICU and are called *progressive care units*.

In certain areas of the hospital there are very specialized rooms. For example, in older hospitals, a woman who came to the hospital in labor went to one room during labor, to the delivery room during the delivery,

A chart rack with names clearly marked on the front and placed according to patient room number marked on the rack.

and then to a post-partum area to recover before going back to her original room. However, most labor and delivery areas now have LDR (labor, delivery, recovery) rooms. The patient in labor goes to an LDR room and remains there until after the delivery and a short recovery period before going to a regular hospital bed before being discharged.

Some hospitals have LDRP (labor, delivery, recovery, post-partum) rooms, and the patient never leaves that room the entire time she is in the hospital. Most hospitals with LDRP rooms also arrange for the newborn baby to stay in the room with the mother rather than being kept in a newborn nursery. The nurses assigned to LDRP rooms take care of both the mother and the baby.

While most hospitals now have LDR rooms, only the larger or newer hospitals will have the full LDRP rooms. Not everyone has LDRP full-service rooms because of limited space or staff.

A twenty-four-hour nurses' sheet is usually located either on the door of the patient's room or on a clipboard attached to the bed. This permits easy access for recording medications, vital signs and any change in the patient's condition. Nurses have access to the electronic record and enter verbal orders and retrieve electronic orders via the computer terminal nearest their patients. Also, the nurse enters her own notes into the written medical record.

Every patient floor also has a stockroom in which there are bins on wheels that contain gauze, bandages, thermometers, tape, antiseptic solution, etc., as well as laundry items such as towels, sheets, washcloths and pillow covers. These items are restocked daily by units on wheels, and the soiled linen is placed in large hampers (on wheels) which are taken directly to the laundry.

A small kitchen is usually locked with an access code lock and contains a refrigerator, microwave, toaster and sink where small meals and liquids may be prepared for patients whose diets are being advanced. The floor kitchen saves a call to the main kitchen for small meals, and also permits nurses, assistants and others to prepare their own meals.

A conference room is designated for the nurses to use for shift signouts, and another conference room is assigned to the doctors so that they may dictate charts, make phone calls and review old records that have been brought up from the record room. There are often one or two waiting rooms or lounges on patient floors with a TV, chairs, table and couches where families and patients may meet or where families and significant others wait for doctors during interventions, procedures and surgeries.

Visitors are restricted to fairly generous hours, and nurses have become accustomed to working around families. The most profound change in the care of the hospitalized patient is that this liberal policy did not evolve out of administrative generosity, but rather out of necessity. Cost containment resulted in major cutbacks in nursing staffing, as well as retraining of unsophisticated workers. The orderly of last week may be doing your EKG this week. This "dumbing down" of hospital personnel is one of the best-kept secrets in America.

Thus, visiting hours are not really casual interactions anymore. The intelligent patient and family participate in the patient's care and assume responsibility for making certain those things that are being done are supposed to be performed. The visitors must ask questions—if they can find a nurse to talk to. The "disappearing nurse" results from overwork and annoyance. A delicate balance exists between those checking on what's happening and the staff trying their best to provide high-quality care.

The purpose for establishing visiting hours was thus to provide time for the patient to get proper rest and to permit nurses time to complete their caregiving chores, such as changing bedding, bathing patients and assisting in other ways, in an atmosphere of privacy. It's interesting to look back to the mid-1970s when visitors were only allowed to see a patient within a defined time period. Also, guests had to register, and only two or three passes were issued per patient to keep the number of visitors to a minimum at any given time.

Visiting hours of course still apply to friends or family who wish just to visit. However, now a family member is permitted to spend the night in the hospital in the patient's room, and a chair can be made into a temporary bed. This allows the parent of a child or the spouse of an adult to room with them during the night and to keep a vigil during the critical hours when oddball things can happen to patients—and nurses tend not to call for help because of the hour.

While ICUs have mechanical noises in an otherwise hushed area, the patient floors are exactly the opposite. During the day, the hallways outside the rooms are often more crowded and busier than at night, filling as first light dawns with ambulating patients pushing their IV poles, parked wheelchairs, attending doctors, residents, medical students, visitors, clergy, food handlers, patients in wheelchairs or gurneys being transported to other areas of the hospital for tests or procedures and lab technicians.

Overhead, the paging system never seems to stop.

Hospital Elevators

Hospital elevators have their own small unique world of sights and smells inside the cramped four walls, filled with equipment, patients, doctors, nurses, visitors, wheelchairs, gurneys and students. Hospital elevators are large in order to accommodate a stretcher. Usually there will be "visitor" and "patient transport only" elevators side by side. Hospital employees use the elevators to move materials, including patients, among the floors.

Patients are always placed in an elevator headfirst, with the foot of the stretcher near the doors. Some elevators open through two doors. The stretcher is rolled onto the elevator with care, as the bump at the sliding-door gap may cause severe pain in patients with fresh wounds and various painful medical conditions. All IVs, oxygen and other paraphernalia are hung from built-in poles on the stretcher or are stored under the stretcher. At times, extra equipment must be rolled alongside the stretcher.

When the elevator doors open, any number of personnel may be pushing their wares out past the sliding doors. The hardware of hospital care and the personnel who transport it include:

- respiratory therapy and their ventilators
- radiology techs with a portable X-ray machine
- OR personnel with laparoscopic, laser and other machinery
- nurses with EKG monitors
- food services folks with food carts, both full and empty
- housekeeping people with carts with sheets, towels, soap, etc.
- orderlies transporting patients
- orderlies transporting dead patients to the morgue using special "hideaway" stretchers
- pharmacy transporting unit-dose medication bundles on carts
- maintenance personnel with ladders, paint supplies, plumbing materials, lightbulbs, etc.
- biomedical engineers with various pieces of high tech equipment en route to repair
- doctors rolling special clinical and research equipment from one place to another

Elevators have emergency phones as well as a lock system that allows the elevator to be held on one floor. For example, suppose a patient in shock must be rushed from the ED to the operating room one floor down. Someone from the ED races to the elevators, punches all of the buttons and locks the first elevator to arrive—including asking people to get off. When the stretcher arrives at the elevator it is unlocked, and the patient plummets to the OR floor.

The Nurses' Station

Some hospitals have begun to use multiple nurses' stations rather than a single location. This permits charts and the covering personnel to be closer to the patient rooms for which they are responsible. Computer

Supplies of bandages, drains, catheters, IV solutions, needles, tape, gauze and instruments are stored for easy access in the treatment and supply area beside the nurses' station.

terminals may be found at the peripheral stations as well as at the main desk. A large board lists each patient, room number and the doctor of record.

The nurses' station is often located midway between all the patient rooms that it is responsible for covering. Next to the nurses' station is the supply room containing bandages, needles, tape, drains, tubing and catheters. There is also a med room next to the station with either a computerized medicine dispensing unit (Pyxis) or a locked drug cart. Also stored together are IV bags, tubing and IV poles.

A floor clerk (or ward clerk) is responsible for answering questions at the desk, directing visitors and answering a multitude of phone calls. The nurses' station also has a chart rack containing the active in-patient charts on all the patients. When an attending doctor makes rounds on the floor, the nurse may or may not accompany him. The good nurses stop what they're doing and follow the doctor to determine the day's workup and treatment plans. This allows time for the doctor to discuss the patients' condition and review new orders with the nurse.

The nursing staff includes registered nurses, LPNs and nursing assistants. The ratio of nursing staff to patient on the floor is 1:5 or 1:6, meaning there is one nursing staff member per every four or five patients. Despite this number, the nurses may become preoccupied with one especially sick patient, leaving the others to fend for themselves.

Managed care has left a huge dent in patient-floor staffing. Conflict may arise from any disruption involving patients, their families and friends, and the nursing staff.

CHAPTER SEVEN

Medical Records, Information Services and Paging Systems

M edical records detail the life history of the sick, the unfortunate and the desperate. Some patients have several volumes (folders) of medical records, each as thick as large-city phone books. Millions of medical records are generated each year in the United States. You can't go to the ER for an ingrown toenail without incurring a new medical document of at least three or four pages. The medical records—containing copies of the patient's history and physical examination, lab studies, X-ray reports, procedures, surgeries, progress notes and nursing notes—must be sorted, coded, filed and stored. The record serves to improve patient care, risk management, quality assessment, research and peer review, and provides documentation for hospital reimbursement. Access to health care depends on access to large databases from a variety of sources and managed care involves the management of endless information.

Patient Medical Records

Medical records are usually referred to as *charts*. The chart is a legal as well as medical document and highlights the history of everything that happens to a patient while in the hospital. When the patient is discharged the in-patient chart is sent to the Medical Records Department, where it is analyzed, coded and then filed in manila folders as a medical record in a secured, safe area with limited access.

Most hospitals use three-ring binders for active in-patient charts in various units so that pages may be added as needed. The chart is divided and organized using insert tab dividers for orders, lab notes, progress notes, nursing notes and charts, X-ray reports and consult reports. Every entry includes the date and time that contact was made with the patient, or when the chart was reviewed.

The Joint Commission on Accreditation of Healthcare Organizations (JCAHO) requires hospitals to keep a record on all active patients. Each record contains four kinds of information: personal, financial, social and medical. At *no* time are documents to be removed from the chart. Everything that is added must remain in the chart, since it is now part of a medical-legal document.

Most hospital charts are laid out in a logical format so that important information can be found quickly. The admission face sheet is in the front, usually followed by physician's orders. The exact order of sections in the chart is not critical and will vary from hospital to hospital.

Anatomy of an In-Patient Chart
- Face sheet (admission sheet) with name, birth date, sex, marital status, next of kin, occupation, physician, etc.
- Insurance policy and numbers, Medicare/Medicaid numbers, etc.
- Physician Orders (for medications, tests, consults, treatment and care)
- History and physical (chief complaint, current medical and family history, past medical history, physical exam, planned tests and interventions and treatments)
- Nurses' "Daily Sheet" (vital signs, treatments, medications, and condition)
- Progress notes (physicians' notes on condition, plans and treatment)
- Lab reports
- X-ray reports
- Pathology reports
- Operation & Procedure reports

- Consultation sheets
- Discharge summary and Orders

Perhaps the most active portions of the medical record are the lab, X ray and progress notes sections, as well as the order sheet—now often replaced by electronic entries via the ubiquitous computer. Some orders are handwritten, as are all physician progress notes and nurses notes.

Progress notes are short, scribbled missives the physician writes regarding the day-to-day changes in the patient's condition, test results and future plans. Progress notes must be dated, timed and signed by the physician. For instance, a progress note may look like this:

10:15 am, 1/24/99:
Patient seems to be in more discomfort. Spiking temps, and abdomen more tender. Will order CT to r/o abscess. Will get blood cultures. Consult for surgery to see.

In a large teaching hospital, more formal notes are often required by the academic departments because the entries also serve as a learning device. For example, a typical progress note format is known as *SOAP notes*. The four categories of information are *S*ubjective—what the patient says and feels; *O*bjective—the observations of the doctor and/or medical team; *A*ssessment—the day-to-day or minute-to-minute assessment of the patient's clinical condition—solid, evidence-based observations; *P*lan—the diagnostic workup and treatment ideas of the doctor or team. In this system, every entry follows this four-point format. Labs, X rays, pathology and other test results are entered under "objective" data.

The chart represents an up-to-date record of the patient's condition, test results and treatment plans, and must always be accessible. When the patient is moved, the chart goes with him from place to place in the hospital while he is undergoing tests and procedures. Thus, important information about the patient is immediately available to the staff performing the procedure—often a doctor not familiar with the patient.

A progress note will be entered into the chart at the time the test or procedure is completed. Because the typed copy of the full procedure report won't be on the chart for days, this cryptic note provides the essential findings of a test or the elements of a procedure. A progress note following a procedure might look like this:

2:45 pm 2/15/99
Patient underwent bronchoscopy to evaluate infiltrate in the lingula of the left upper lobe. Mucosa of the lingular bronchus was inflamed. No tumor seen. Brushings and biopsy obtained. Patient tolerated the procedure well and returned to the floor in good condition. Cultures and histology pending.

Formal dictation of the bronchoscopy is done at this time as well, using a dedicated dictating system located on all procedure units, but it is the brief written note that informs anyone who reads the patient's chart what was done to the patient. If the patient develops new symptoms (for example, a mild sore throat), the chart would suggest it might be secondary to the bronchoscopy performed that day rather than due to strep throat.

The nurse records the events of her day as they relate to specific patients in the patient's chart in a section for nurse's notes or the nurse's *daily sheet.* The daily sheet is a twenty-four-hour record documenting vital signs and the nurse's assessment of the patient's condition. The daily sheet may be a three-page foldout record. The active daysheet is kept on the door of the patient's room or clipped to the bed. Every time vitals are measured, drugs are given or special care is provided, it is recorded in the daily sheet. At the end of twenty-four hours, the sheet is added to the chart, and a new twenty-four-hour daily sheet is started.

Charts are usually kept in a chart rack at the nurses' station, although some hospitals keep the charts on the door of the patient's room. Chart racks may be a rotating circular contraption with slots like spokes, or they may be slots in shelves marked with the patient's room number. The charts are kept in these slots unless being used on rounds by doctors, referred to or written in by nurses or when the patient is transported to another part of the hospital. When doctors make rounds on their patients, they take the charts with them, and occasionally the nurse assigned to those patients will accompany the doctor to discuss the patient's condition and review orders.

Charts are always being reviewed and brought up to date as new information is added; it might be anything from lab slips to X-ray reports.

When chart rounds are made, the attending staff, residents and medical students on their service sit together in a small conference room and review the updated information in the chart of each patient on the service. This setting permits a more casual review of the patient's progress and is often accompanied by bedside rounds or patient rounds after all of the charts have been examined.

It should be mentioned that while charts represent the information center for each patient, they are also a constant source of irritation. Doctors must diligently keep progress notes up to date and sign all phone orders. Also, the Attending must co-sign medical students' orders and, when the patient goes home, dictate a lengthy discharge summary. Chart maintenance becomes an endless task, and every physician develops a backlog of charts, which eventually pile up in the record room where they await the doctor's attention.

Thus, at the time of the patient's discharge, the chart travels from the floor to the Medical Records Department to be completed. It is coded for proper billing, analyzed for signatures and completed discharge summaries, and then put into a folder and filed in a secure place.

Chronological Sequence From New Chart to Completed Record at Discharge

1. Three-ring binder with tab dividers is labeled with patient's name.

2. Face Sheet (Admission Sheet) is completed in Admitting Department.

3. The dividers separating orders, physician's progress notes, history and physical, lab results, X-ray reports, reports of surgeries-procedures-consults and nurses' twenty-four-hour daily sheets are added to the chart when they are completed.

4. Discharge summary and discharge orders are the final sheets to be added at the time of discharge from the hospital.

5. Chart is sent to the Medical Records Department for completion.

6. Entire chart is removed from three-ring binder and placed into a manila folder.

7. *Analyzed*: The chart is analyzed to see if everything has been completed, that every note and order is signed, and that all required papers are completed and in the chart.

8. Charts that are found to be incomplete must be completed by the physician within a specified period of time. Notice is given to the physician to complete the chart.

9. *Coded*: Chart is coded for hospital stay, diagnosis, tests and treatments for billing and for future review of diseases, complications, and treatment.

10. The completed medical record of that hospitalization is filed in a secured, locked area.

Once an in-patient medical record has been completed, the original record is stored until it is requested for patient care or Quality Assessment review, or to copy for outside use. When the ER asks for a medical record on a patient who has been treated at the hospital previously, the chart is removed from its secure home in medical records and transported to the ER. This also occurs when the patient is being readmitted to the hospital. *Copies* rather than the original record are sent to any legitimate individual outside of the hospital who requests them.

Keeping Medical Records

Federal and state laws and local regulations dictate how long a hospital must retain a medical record. A general rule of thumb advocated by the American Bar Association is at least ten years. For minors, medical records are kept for twenty-one years. For the most part, it is the state hospital licensing agency that spells out the length of time medical records must be kept. The big issue is space, although computers have solved some of the storage problems. Hospitals expecting to receive federal funds and to participate in federal reimbursement programs must meet rigid record-keeping requirements. For a given state or locale, one of the following four categories is usually identified:

- records must be kept for ten years
- records may be kept for less than ten years
- records must be kept for prolonged periods of time
- special requirements for certain parts of the record

Statutes of limitations enter the discussion of length of retention of records. These issues depend on whether the cause of action, for example, is tort or contract law. If someone waited until they reached the age of

---

Medical Records May Be Stored As:
- paper
- microfilm
- computer disc

---

majority, say eighteen, the statute of limitations would probably be twenty years, providing two years beyond the age of majority in which to bring suit.

Medical research is another reason for prolonged retention of medical records, especially if new treatments are used that may require an extensive review of a patient's evaluation and treatment. Some agencies suggest retaining records up to seventy-five years for research institutions, particularly if litigation may arise in the distant future. Besides computer storage, some hospitals also use microfilm.

The destruction of medical records occurs when the retention period is completed or after the record has been converted to microfilm or computer disc. Burning and shredding are considered the most effective methods of destroying the medical record, but some states specify the method they mandate. Whatever the method of destroying the record, the following considerations are important:
- the hospital understands the method of destruction
- safeguards against any breach of confidentiality
- indemnification provisions
- certification that the records have been destroyed
- permanent retention of the documentation of record destruction

The Medical Records Department

The Medical Records Department is a large, secure area of the hospital, usually centrally located on or near the first floor for easy access. The configuration of the department depends on the size of the hospital: Smaller institutions have a designated room with minimal staff assigned to retrieve, assemble and store charts. What characterizes every medical records department is a room filled with manila folders, stacked by physician name. Pile after pile of incomplete records awaiting documents, dictation and signatures.

A clerk-receptionist sits at a front desk and asks doctors, whom they don't recognize, for identification and hospital number in order to obtain the necessary charts for them to complete and sign. By calling ahead, the Medical Records clerks can put charts into a stack with the doctor's name on a large tab. In the working area of Medical Records, where dozens of piles of charts flood the area, the doctor of record completes her charts. It's an unhappy room away from the main working area, with small cubby areas or cubicles with desks, dictating machines and telephones for the doctor to use for signing progress notes and orders, and for dictating consultation forms and discharge summaries.

The Medical Records Department is responsible for analyzing all charts at the time of discharge to make certain they have been properly completed and coded for billing, and then they store the charts in a secure manner. If a record is requested, the clerks obtain a consent form authorizing release of the medical record, signed by the patient. The medical records department is also responsible for copying the record and sending it to attorneys' offices, other hospitals or physicians' offices. A final responsibility is to ensure medical records security.

Personnel of the Medical Records Department

- **THE MANAGER OR DIRECTOR** is responsible for overseeing the department and for the security of medical records requiring "lock-up." This individual also is responsible for contacting the medical staff when they fail to complete a chart within a specified time. Other duties include verifying the legitimacy of requests for records, compliance with research needs and providing Q/A committees with information.

- **ANALYZERS** are responsible for reviewing the entire chart of each patient at the time of discharge. Analyzers make sure every part of the chart has been included, and that everything has a signature where needed.

- **CODERS** have to add the proper code for the patient's hospitalization and treatment, for every procedure and for the final diagnoses (see page 221 for "Coding"). Without proper codes, the hospital will not receive payment from third-party payers. Also, medical codes are needed to retrieve statistical data regarding treatment and complications.

219

- **CLERKS** are responsible for filing completed charts, retrieving and copying medical records and refiling those that have been pulled. Records are pulled if a patient is currently in the ER or if a patient is readmitted to the hospital. The record or, in some cases, a copy is sent to the ER or to the floor so that the complete medical history can be reviewed. Clerks also make copies of medical records—if requested by appropriate parties—to be sent out of the hospital. Clerks confirm that a consent form has been signed by the patient before any records are released.

Analyzers

Proper completion of all charts is an absolute rule at every hospital. There are rigid rules established by the Joint Commission on the Accreditation of Healthcare Organizations (JCAHO) and adopted by every hospital staff by-laws. The penalties for not completing charts in a timely fashion are severe. According to standards set by the joint commission, charts must be completed by thirty days after discharge.

Most hospitals require charts to be completed within fifteen days, well under the required thirty-day limit. Physicians are contacted by the Medical Records manager as soon as the analyzers find incomplete charts, and again seven days after the patient's discharge, and instructed to complete the chart. On the thirteenth day, the physician is informed the chart must be completed. The following day—the fourteenth day after discharge—the physician may be suspended from the medical staff by the Medical Records Department manager if the record has not been completed.

Once charts have been completed, the suspension is lifted. During the suspension, the physician is not allowed to admit new patients. If there are three or more suspensions in the same year, a physician may face removal from the medical staff.

The most common reason for incomplete charts is failure to complete or to sign the discharge order or discharge summary. The next most common reason for an incomplete chart is unsigned orders. These are usually orders that were called to the floor. The nurse recorded the oral order and implemented it, but the physician must eventually sign the orders.

Clerks

Many Medical Records departments are open twenty-four hours a day, but every hospital must have twenty-four-hour access to patients' medical records. The Medical Records Department in smaller hospitals may not require twenty-four-hour staffing, but there must always be someone in house with access to the records. Usually there is an assigned nurse supervisor with a key or an access card who is authorized to pull medical records if they are needed during off hours, usually for a patient in the ER. Clerks must also refile records that have been pulled and then returned to Medical Records.

Clerks are also responsible for copying medical records and sending the copies to the appropriate places. Copies of medical records can only be sent out after the hospital has received a consent form signed by the patient authorizing release of medical records.

Coders

Different codes are used both by the hospital and by doctors to determine what charges to submit for services rendered. The job of the coders is to assign proper codes to the charts. Prior to the 1980s, "cost-based" reimbursement ruled the medical roost: The hospital was paid what it billed. In 1983 the government introduced *DRGs*, or *diagnosis-related groups*. As a method of restricting how much the federal government would pay for Medicare, the DRG specified an exact amount of money to be paid for a service, no matter what it cost the hospital. Other codes have arisen since—new ways to restrict payment to physicians and hospitals.

Medical records are open to reviews for quality assurance. The data from multiple charts allows reviews for antibiotics, infections, post-operative complications and deaths. For instance, if a hospital wanted to review all cases of deep vein thrombosis (DVTs) and evaluate the success rate of treatment versus the complications, the information can be quickly obtained from a computer using the correct diagnostic codes (ICD).

Commonly Used Codes
Diagnosis Related Groups (DRGs)

DRGs permit payment by the government of a specific dollar amount for the treatment of an illness in a specific diagnosis group; e.g., pneumonia. It's the average of what it costs to treat most similar cases. If a complication prolongs hospitalization, the hospital does *not* get paid more for expending additional resources on the patient. The hospital loses money instead. The system rewards cost-effective care, but it also sometimes forces discharge from the hospital earlier than may be medically indicated.

International Classification of Diseases (ICD)

This code is used to label the final *diagnosis* and all co-morbid conditions. For example, this might be ruptured appendicitis. The ICD code is used along with secondary and tertiary codes to evaluate the "mix" of cases and the severity of illness. If a diabetic with asthma and hypertension develops acute appendicitis and has complications after surgery, the hospital may document the co-morbid conditions as a reason to be paid more than for an uncomplicated case.

Current Procedural Terminology (CPT)

This code is used to identify *medical services and procedures* performed by physicians. These codes are widely used by government and private health insurance programs, and are useful for administrative management purposes, such as claims processing, and for creating peer review guidelines. The codes use descriptive terms to identify services using uniform language for office and hospital care. For instance, if a CT scan is used to establish appendicitis, the CT scan is identified with a specific CPT code by which reimbursement is determined.

The Purpose of a Medical Record

While the obvious reason for the in-patient medical record (chart) is for documenting chronological medical condition and treatment of the patient, numerous other uses for medical records have evolved. The complex relationship between the expanding number of health care professionals involved in treating a patient and the growing number of enlightened consumers of medical services mandated better record-keeping. More data evolved from increasingly convoluted interventions, both diagnostic and therapeutic, and this information formed the basis of the new medical record. Secrecy and concerns for confidentiality kept medical records primitive at the beginning of the twentieth century, but as we begin the twenty-first century, complex documentation of health care is the standard, and confidentiality is an old problem with a new twist.

The purposes of the medical record are considered primary and secondary.

- to document the planning of all aspects of medical care (medical/legal) and record the completion of that care and its consequences
- to document communication among the various members of the medical team treating a patient
- to aid in medical education
- to provide data for clinical research
- to allow quality assessment and peer review committee evaluation
- to provide a legal document for the subsequent defense of the hospital and/or physician in cases of medical malpractice

The Language of the Medical Record

Young doctors and medical students are encouraged to not engage in "chart fights," a time-honored way physician egos have clashed in the past—to no one's advantage. The conflict begins when one doctor records his opinion about what the best treatment or test should be for a patient. Rather than follow the recommendation, another doctor writes down her opinion and why she disagrees with the first physician, often using disparaging language and claiming a superior grasp of the issues. Back and forth rages the dispute, often for days, with the various players making rounds at different times and informing the patient of the incomprehensible position the "other" doctor is taking.

This medical record becomes a gift served up on a silver platter by the confused (and by the end of the case, angry) family to any mediocre lawyer who happens to stumble upon it. The solution? Doctors, nurses and other allied health care workers should restrict themselves and their comments in the record to objective statements. A suggested list of guidelines includes:

- Enter facts in an objective manner.
- Opinions that bear directly on patient care should be provided only by the treating doctors.
- Opinions should be labeled as such so they will not be confused with data culled from the literature; evidence-based medicine versus judgment must be spelled out, as both are viable approaches to the care of the patient.

- Only use abbreviations that are understood by all members of the team; avoid disparaging terms and abbreviations.
- Deprecatory comments about other providers or the patient are to be avoided.
- A solid medical record is objective, brief and accurate.

The Day-To-Day Medical Record

Data is entered into the medical record by numerous individuals, but no one should include data that is speculative or unsubstantiated. The chain of connection of information must always be confirmed; that is, the reality of what happened in managing the patient must be properly documented, with no embellishment or distortion. This concern includes two areas.

- **VERBAL ORDERS** are a way of life in most hospitals, despite efforts to insist on all written orders. Called at home, from another part of the hospital or the office, the physician many times must conduct the care of his patient from a distance. The order is verbal and must be signed within twenty-four hours.

- **CORRECTIONS OR OTHER ALTERATIONS OF THE RECORD** must be done immediately and by the proper personnel. In teaching institutions, the Attending physician or the resident may correct orders and progress notes written by more junior residents and medical students. This is legitimate and expected. Corrections in this setting serve the principles of both medical education and patient care. However, the chart or electronic record of any case under litigation must *never* be tampered with. Precedents in the courts exist that spell out the disastrous consequences of attempting to cover up negligence by rewriting orders or notes.

Other Patient-Related Hospital Records

Information that bears directly on patient care, and information that is confidential, finds its way into the *primary medical record* from many sources all over the hospital. It seems unlikely that any one person possesses a grasp of the entire information system, but a multitude of components of the record system are needed to provide complicated care. Multidisciplinary care necessitates massive amounts of data. The following list provides an estimate of the major hospital departments that record patient-sensitive information (Bruce, J. *Privacy and Confidentiality of Health Care Information*, 1984):

- radiology—diagnostic
- radiation therapy
- clinical laboratory
- pathology—histopathology, genetics, necropsy
- social services
- occupational therapy
- physical therapy
- psychology lab
- nuclear medicine
- interventional radiology
- interventional cardiology
- cancer registry
- patient information services
- patient accounts
- risk management
- research programs
- surgical services
- critical care services

Incident Reports

The tricky task of reporting and documenting adverse incidents and in-house accidents requires specific rules and regulations for every hospital. An *incident report* is a factual document that describes where something happened, what exactly happened, who it occurred to and when it took place. For instance, if a patient who slipped and fell had sustained a laceration while being moved into bed, an incident report would have to be filled out and signed by those involved. The intent is to review adverse occurrences and improve patient care as well as staff and other personnel safety.

In some states the incident report is available for pretrial discovery in cases of litigation. Thus, the risk manager and the hospital's attorney should review all incident reports of consequence, as determined by the hospital administration.

Medical Record Security

The Medical Records Department is one of the three most secure and guarded areas of the hospital. It is important that no one have unauthorized access to a medical record as a matter of privacy as well as to guarantee no part of the record will be altered or deleted. For instance, if a nurse stole drugs for her personal use, she might want to alter the chart to make it seem as if the patient had been given the drugs. Or if a surgeon made a gross blunder during surgery, he might want to change the operative note to cover up his mistake. Or a doctor might want to delete or alter something in the chart if there was a pending malpractice suit. Or someone might wish to obtain medical information to blackmail another professional or damage his career.

One of the times the original medical record can be removed from the Medical Records Department is when the medical record has been subpoenaed and will be viewed in a court of law. Then it must remain in the custody of the manager of Medical Records, who must accompany the medical record to court and confirm that it is the original and unaltered record.

When a physician goes to Medical Records and asks to see a record, he will be asked his name and hospital ID number. Also, Medical Records will check to ascertain that his name is on the medical record before allowing him to review it. If he was never involved in the treatment of the patient, he may not be allowed to review the records.

However, if a physician assigned to a review committee wishes to review the records of patients with a certain disease (those with the same ICD codes) in order to make an analysis, those charts will be pulled and reviewed or copied. If a medical student wishes to review a record, the student must have written permission from the Attending staff physician.

Security of original files occurs through the use of several mechanisms:

- centralization of original records
- use of requisition forms and countersignatures for access
- use of a charge-out (sign-out) system to keep track of record location and time of use, and to avoid record loss
- use of reproductions (photocopies) of the original record preserves the original but poses a problem regarding the need to return and destroy all extra copies of patient-identifiable information

A questionable advance in medical records security is the process of converting the written page to electronic information. Clerks scan page after page of the medical data and put the entire record into a computer file. Physicians may review the record, but since the record can only be viewed onscreen, information contained within the record is safe—it cannot be changed or altered. Also, there are master and backup copies that also ensure records have not been altered. Most larger hospitals are beginning to computerize medical records. In the future, even active in-patient charts will be computerized.

Electronic communication has eased the way healthcare information is collected, stored and transmitted. Computerized medical records can be accessed almost instantly for improved patient care and improved record management. However, this system allows more people access to private records. Privacy and confidentiality are proving to be much more complex in the computerized world than in the realm of the great paper chase!

Concerns for medical privacy led to the introduction of the Medical Records Confidentiality Act and various state statutes aimed at ensuring privacy with respect to medical records and healthcare-related information. Most states require legal authorization for the release of specific records such as those pertaining to

- HIV testing and therapy
- sexually transmitted diseases
- records of psychiatric treatment
- the treatment of children
- child abuse
- substance abuse

"Lock-Up"

When an in-patient dies from questionable or unusual circumstances in the hospital, his hospital chart goes immediately to the Medical Records Department for maximum security, or what some hospitals call *lock-up*. This prevents anyone from seeing or altering the chart in any way. It is no longer active. No one may review a lock-up medical record without a manager or director in attendance at the time.

Occasionally there is an unannounced audit of lock-up charts. This is to guarantee that nobody has had access to them and that every chart listed as a lock-up is indeed still secure. Lock-up charts may be reviewed in the presence of the Medical Records Department manager.

Reasons for a Medical Record Lock-Up
- for personal reasons (e.g., sexually transmitted disease, abortion or AIDS)
- sudden, unexpected death of an in-patient
- pending lawsuit
- questionable, unethical medical practice by doctor or nurse
- if a crime is suspected, with possible police involvement in the case

Privacy and the Medical Record

While the security of medical records is a hospital systems problem, the issue of privacy extends beyond the walls of the institution. The medical record is never made public, but may be accessed by certain parties without the patient's consent. Nevertheless, the protection of medical information is a major issue today, especially with electronic data storage and transfer. As medicine moves into the next century, computers will no doubt become the exclusive domain for storing medical records.

This method of storing sensitive information sets up serious opportunities for breaches in confidentiality, and thus the threat of litigation.

When a patient reaches the hospital, personal information is captured in the permanent record and becomes available to a multitude of both legitimate and dubious eyes. In the early 1900s, doctors kept your medical condition a private matter. In fact, privacy was such an important issue early in the century that medical documents were inadequate, and in many cases useless.

In a recent study, it was estimated that as many as *seventy* hospital personnel have an opportunity to access a supposedly confidential medical chart.

Seventy!

Doctors, nurses, aides, orderlies, secretaries, physical therapists, occupational therapists, X-ray techs, OR techs, medical and PA students, nursing students, kitchen help, police, ambulance drivers and delivery service personnel—all have a chance to see your inadvertently opened three-ring binder (or may feel uninhibited about flipping it open and reading it). This is an in-house problem of confidentiality with a paper record.

The problem of patient confidentiality in the hospital is no less severe with electronic records. A survey at UCLA revealed that a third of doctors, nurses and "other" hospital employees questioned were concerned that medical record confidentiality was a problem. Twelve percent of the nurses and eleven percent of "others" admitted to inappropriately accessing computer information. Twenty-five percent of nurses and "others" observed other hospital personnel looking at confidential computer information. And while a third of the nurses intervened to stop the wrongful access, only twelve percent of doctors took action.

Obviously there is a serious potential for, and in most hospitals a real problem with, misuse of electronic information storage and retrieval. Added to the sleazy computer access conundrum is the quandary of casual conversations—the hallway, cafeteria or elevator disclosure of medical information among healthcare professionals.

In the near future, the written chart and paper medical record may become a relic of the past. Instead of doctors having to leaf through dozens of chart pages, they can review the entire medical record on a computer screen. No doubt the computerized chart will speed up coding and billing, as well as the physician's ability to review lab data in graph form. If proper precautions are taken, electronic storage may add to the security of the chart.

In an article in *American Medical News* (August 24, 1998), Health and Human Services (HHS) Secretary Donna Shalala spoke about the issue of a patients' privacy, noting that computerized medical information speeds the process of transmitting information between doctors and accelerates the process of patient billing. However, before accepting a mandatory ID number as proposed by the government, one has only to look at how Social Security numbers have become ubiquitous to anticipate the potential for unsafe medical records. The loss of privacy and confidentiality would have a profound effect on the patient-physician relationship.

Physicians have taken a leadership role in speaking out in favor of strong safeguards for patient privacy and confidentiality. The House of Representatives passed a bill in the late 1990s outlining rules for medical record information disclosure that requires insurers, employers and providers to allow patients to inspect and copy their medical records. The bill requires privacy safeguards be established to protect the confidentiality of medical records.

Health and Human Services submitted to Congress recommendations for federal health record confidentiality legislation that would guarantee rights for patients and define responsibilities for record keepers. The recommendations cover the confidential treatment of personal health information as well as penalties for its misuse.

Guidelines for Improved Medical Record Confidentiality

If a patient's confidentiality is violated, the person responsible is at risk to suffer civil penalties. We know these violations happen. How do we prevent it? The following suggestions have been made by Jerry Blaine, M.D. and Bonnie Johnson, RN, JD, from the Lahey Clinic Medical Center:

- Use passwords for all authorized personnel and change them regularly.
- Educate employees not to disclose their passwords.
- A screen saver with a designated password should be used for any office or home computer that may be left unattended for periods of time.
- Hospitals, other medical institutions and doctors' offices must have policies to purge files on a regular basis, particularly if a computer is sold or given away.
- Create restricted access to special records such as HIV/AIDS patients and those of employees, families of staff or VIPs.
- Educate employees that they are on a need-to-know basis, and that it is wrong to search private records through the computer.
- Limited access policies must be established for ancillary systems such as pharmacy or the lab where sensitive information is available.
- E-mail is *not* secure and should not be used to transmit sensitive information.
- Cellular phones are *not* secure and are viewed as radio transmitters; no privacy should be expected.
- The Internet is *not* secure and should not be used to transmit confidential data; encryption should be considered when applicable.

The contents of medical records may be disclosed or reviewed *without* a patient's written consent in the following situations:

- to medical personnel during a medical emergency (patient care)
- to qualified personnel to conduct scientific research or to evaluate the quality of medical care; audit reports
- if authorized by a court order showing good cause

- to determine benefits entitlement
- in situations affecting health or safety (psychiatric information)

Releasing Medical Records

According to the AMA's Code of Ethics, failure to release medical records—for whatever reason—violates the patient's continuity of care. And failure to release records to a patient could cost the physician his license. Most states have laws authorizing patient access to their own medical records. The legal requirements for the release of medical records are as follows:

- The patient's consent for releasing medical records must be in writing before releasing.
- Medical records can only be released with the patient's written, signed consent.
- Medical Records personnel should examine the signed consent form to ensure that the signature is in fact that of the patient.
- For release of records for minors or those deemed incompetent by the court, the parent or legal guardian must sign the consent.
- If the patient is deceased, the record must be signed by the executor or administrator of the patient's estate.
- The consent must identify the specific information or medical records to be released.
- The reasons for or purposes of the release must be specific.
- The consent must specify the persons to whom the information or records are to be released.

A patient may fax a signature authorizing the release of her medical records. However, she will be questioned as to whom and why the records are being sent. Also, the records room staff will check the faxed signature to see if it matches the consent for treatment form on the face sheet of the record.

If another hospital calls and asks for a medical record to be faxed to them because the patient is being admitted there or is being seen in the ER, the Medical Records Department will call the other hospital back to confirm that they in fact called for it.

The Emancipated Minor

Discontinuation of the parent-child relationship—as reflected in abandonment or mutual agreement—permits a minor to represent herself. Evidence of the young person's maturity and ability to understand the implications of one's actions are usually adequate to permit independent decision-making by a minor. Some states have statutory requirements permitting minors to consent for themselves in the following situations (Bruce, J. *Privacy and Confidentiality of Health Care Information*, 1984):

- treatment of venereal disease
- treatment for drug addiction
- treatment in connection with pregnancy or childbirth
- procurement of family planning information and services
- blood donations
- treatment of a child whose parent is also a minor

Confidential Medical Information

Is the sort of informed consent used in informing a patient of a procedure or intervention the same for the disclosure of patient-identifiable data from a hospital record? Hardly. When a patient signs consent to release sensitive information about his health status or the care which has been provided, he cannot know with absolute certainty where that information is going to end up. Legitimate requests for confidential medical information can be made by the following:

- **OTHER HEALTH CARE INSTITUTIONS** if there is a compelling reason, such as the patient is in need of emergency care or is being transferred to the institution requesting the information
- **INSURANCE COMPANIES** health, life and disability policies require medical information for the individual, and the hospital must have policies regarding the outflow of patient-identifiable information to outside insurers, including third-party healthcare insurers
- **EMPLOYERS** much health insurance is employer-based, and information flows freely to them
- **HOSPITAL ACCREDITATION, LICENSURE AND CERTIFICATION REGULATORY BODIES** to comply with a variety of regulations, such as the Department of Health and Human Services, via authority from the Social Security Act, may review health records for Medicare nursing home patients

- **GOVERNMENT PROGRAMS** the U.S. government is the biggest requester of patient-identifiable information, and a variety of government agencies have dossiers on individual citizens; this includes health information
- **LAWYERS IN MEDICAL MALPRACTICE CASES** hospitals should have policies spelling out how much information an attorney may gather and how that process will be carried out; proof of a client-attorney relationship is mandatory, including the patient's signed consent
- **THE INTERNAL REVENUE SERVICE** the Tax Reform Act of 1976 restricts the IRS to gathering only that patient-identifiable information needed for tax-calculation purposes and restricts the exchange of this information with other agencies
- **THE FBI** the FBI may collect information on presumably dangerous individuals, as well as for security clearances and pre-employment health clearance for applicants
- **THE CORONER OR MEDICAL EXAMINER** to access cause of death, it is routine for information to be passed on to the ME

Information Services

Information Services is the hospital department responsible for the institutionwide communications network. It is the neural system that keeps people in contact with each other. Information Services is responsible for phones, overhead paging systems, pagers and beepers, as well as all computers and fax machines, within the hospital. People in this department are also responsible for installing new software and training others how to use it, and for the upkeep of the electronic information network.

Hospital operators receive calls from both inside and outside of the hospital. They will direct outside callers to the correct patient's room, or contact the proper employee or other personnel through their beeper or by paging them overhead. Also, family members calling the hospital will be given the room number of any in-patients. However, information regarding the condition of a patient will only be given to family members—and *not* by the paging operator.

Pertinent medical information is *never* given out by the hospital operator, as it once was when fewer patients formed the hospital population and life was simpler. Now families obtain information from specific floors and units.

Paging Systems

Paging systems within the hospital consist of both an overhead speaker system that everyone in the hospital can hear and personal pagers. Almost everyone involved with the running of the hospital has her own personal pager and can be reached anywhere on the hospital campus. Usually the operator will first try to reach someone by pager. If the pager is not answered, the operator will page on the overhead speaker system.

In addition, the hospital paging system permits those physicians who are employed full time by the institution to be reached citywide. Private doctors hire private companies to handle their communication needs, although in some areas of the country the local Academy of Medicine performs the citywide paging system. Usually, patients cannot call their doctor at home, but rather must reach him through his *answering service*, as the paging system is called.

Hospital operators will page a doctor "overhead" through the speaker system if she has not answered her beeper. Sometimes the beeper may be turned off, the battery may be dead, or the doctor left the beeper in a white coat or a locker.

Hospital operators also use the overhead speakers to page for all emergencies. This saves valuable time if someone's life is at stake. When a *STAT* page is announced overhead, the appropriate personnel can respond without wasted time. For routine pages, the announcement is usually repeated twice. For example:

> *Doctor Shermis, please call 8909.*
> *Doctor Shermis, please call 8909.*

If the emergency is more critical, the page will be for a patient's room. This instructs the doctor or others to go directly to the patient's room rather than taking time to call the nurses' station. If a patient is choking, bleeding or having difficulty breathing, time is of the essence.

> *Respiratory therapy, room 7702, STAT!*
> *Respiratory therapy, room 7702, STAT!*

Codes

Codes may be used to alert the hospital's general population of an impending disaster, or the medical staff of an emergency. Most codes are for the medical staff and are familiar to most people. The most common code and most ominous in the hospital is *CODE BLUE.*

CODE BLUE signals a cardiac arrest, usually accompanied by respiratory arrest. This code requires immediate attention or the patient will die. Every second counts, and the page CODE BLUE sets into motion a flurry of activity from the code team. The code page directs the code team to a specific patient room or area of the hospital to ensure the fastest possible response time.

Some hospitals use *CODE-99* instead of CODE BLUE, but they mean the same thing. Under new JCAHO guidelines, CODE BLUE has become the standard code. In larger hospitals, the code teams are divided into pediatric and adult codes. These two categories require different-size instruments, different drug dosages and different handling of the patients. With two separate teams, each team is familiar with the patient population they are dealing with, know the drugs and dosages by heart and don't have to delay response while they adjust for adult versus pediatric patients.

For emergency codes, the announcement is repeated three times. The overhead page in a larger hospital would be like this:

> *Attention Memorial Hospital. CODE BLUE, room 413. Adult code team respond.*
> *Attention Memorial Hospital. CODE BLUE, room 413. Adult code team respond.*
> *Attention Memorial Hospital. CODE BLUE, room 413. Adult code team respond.*

If the code is for a baby or child, the announcement would be "Pediatric code team respond." When a CODE BLUE is announced, every doctor and nurse in the hospital does *not* take off in a panic to assist. This would lead to chaos for the rest of the hospital, as well as in the patient's room. There would be far too many people to work effectively as a team. Instead, hospitals form code teams that function as a unit. They move quickly and efficiently to try and resuscitate the patient.

Code Team (For CODE BLUE or CODE-99 Response)

- doctor (internal medicine, cardiology or anesthesiology resident)
- possibly a second doctor to assist
- two nurses from a critical care unit
- respiratory therapist

Who comprises a code team will vary from hospital to hospital, but most code teams are made up of similar personnel. A doctor heads the code team and is usually an internal medicine, cardiology or anesthesiology resident. There may be a second physician on the code team to assist. There are two nurses, usually from a critical area such as the intensive care unit (ICU), and a respiratory therapist.

The respiratory therapist, anesthesiologist or anesthesia resident establishes an airway and properly ventilates the patient. The two nurses start IVs, administer drugs and run EKG strips. The doctor leading the code team monitors the EKG, directs the drugs and dosages to be given, and will perform either closed chest cardiac compression or defibrillation. A surgical resident is usually available for the placement of central lines, performing venous cutdowns if needed or performing an emergency airway (crycothyroidotomy).

The team members are usually scattered around the hospital when the CODE BLUE is announced, but they race to the room, arriving within seconds of each other, and begin a coordinated, efficient and (usually) smoothly orchestrated resuscitation in an attempt to save the patient. This is one of the few times you will see doctors and nurses racing up and down stairs and through hallways.

There are other codes paged overhead. These are *Disaster Codes* that may affect everyone in the hospital. Disaster Codes are announced on the overhead speakers and are usually given a color (or name) so as not to alarm patients and their families, but instead to alert the hospital staff who know the codes and are trained to take appropriate action.

The name or color given to disaster codes will vary from place to place. Most hospitals try to use standard codes that will be readily understood by the staff.

For instance, CODE RED means there has been a fire reported within the hospital. When this code is announced, hallway doors close, alarms

will ring in the corridors and floor managers are supposed to take steps
to ensure the control of the fire and the safety of everyone there. Disaster
Codes are also announced three times.

Attention Memorial Hospital. Code Red, second floor, north wing.
Attention Memorial Hospital. Code Red, second floor, north wing.
Attention Memorial Hospital. Code Red, second floor, north wing.

Hospital Emergency Codes

Code Purple	missing patient
Code Black	bomb threat
Code Orange	chemical spill
Code Green	evacuation of the building
Code Red	fire
Code Yellow	medical disaster (plane wreck, earthquake, bombing) influx of injured victims of disaster
Code Blue	medical emergency—cardiac arrest (some places still use CODE-99)
Code Adam	missing child/infant abduction
Code S	suicide threat
Code Magenta	radiation incident
Code White	snow emergency (varies depending on locale)
Code Grey	severe weather—tornado warning

CHAPTER EIGHT

Mistakes, Complications and Accidents

A lmost everyone finds themselves in a hospital at least twice in a lifetime, first to be born and then to die. Most will be hospitalized a few more times, and even more will be treated in an emergency room. Hundreds of millions of patients are treated yearly by more than 600,000 U.S. doctors, and many more nurses and ancillary medical care personnel.

The number of treatment interactions is literally countless. It would be foolish to assume that mistakes won't be made.

Modern medicine is built upon the miracle of technology. MRI scanners can see inside the entire body, CT scanners generate 3-D color images of bones, organs and vessels, lasers open clogged arteries, gene therapy permits novel treatment, organs are routinely transplanted and computer chips restore vision. These are just some of the recent breakthroughs in medicine. The technology explosion of the past three decades has advanced the frontiers of medicine more in those remarkable thirty years than has the entire combined knowledge of medicine over the past ten centuries.

So, has all this new technical advancement made the practice of medicine perfect and error free? Can patients depend on computers, monitors and medical staff to guarantee no mistakes will be made?

The obvious answer is no. Mistakes are made. Hospitals work miracles every day, but mistakes do happen.

Mistakes

The AMA patient safety board estimated a staggering 180,000 deaths last year from medical mistakes, equipment malfunction and complications.

Those 600,000 doctors and 2 million nurses order more than 150 million X rays and 30 million laboratory tests annually, and prescribe more than 100 million drugs each year. Unfortunately, with fallible humans performing these tasks, errors occur with annoying regularity.

Computers, complex machines, monitors and electronic devices do occasionally fail. However, most of the mistakes are indeed human error. With the huge numbers of hospital staff, patients, examinations and prescriptions involved, it is unreasonable to assume that mistakes would not be made.

How serious is the problem? The AMA patient safety board estimated a staggering 180,000 deaths last year from medical mistakes, equipment malfunction and complications. How many more individuals are injured or maimed is not really known. Most people never hear about the much more common mistakes: injuries or burns from medical equipment, medication errors, overexposure to radiation, and surgical equipment left inside patients after surgery. How many allergic reactions occur because someone wasn't paying attention to a medical bracelet? How many patients have received an operation that may seem to have been proper but, in fact, was not the most suitable for a given condition?

A major area where mistakes are made is when doctors perform invasive procedures and interventions. Procedures can range in magnitude from inserting a central venous catheter to performing an organ transplant, or from placing a guide wire into a breast before biopsy to open-heart surgery. In spite of meticulous methods to prevent such errors, surgeons still in rare cases leave surgical sponges or surgical instruments inside the patient when they close the incision. Common to all of these interventions is the need for a skilled physician to execute these procedures in a delicate manner.

Mistakes fall into a variety of categories. For example, there are mistakes of ordering the wrong drug dosage or the wrong drug, or the right drug and dosage may be administered to the wrong patient. Equipment failures are not uncommon with new high-tech laparoscopic procedures, there are injuries and burns from medical equipment, and surgical errors are made by human hands. Mistaken identity (the wrong patient) still occurs, and wrong-side surgery punctuates adverse outcomes with regularity. At the opposite end of the age scale, baby mixups in the nursery still happen.

Most of the mistakes are minor ones, but some are tragically life-threatening or fatal.

Hospitals have Quality Assessment (QA), Credentials, and Risk Management committees to review mistakes that have been reported to them. By reviewing charts that reflect care already provided, these committees can retrospectively uncover mistakes that are not yet reported and discipline the medical personnel involved. The purpose of these committees is to learn why mistakes occurred and to prevent or minimize them in the future. If a nurse or physician is responsible for the error, the committees' role is to inform them of the mistakes and require some type of monitoring of the individual's behavior for a period of time, or, in severe cases, even recommend the doctor or nurse be removed from the staff.

One method of dealing with what seems to a case reviewer to be a major omission or commission of an error is to request a written response by the physician of record. This allows the doctor to review what was done, rethink the overall strategy used in managing the patient, and then provide the QA committee, for example, with a letter indicating if another approach might not have been more efficient.

Mistakes
It's the Wrong Side!
The patient is already asleep on the table, an endotracheal tube projecting from his mouth. Monitors are attached to his forehead, finger, chest and forearm. His oxygen saturations, end-tidal CO_2, heart rate, blood pressure and pulse rate splash across a large, beeping video screen.

The surgeon, fatigued from spending three hours in the middle of the night doing emergency surgery for a ruptured spleen, scrubs his hands and walks into the OR, where six other members of the surgical team are already waiting. The surgical assistants are gowned and waiting. An anesthesiologist and nurse anesthetist are performing final rituals with tape, tubing and wire. The scrub nurse is working from a large table set with glistening instruments. And the circulating nurse is counting, opening, untangling, positioning and writing. The leg has been shaved, washed, painted with iodine, and draped with sterile towels. Only a small area of brown-stained skin is visible.

The ninety-minute surgery goes smoothly. After the skin is sutured, the stump is bandaged. The nurse pulls off the drapes—and only then does the surgeon realize what has happened.

He's just amputated the wrong leg!

Could such a horrible mistake actually happen? According to the *American Medical News*, there were 982 reported such cases in the past twelve years, an average of seventy-seven wrong-site surgeries per year.

It's easier to make this mistake than you might think.

Usually, the surgeon speaks to the patient just before surgery and, while he scrubs, the anesthesiologist puts the patient under. X rays of the patient are hung on the view box in the room, and the circulating nurse scrubs the area and covers it with sterile drapes, leaving a small area exposed for the surgeon. Many times the surgeon drapes the patient himself after the circulator has prepped the patient with antiseptic solution.

The surgeon is assisted with his sterile gloves as he talks to the team, adjusts the lights and begins the surgery. Not surprisingly, the surgeon assumes everyone in the room knows which is the correct side, and that the circulating nurse prepped (and draped) the correct site.

In the rushed atmosphere of the operating room, personnel can make mistakes.

An operation performed on the wrong person or wrong body part can be devastating for the surgeon as well as the patient. Such a mistake might destroy a physician's hard-earned reputation—or even end his career.

This preventable error doesn't just happen to insensitive or poorly trained doctors. Outstanding surgeons—general, thoracic, orthopedic and neurosurgeons—all have made the tragic mistake of operating on the wrong side. A whole array of things can happen to distract the surgeon and the circulating nurse from performing a double-check prior to surgery. Scrubbing, anesthesia, draping, checking of instruments and calls to the OR room and from other doctors all add to the confusion surrounding surgery. Sometimes the patient must be placed on his side or abdomen for surgery, making side identification even more confusing.

The JCAHO reviewed several cases of wrong-site surgery and identified four risk factors:

- more than one surgeon involved in the case
- multiple procedures on the same patient during a single trip to the
  OR
- an unusual start time, or pressure to hasten the preoperative
  procedures
- unusual patient characteristics, such as obesity or deformities

A handful of slipups made headlines in the 1990s. In Florida, a surgeon
amputated the wrong foot of a diabetic patient. A surgeon at a prestigious
New York cancer center operated on the wrong side of a patient's brain.
Another doctor removed the wrong breast for cancer. *Wrong-site* surgery
has been reported with brain surgery (wrong side of brain operated on),
lung surgery (wrong lung removed), breast surgery (wrong breast removed or biopsied) and extremity surgery for joint replacement, reconstruction or amputation. Data show that one in four orthopedic surgeons
will operate on the wrong site at some point in their careers!

Surgeon, Sign Your Site
There is a campaign underway now, launched by the American Academy
of Orthopedic Surgeons (AAOS), to prevent wrong-site surgery. Surgeons will sign their initials directly on the operative site after confirming
it a final time with the patient prior to anesthesia. One earlier approach
was to put an *X* on the site, but sometimes this area was under the drape
and not seen, or some well-meaning person would put another *X* on the
wrong side. Also, some hospitals have the surgeon write "No" on the
nonoperative site.

Double-checking the X rays, chart and consent form are all insufficient
to prevent the error. The surgeon's signed initials more reliably assure
everyone that the surgical site is correct.

This campaign by the AAOS designed to end wrong-site surgery is
called *Sign Your Site.*

Patients can contribute to the safety of their surgery by reminding the
surgeon in pre-anesthesia holding which side is the proper one. But it is
the surgeon's ultimate responsibility to check the chart and the appro-

priate X rays (which should be up on the view box in the room), and then the patient to confirm the correct site for surgery.

The incorrect labeling of biopsies, X rays, laboratory tests and blood can also prove to be deadly mistakes. A biopsy labeled "left" when it should have been "right," or a biopsy labeled with the wrong patient's name on it, may cause a potentially huge problem for both the doctor and the patient. Blood samples with the wrong patient's name, or laboratory slips with the wrong name, can be deadly errors.

When specimen errors occur, they are almost uniformly clerical in nature.

Awake During Surgery!

According to an article in *U.S. News & World Report* (October 12, 1998), a woman slowly regained consciousness on the operating table during surgery. She was confused. Why wasn't she in the recovery room? Then she realized that her surgery wasn't over.

In fact, it had barely begun.

Another woman woke up while under anesthesia during an abdominal operation. She realized things were going badly when she felt the scalpel cutting into her abdomen, but was unable to move. A muscle relaxant had been given to paralyze her. She tried desperately to move, to tell them she was awake and feeling everything, but to no avail. Then, because of the added stress, she suffered a cardiac arrest.

The anesthesiologist had administered a muscle relaxant that left her unable to speak or even blink her eyelids. But the anesthesiologist had forgotten to fill the canister that dispensed the inhalant that extinguishes consciousness and eliminates pain. Afraid and in great agony, the woman had no way of communicating to anyone.

Over the next 45 minutes, she felt every slice of the surgeon's knife.

It's every patient's worst nightmare: The thought of undergoing surgery with inadequate anesthesia, of feeling the cut of the surgeon's knife but not being able to tell anyone that you're not unconscious. Waking up during surgery under general anesthesia is called *awareness*. The director of anesthesiology in a New York hospital believes that as many as 200,000 people a year may awaken, but many patients don't report it. Awareness during surgery is due to an inadequate level of anesthesia as a result of failure to maintain adequate blood drug levels. The range of awareness

varies from being pain-free but fully awake to being in intense pain and
paralyzed, unable to communicate to anyone. Patients reported that anxiety, fear or severe panic were because of paralysis.

The objectives of general anesthesia include:

- unconsciousness
- suppression of reflex responses
- muscle relaxation
- suppression of pain

The anesthesiologist walks a tightrope between too much and too little
medication. On the one hand, he does not want to fail to provide adequate
anesthesia to even one patient. On the other hand, he is concerned about
endangering his patients with overmedication.

Chances of awareness during general anesthesia are reduced with in-
novative new state-of-the-art brain wave monitoring devices that measure a person's state of consciousness and measure pain. With one device,
a sensor is placed on the patient's forehead to track brain wave activity, a
measure of level of wakefulness. Another new device tracks electrical-
muscle activity of the forehead to detect if the patient is experiencing
pain.

The new system, called the *Bispectral Index* (BIS), offers the first direct
method of measuring the effects of anesthetic and sedative agents on
the brain, using an enhanced EEG (electroencephalogram). The BIS
monitor converts the brain wave pattern into a "depth of sedation" number between 0 (indicating no brain activity) and 100 (fully awake). The
target number for an anesthetized patient is approximately 50 to 60.
Anything below 50 means the patient been so deeply anesthetized that
there will be delay in waking up from anesthesia, and increases the risk
of anesthesia. Anything above 60 means the patient is only mildly anesthetized; the higher the number, the closer to waking up.

The marvel of this system is that now the anesthesiologist can determine the exact range of level of anesthesia to administer so that the patient
does not wake up during surgery, and still ensure that the patient is not
too deeply anesthetized. When BIS is utilized to determine the proper
amount of anesthesia, patients wake up from surgery much faster and
have far fewer secondary complications and complaints. Many anesthesi-

ologists believe that BIS monitoring during surgery should be used routinely.

Patients contemplating surgery can ask for one of these monitoring devices to be used (if the hospital has one). The patient can also ask for the family physician or a second anesthesiologist to be present during surgery. Unfortunately, insurance would probably not pay for this, and the extra expense would be the patient's responsibility.

Giving the Wrong Drug

Medication errors are more common than one might think. It is estimated that 140,000 deaths a year are related to drug mistakes involving dosage or the incorrect drug, or from fatal drug interactions. Mistakes can happen anytime during the treatment process, which includes the prescribing, preparation, distribution/delivery and administration of drugs, any one of which can result in a patient receiving the wrong medication. A study from Boston showed 6.5 adverse drug events—errors or adverse reactions—involving drug administration for every one hundred patients treated.

Six and a half drug problems per one hundred patients!

According to a study in *JAMA* (October 1996), every day in an American hospital, a patient dies because someone makes a mistake in the prescribed medication. The errors were both from the wrong drug or the wrong dosage. One study found four clinically significant dispensing errors for every one hundred prescriptions. In-hospital errors occurred at the rate of one error per patient per day!

Inadequate staffing and increased workloads in pharmacies are causing chaos. Prescriptions are up dramatically. And HMO third-party payers are imposing ever-lower reimbursement rates on pharmacies so that they must churn out high volumes to make a profit. One study found a direct correlation between pharmacists' workloads and error rates.

An article from *Reader's Digest* tells the tragic story of a seven-year-old who took the first pills of a prescription for Ritalin, used to treat her attention deficit disorder. In an emergency room later that day, the doctors discovered she hadn't gotten Ritalin, but instead a high dose of a diabetes medication that was sixteen times the normal dose for an adult. Her blood sugar plummeted and, as a result, she suffered permanent brain damage.

Prescription Errors

Illegible handwriting and misinterpretation of medication orders accounted for 15 percent of prescription errors. The illegible scrawl of many doctors has been the butt of jokes, but research shows it can have deadly results if the wrong drug or dose is given.

Most medication errors result from errors at the ordering stage, but many also occur when the drugs are administered.

A study in *JAMA* found that 66 percent of physicians had at least fair handwriting, but 17 percent of physicians had illegible handwriting. And even orders written with good handwriting can be misinterpreted.

Another reason for mistakes is the hundreds of drugs with similar names, causing confusion and inappropriate interchange.

Similarly Spelled Drugs Creating Medication Errors

Quinine	Quinidien
Lamotrigine	Lamivudine
Vinblastine	Vincristine
Platinol	Paraplatin
Sulfasalazine	Sufladiazine
Indapamide	Isradapine
Levoxine	Lanoxin
Norvasc	Navane
Hydroxyzine	Hydralazine
Losec	Lasix
Clonopin	Clonidine
Xanax	Zantac

Seemingly unimportant actions can lead to medication errors. Most hospital pharmacies and nurses use NCR copies of physician orders. As a result, the second and third (often faintly inscribed) copies of an order are used as the "working copy." Also, abbreviations can lead to dispensing both the wrong drug and the wrong dosage. Because of this, abbreviations are discouraged when prescribing medications.

One of the particularly dangerous abbreviations is the use of *U* as an abbreviation for *Units*. This has caused severe medical errors when the *U* was interpreted as either a *4* or a *0* (zero).

Confusing Drug Abbreviations

5-FU vs. 5-FC	Fluorouracil vs. Flucytosine
ARA-A vs. ARA-C	Vidarabine vs. Cytarabine
CPZ	Chlorpromazine vs. Compazinereg
OD	Once Daily vs. Right Eye
"gr"	Grams vs. Grains (65 mg/grain)
"ug" vs. Mg	Microgram vs. Milligram
ASA vs. 5-ASA	Aspirin vs. 5-aminosalicylic acid
T3 vs. T3 vs. 3TC	Lithyronine vs. Tylenol/Codeine vs. Stavudine
Q.D. vs. QID	Daily vs. Four Times a Day
TIW vs. T/W	Three Times a Day vs. Twice a Week
D/C	Discharge vs. Discontinue

The Wrong Dosage

Giving the wrong dosage of a drug can be just as dangerous as giving the wrong drug. When the wrong dosage is given to the patient, it is usually by a factor of ten-times or one hundred-times the intended dose. That is because the decimal point is either misinterpreted or the dosage is incorrectly written. A leading zero should always precede a decimal expression of less than one. And a terminal or trailing zero should never be used after a decimal. Tenfold errors in drug strength and dosage occur with decimals due to the use of a trailing zero or the absence of a leading zero.

For example, *10.0 mg* could be interpreted as 100 mg (trailing zero), or *.5 mg* could be interpreted as 5 mg (absence of leading zero). These should have been written as *10 mg* and *0.5 mg* to avoid this mistake. These decimal point errors result in tenfold dosage errors that can prove to be fatal. The following case is just such an example of a tenfold error from decimal point.

A *New York Times Magazine* article (June 15, 1997) relates the story of a two-month-old baby whose parents took him to the outpatient clinic for a checkup. He seemed healthy and was growing well. But the doctors heard a heart murmur and discovered a ventricular septal defect, a hole between the pumping chambers of his heart. The baby was showing signs of early congestive heart failure, which the doctors decided to treat with Digoxin. The surgeons decided to admit him and treat him medically, wait until he was a year old, and then operate.

The baby's weight was used to carefully calculate the correct dosage of Digoxin. The order in the chart was for .09 milligrams. The dosage administered was 0.9 milligrams, or tenfold more than the amount calculated. There was an entire chain of events that led to the wrong dosage being administered. The nurse who finally administered the drug as ordered worried that the dose was wrong and asked a resident to recheck the dosage, asking if that was in fact the dose that he wanted her to give the baby. The resident at that time (not the one who originally ordered the drug) did not notice the difference in the decimal point between .09 mg and 0.9 mg. The order should have been written *0.09* rather than *.09*.

It took twenty minutes for the entire tenfold dose to drip through the IV tube. Minutes later the baby began to vomit, the first sign of drug overdose. The nurse's fears confirmed, she immediately gave him an antidote of Digibind, but it was too late. The baby died soon after. Everyone involved was devastated, the loss indescribable to both the staff involved and to the parents.

The same article also told of the death of a young, thirty-nine-year-old health columnist for *The Boston Globe* who died not from her breast cancer but rather because of a fourfold miscalculation in the amount of Cytoxan she was given at a hospital to battle her breast cancer. She died because the total dose to be given over four days was instead given on *each* of the four days, an error that was not discovered or corrected by doctors, nurses or pharmacists.

Another potentially deadly complication of administering several concurrent medications is the harmful reactions between different drugs. The hospital's computer system automatically searches for possible dangerous drug interactions. One drug alone, called *cisapride* and used to treat gastrointestinal problems, accounted for nearly 71 percent of dangerous drug interactions.

When it comes to drug errors, be it wrong drug or dosage, physicians have traditionally received most of the blame. Because physicians choose most medications, write the prescription and sign it, they are the ones who take the fall when things go wrong. But studies reveal that physicians

---

Common Types of Drug Errors
- illegibly written drug orders
- poor communication of oral orders on the phone
- wrong drug, the result of look-alike packaging, soundalike names of drugs, mishandling error or misread order
- wrong dosage
- wrong interpretation of abbreviation
- wrong patient
- wrong directions
- giving drugs with harmful interactions

---

aren't always the culprits. It is estimated that up to 28 percent of all drug mistakes could have been avoided if there had been some system in place to prevent errors.

Many hospitals use electronic ordering, and physicians are becoming computer literate. This dramatically decreases errors resulting from illegible handwriting and misinterpretation of the order, as well as improving the doctor's ability to cross-check for harmful drug interactions. Computerized physician order entry has cut serious medication errors by more than half.

Wrong Information on Chart

The number of times reports, tests, lab slips, pathology reports, EKGs and consultation sheets get attached to the wrong chart is difficult to uncover. Many times the error goes undetected unless someone happens to flip through the active chart and spots a sheet with someone else's name on it. The volume of paperwork that arrives daily at the floor for charting is staggering.

The amount of reimbursement to hospitals has been slashed by HMOs, forcing hospitals to make drastic cuts in staffing. This has left vital areas of the hospital understaffed, and has led to increased stress on those working harder, poorer patient care and serious medical mistakes. Charting the volumes of paperwork generated on in-patient care creates even more of a burden and is also subject to errors.

A common charting error that occurs in most hospitals is when patients with very similar names, different middle initials or the same full name are in-patients at the same time. Anna Smith might be confused with

---

Estimated Number of Yearly Mistakes

- wrong-site surgery—77 per year
- awake during surgery—200,000 per year
- wrong drug/dose given—1 error per in-patient every day, 1 in-patient death every day
- switched babies—2 to 3 times a year
- stolen babies—15 per year

Anita Smith; Leonard Williams confused with Leonard Williamson; and Sarah F. Carter confused with Sarah E. Carter. Similar or same names is a very common cause for mischarting lab slips and medical reports.

Most larger hospitals are now in the process of computerizing data that is added to the appropriate chart, saving time and reducing errors. For the computer, given enough ancillary data, even patients with exactly the same name should not present a problem for correct charting.

Misinterpreted Orders

Orders may be misinterpreted for a number of reasons. Verbal orders or orders given over the phone may be either not understood or written down incorrectly. The mistake is usually picked up when the doctor signs the phone orders the next morning, but unfortunately there are occasional times when it is too late. Serious (or even fatal) results may have already happened.

Illegible or incorrectly written orders can lead to misinterpretation. Also, the way the order was written may lead to misinterpretation. (See the discussion on page 247 about wrong drug dosages.)

Switched Babies

Every new parent's nightmare is the fear of having a switched-at-birth baby and the anguish of taking home the wrong baby. Parents want to know it is their own baby they are taking home from the hospital, not someone else's.

Over 4.5 million births take place each year in the United States at approximately 3,500 birthing facilities. While short hospital stays are usually uneventful, every once in a while there is a tragic birth-related story. Someone snatches a newborn from a hospital nursery, or parents take the wrong baby home. Protecting newborn babies from mixups or abductions has become a primary concern for hospital nurseries. Extensive effort is put into preventing switched-baby errors. However, even when every precaution is taken, switched newborns are reported two or three times a year.

Hospitals follow a common safety procedure in which babies and their mothers are assigned identical (numbered) identity bracelets immediately after birth. The baby gets two: one on the wrist and one on the ankle; the mother gets the larger one on her wrist. The bands cannot be removed accidentally, and have to be cut off. During feeding, the mother's nameband is checked against the baby's band, and both are recorded to make sure there is no mixup.

In addition, the father or support person is also banded. Further, babies are footprinted and the mom's fingerprint goes on the ID card.

But in spite of this complex system of checks and counterchecks, mixups still occur, although rarely. Three such cases made the news recently.

The first case was that of Kimberly Mays, who was switched with Arlena Twigg at a hospital in Florida when they were born in 1978. The swap was realized ten years later in 1988, when Arlena died of heart disease and tests showed she was not the biological child of the parents who took her home. The case drew national attention and was the subject of intense custody battles.

The second case was that of two newborn baby girls, Rebecca and Callie, who were also sent home with the wrong mothers. According to *USA Today*, the two mothers spent hours walking off labor pains together in the hallways of the maternity ward. One was twenty-seven years old and the mother of three, the other a sixteen-year-old having her first baby. They talked about the agonies of labor. Three years later, when the baby girls were three, the mistake was discovered after one of the girls underwent genetic tests. DNA results proved that the girl was not the older mother's biological child. The hospital immediately began the task of tracking down the other parents, who also had the wrong child. In a tragic development, the younger parents died in a car crash on the Fourth of July, leaving that girl to be raised by grandparents.

The third case involved a mother whose baby died at a university hospital. She was given the wrong remains. Fortunately the mistake was discovered before the baby's body left the hospital. The baby was born prematurely with multiple birth defects in another town and was transferred to a university hospital for treatment—where it died. The mother went to the hospital to take her baby's body back home for burial, but she was given a plastic coffin containing the body of another infant. The mixup wasn't discovered until the mother asked for her baby's blanket, which hospital employees found in the morgue next to the body of her daughter.

Hospital officials confirmed the account of the incident and blamed the switch on failure to check the cardboard tag affixed to each body bag.

Stolen Babies

Even more frightening than switched babies is the terror of having a newborn baby or infant stolen from the nursery.

The three areas of greatest security risk within a hospital are the pharmacy, the newborn nursery and medical records. Of these, the most protected and secured area is the newborn nursery because of the fear of baby kidnapping. The FBI documented 145 infant abductions over the past ten years. Of those, eighty-three were stolen from hospitals; sixty-two infants were abducted from other locations such as residences, daycare centers or shopping centers.

Baby stealing has become the number one concern for newborn nurseries, and most hospitals have a security system in place to prevent the abduction of recent arrivals. Nurses in the newborn nursery are taught that their most important duty is to be on the alert for the safety of the babies to avoid both mixups and baby stealing.

Hospitals take nursery security so seriously that administrators won't talk about it for fear of giving away secrets. Obviously, the degree of security for nurseries varies from hospital to hospital. More than thirty hospitals across the country are now using a new device, a tiny quarter-sized transmitter that is attached to the baby's umbilical cord. It can only be removed with a specially made tool. If the newborn travels too far from the mother, an alarm will sound, notifying the nursing staff and hospital security to guard all doors.

In other hospitals transmitters are attached to the baby's ankle or wrist. Not long ago when someone tried to snatch a baby from a hospital in Buffalo, New York, the device alerted hospital security. The would-be baby snatcher was caught before he could reach the hospital exit.

> ### *Three Areas of Greatest Security in a Hospital*
> - Pharmacy
> - Newborn nursery
> - Medical records

Some medical centers use a lockdown unit in which people can only access the maternity ward with a special code punched into the secured door. All other doors to the ward are locked and secured with an alarm. Surveillance cameras are present in every hall of the nursery. There are additional security procedures, but those are not made public. The problem for the hospital is to strike a balance between security and openness; to be family-oriented and friendly, yet at the same time to be safe. After all, it is a hospital, not a prison.

Most hospital baby kidnappings occur during normal working hours, between 8 A.M. and 6 P.M. Monday through Friday. The reason for this appears to be ease of movement. Abductors disguise themselves as employees and slip in and out virtually undetected. Infant abductions usually are carried out by women who are not criminally sophisticated. However, they demonstrate an ability to carefully plan the abduction and convincingly play the role of a hospital employee or health professional, and will resort to deadly force if necessary.

At a Kansas City hospital, a young woman entered a mother's room on the pretext of telling her about a drawing in which she could win baby clothes. According to the FBI, the woman then abducted the hours-old baby girl when the mother fell asleep after being sedated. According to the security videocamera, the woman left with a male companion holding the baby in an infant carrier. Earlier that same day, the security cameras caught the same two near the elevators of the maternity floor, a hint that the couple might have been shopping for a baby. Three days later, the couple was captured, and the baby was returned safely to her mother.

In Jacksonville, a newborn was abducted from her mother's side in a hospital by a woman wearing hospital scrubs and a wig. Another woman had visited three hospitals while wearing maternity clothes prior to finally abducting a baby.

Profile of Baby Kidnappers
- usually women (141 of the 145 cases in the past ten years)

- average age twenty-eight
- the need to present their partner with a baby often drives the offender
- some use the baby to prevent partner from leaving
- several used a fake pregnancy to force marriage and had to produce a baby
- hospital kidnapping usually occurs between 8 A.M. and 6 P.M.

Making the Wrong Diagnosis

Math is reproducible: There is only one answer to a particular equation or problem. Errors in calculation can be identified and corrected.

Not so in the practice of medicine. Clinical medicine involves a series of steps in which all the appropriate facts are gathered (clinical findings on physical exams, lab tests and imaging studies). A conclusion is formulated and a diagnosis suggested based on an interpretation of all the evidence. This process is always *subjective*. A different doctor may arrive at a different diagnosis.

For example, a patient presents to the ER with a severe headache and nausea. You, the treating physician, perform a clinical assessment and review a few lab studies, which are all normal. You make a diagnosis of stress-related headache. Another doctor says it's a migraine. And a third insists it's a subarachnoid hemorrhage.

Who's right? What do you do next? And what are the consequences of being wrong?

If it is an intracerebral bleed, further emergency workup and immediate treatment of the patient are critical. Delay of treatment could spell death. If you decide it's a migraine and admit the patient to the hospital for better pain control, and only later realize it is a subarachnoid bleed, did you make a mistake?

What if this patient was the seventh one today you've seen with a headache; the others were sent home from the ER on pain medication and instructions for followup with their primary care doctor. If you miss something dangerous in this patient who is presenting to the ER with *exactly* the same symptoms as the others and none of them have any positive physical findings, did you make a mistake? Is it an error in judgment?

Can the path to the correct diagnosis be traveled without error 100 percent of the time?

Without a doubt, missing an important diagnosis represents a deviation from accuracy. The issue is one of *degree* in medicine. And the whole topic of mistakes and errors can only be understood as it applies to the clinical situation from the perspective of patient expectation.

The patient does not expect the doctor to miss the diagnosis. That's why she went to that physician. His reputation is stellar. Which means what?

A sound clinical reputation reflects the prior practices of a doctor who is usually right. But not always. Most of the doctor's patients have done well and his errors have been few, their impact on patients presumably slight.

In reality, this is not how most patients view their doctor's actions. Patients do not wish—and in fact refuse in most cases—to accept that their physician does make errors and may make one with them. The expectation is that the case will be solved and the patient will be cured.

More often than not after a bad result, a family member (usually one who was not around during the agonizing days of decision-making and terminal care) asks why things didn't turn out better. The implication is: If we can put a man on the moon, why couldn't you get my mother through an operation for colon cancer?

The answers as to why some patients do poorly are varied.

Complications

Unlike an error or mistake, a complication is considered an unwanted but acceptable result of a clinical procedure. Complications are acceptable, recognized risks of a medical treatment, procedure or medication. These are risks most patients are willing to face when there is a reasonable chance for improvement or healing. Just as anyone who flies commercial airlines know there is a very, very slight risk of dying in a crash, they also know that the chances are so minimal that those risks do not outweigh the advantages of air travel.

Almost every working person in the United States owns a car, even though it is well known that 45,000 people a year die in highway accidents. Obviously, that number of deaths is considered an acceptable risk to those who drive.

Medicine also carries defined risks and complications.

Procedures, tests and surgery have risks associated with them. These risks usually involve unforeseen complications, such as infection, bleeding, failed sutures, cardiac or pulmonary problems. We accept them because we think the benefits outweigh the risks.

Drug Reactions

Listed on every drug insert are the possible reactions that may arise from using the prescribed drug. This is not a drug *interaction* from combining with another drug, but rather a possible complication of taking that particular drug. A reaction is not an error in prescribing or administration, but rather a complication of the drug itself.

Many complications may be as simple as hair loss, upset stomach, restlessness or fatigue. However, others can be life-threatening. These might include cardiac arrhythmias, massive hemorrhage, bone marrow dysplasias or failure of vital organs such as kidney, liver or pancreas.

Drug reactions are complications of medical treatment: They are not mistakes or errors. But they do contribute to patient injury and death. Again, these adverse reactions are known risks associated with taking a particular drug.

Blood Transfusions

Blood transfusions—or any other form of blood-component therapy involving other blood-derived products—are often needed to save a patient's life. As with drugs and procedures, there are recognizable (and accepted) risks with receiving typed and cross-matched blood. Sometimes *transfusion reactions* still occur, which refers to adverse immune responses and other complications related to receiving someone else's blood.

Blood and blood products may carry viruses and bacteria that can cause severe illness or death, including but by no means limited to HIV and hepatitis C. These adverse reactions are not mistakes, but they represent a spectrum of complications that can occur even with well-screened blood donations.

There are numerous studies underway to figure out how to prevent both the spread of infections through blood transfusions and the immunological responses.

CURRENT RISKS OF BLOOD TRANSFUSION

Adverse Reaction	Estimated Risk Per Unit of Blood
IMMUNOLOGICAL	
Fever	1:100
Nonfatal hemolytic	1:25,000
Fatal hemolytic	<1:1,000,000
INFECTIONS	
Hepatitis B	1:250,000
Hepatitis C	1:500 to 1:3,000
HIV	1:40,000

Infections

Some of the deadliest drug-resistant bacteria, viruses and fungi flourish almost exclusively inside hospitals—even in the cleanest hospitals. Infections are by far the leading cause of morbidity and mortality in a hospitalized patient. Approximately 220 people die in hospitals each day in America from infections contracted inside the hospital; approximately 80,000 patients are killed each year by hospital-borne infections. Some patients carry with them contagious viruses and bacteria that may be spread to other patients.

It is estimated that up to one-third of all hospital-borne infections could be prevented through better care. However, contracting an infection in a hospital doesn't necessarily mean the infection occurred because of bad technique. It depends on the patient's basic immune resistance as well.

Hospital infections are most likely to attack premature babies, the very old and the critically ill. Many cancer patients in hospitals die not from the cancer but from a pneumonia their depressed immune system cannot fight off. Invasive procedures or surgery is also a source of contamination and infection.

Hospital-borne infections are termed *nosocomial* (Greek for *in the house*) infections. They happen for a variety of reasons:

- Prophylactic antibiotics are not given at the right time (usually two hours before surgery), allowing infections to flourish at the surgical site.
- Healthcare workers who don't wash their hands or wear clean gloves can transmit diseases from infected patient to others.
- Naturally occurring microbes in the body find their way to places

they shouldn't be through surgical wounds, IV sites, catheters or the lungs (pneumonia).

Feeding tubes, breathing tubes, invasive surgery, IV lines, bladder catheters and central venous monitoring lines all present ways for microbes to enter the body, bypass a patient's natural defenses and begin an infection. Infections can be found localized in body-cavity or soft-tissue abscesses, within the urinary tract, in the bloodstream (leading to sepsis), in lung tissue (causing pneumonia) or diffusely within the peritoneal cavity of the abdomen (causing peritonitis).

Infections related to surgery vary from approximately 2 percent to 10 percent, depending on both the pre-operative condition of the patient and the type of surgery being performed. Surgical wounds are classified into three groups according to the type of case:

1. clean (elective surgery with skin prep)
2. clean-contaminated (elective colon surgery with appropriate bowel and skin prep)
3. contaminated (emergency surgery for a gunshot wound of the abdomen with bowel disruption)

Risks of Infection for Different Types of Surgery
(Source: National Nosocomial Infection Surveillance 1996 semiannual report.)

low-risk cardiac surgery	1.8%
high-risk cardiac surgery	4.3%
high-risk bypass with leg vein graft	5.4%
low-risk colon surgery	4.2%
high-risk colon surgery	10.8%
low-risk abdominal hysterectomy	1.5%
high-risk abdominal hysterectomy	6.1%
low-risk C-section	3.4%

Endoscopy and Infections
More than fifteen million Americans get prodded with flexible endoscopes each year. These sleek devices have huge advantages over scalpels. But, according to an article in *Newsweek* (March 1, 1999), they may be a cause of spreading infection from patient to patient.

The basic problem with scopes is that, unlike most surgical equipment, fiber-optic endoscopes can't be heat-sterilized. The delicate tubes, valves and optics would disintegrate under the high temperatures and pressures. Instead, technicians painstakingly scrub the scopes with tiny brushes, and then disinfect them by soaking in chemicals for twenty minutes. An FDA-funded study found that almost 25 percent of institutions had culturable bacteria in "cleaned scopes."

Blood and bodily material can lodge in the tiny channels and are almost impossible to clean out with traditional cleaning methods. A new high-tech washing machine has been developed that blasts the scopes with a compound called *peracetic acid*. This washing follows intense scrubbing. The peracetic acid eats through any remaining debris.

Another approach that has been developed is to create a barrier between the endoscope and the patient. A firm called Vision Sciences has developed a "sheathed" endoscope—kind of like "a scope with a condom." Some doctors have found the sheathed scopes harder to handle, but the reduction in risk and ease of cleaning compensate.

According to the article, the surest way to avoid infection is to seek out a facility that either sterilizes with peracetic acid (20 percent of hospitals do this) or one that uses sheathed scopes. However, the article also emphasizes that the one thing patients should *not* to do is avoid endoscopies out of fear of contamination. Endoscopy could save their life.

Antibiotics and Superbugs

According to an article in *Asbury Park Press*, fifty years of antibiotics misuse has created drug-resistant superorganisms that defy conventional treatments. These drug-resistant bacteria are the modern day Frankenstein of the medical profession. They were inadvertently created by doctors through the overuse and misuse of broad-spectrum antibiotics. The big three of the drug-resistant monsters are:

- **VRE** *vancomycin-resistant enterococci*. VRE is considered the worst of the lot because it is resistant to almost all antibiotics.
- **MRSA** *methicillin-resistant staphylococcus aureus*. MRSA is much more aggressive than VRE, but still treatable with vancomycin.
- **PRSP** *penicillin-resistant streptococcus pneumonia*.

In *The New England Journal of Medicine* (February 19, 1999), T.L. Smith et al. described for the first time a newly resistant *staphylococcus aureus*.

The terrible methicillin-resistant *staphylococcus* became resistant to the only antibiotic treatment known to be effective against it. This new dilemma raises the question of whether it might not be possible for this bacterium or others like it to cause as much death and morbidity as the *staph* infections before the era of antibiotics.

The fear is that there may soon be an ultimate superbug that is aggressive, highly contagious, deadly and resistant to everything.

Sepsis

In a cramped and airless conference room down the hall from the ICU, a half-dozen doctors and medical students slump around a conference table. All are glum. One of their patients has sepsis.

An article in *Discover* (November 1993), details the complications of sepsis in the hospital. Sepsis is a generalized bloodstream infection, with showers of bacteria delivered to bone, lungs, liver, kidneys and brain. All doctors—particularly those involved in critical care—know and dread the sudden temperature change, the clammy skin, the drop in blood pressure and the racing pulse that signal the onset of sepsis.

These doctors are all too aware of the deadly domino effect of sepsis. Blood vessels start to leak, allowing blood plasma into tissue and vital organs. Bacteria invade the bloodstream, and the whole body system spirals into the chaos of septic shock. Temperature rises or drops, blood pressure plunges and organ systems rapidly shut down.

Sepsis refers to the generalized effects of severe infection.

Sepsis is the leading cause of death in noncoronary intensive care units, and ranks thirteenth among causes of death in the United States. There is no effective drug treatment once the *systemic inflammatory reaction syndrome* begins, and the mortality rate is approximately 50 percent. Sepsis is on the rise and kills 175,000 intensive care patients annually.

There are many routes into the body for the bacteria that initiate sepsis. In the ICU, catheters, monitoring lines in femoral and pulmonary arteries, mechanical respirators and feeding tubes all provide entryways for large numbers of bacteria to invade the body, overwhelm the immune system and cause deadly sepsis.

Complications of Surgery

Surgery is often performed in an area of the body where the tissue is already markedly diseased with infection, scar tissue or cancer. Some tissues are dead (*necrotic* or *gangrenous*) from lack of blood supply (infarcted bowel, for instance). When the surgeon removes a segment of bowel and then sutures or staples the two ends together, healing usually occurs with no further complications. However, cancer or infection may have already spread to the sutured area, or the technical aspects of the operation may have been especially difficult and the blood supply to the ends of the rejoined intestine may be inadequate.

The result may be a leak from the *anastamosis*, or the joined ends of bowel. Sutures may simply fall out of the tissue, resulting in an opening. The leak leads to either *diffuse peritonitis* or a *localized abscess*. Both of these conditions may result in sepsis and multiple-organ failure.

When a cardiovascular surgeon performs a coronary artery bypass graft (CABG), there may be bleeding at the sutures, or inflammation may cause clots to form with consequent occlusion of the graft. These are complications known to happen with certain procedures. Redoing the surgery then becomes mandatory. Every effort is made to keep these complications from happening, but they still occur at a very low but predictable rate.

Human tissue is a biological variable, and its reaction to surgery cannot be completely predicted.

If you plant one hundred identical flowers and nine die, are you a bad gardener? You planted, fertilized and watered them identically. So the problem is not you as gardener, but rather the biological variability of that species of plant.

Complications of Procedures
Sometimes unforeseen things happen during diagnostic or therapeutic procedures. These complications may be due to tissue variability from one patient to the next, or may be an unforeseeable event that occurred during the procedure.

An example of this is balloon angioplasty. When older people develop peripheral vascular disease, the lumen of some arteries may fill with plaque, causing the blood vessel to markedly narrow and decrease blood flow to the extremities or organs. This can be treated by inserting a graft that bypasses the narrowed area; alternatively, a catheter with a balloon tip can also be inserted into the narrowed area, the balloon inflated and the vessel reopened (angioplasty).

Balloon angioplasty has proven to be an efficient method of treating vascular stenosis (narrowing). However, in a small percentage of patients the balloon may cause the vessel to rupture, leading to massive bleeding. Immediate surgery is then needed to repair the disrupted artery.

This complication is most likely related to the status of the vessel and surrounding tissue. The diseased, frail tissue ruptures.

Thus, complications related to interventions and surgery are due to:
- technology (equipment) failure
- tissue failure (too much disease)
- operator error

Accidents

Most accidents in the hospital are minor ones and include patients falling out of bed or in the bathroom, with fractures, cuts and bruising. However, sometimes the sophisticated and complex technical equipment that defines modern medicine fails and causes injury or death to the patient. Device-related adverse events ("accidents") are reported to the FDA or the manufacturer, who then decides if these are merely isolated events or if there is a series of similar problems with the device that might constitute a design flaw.

There are a multitude of medical devices, which vary in their complexity and their risk potential. These devices include ventilators, heart valves, pacemakers, X-ray machines, MRI scanners, infusion pumps, implants, laparoscopic equipment, biopsy equipment, catheters and monitors. They also include less complicated things such as sutures, thermometers, medical gloves, surgical instruments and prostheses.

Problems can include malfunction, manufacturing defects, product instability or design flaws. Clinical problems include tissue reaction or allergic reaction to the device. Dozens of patients had severe allergic reactions to the latex used in sterile gloves and in some catheters. Several deaths have occurred because of this problem before it was discovered that allergy to latex was the culprit.

Here are some examples of device malfunction or failure.

One dangerous design flaw involved connectors for internal feeding pumps that were inadvertently attached to inflation cuffs in endotracheal tubes. The cuff and feeding tubes were designed to be interchangeable. Some patients drowned when the feeding solutions were pumped into the endotracheal inflation cuff, bursting the patient's lungs.

An eighty-one-year-old woman was undergoing surgery for a left hip replacement. The surgery was proceeding routinely until the surgeon placed bone cement in the acetabular (hip joint "socket") area in preparation to fitting the hip implant, something he does routinely every day. But this time the patient had an unknown allergy to the cement and plunged into anaphylactic shock and died.

During a routine angioplasty procedure in a hospital, the tip of the transluminal angioplasty catheter became detached. The patient underwent surgery to remove the wire tip of the catheter from the heart.

A flash fire occurred during a blepharoplasty (cosmetic eye surgery) being performed on a forty-year-old man. The patient was receiving oxygen via nasal cannula. The surgeon was cauterizing with an electrosurgical cutting and coagulation device when the flash occurred. The patient's eyelashes, face and cornea were burned.

During MRI exams, metal within the patient's body or on the patient's skin can cause burns from electrical current induced in the metal. Patients have suffered severe second- or third-degree burns when EKG leads were applied for monitoring during anesthesia for an MRI examination. The burns occurred even though the leads were placed correctly without being coiled.

Reports of damage to the optic nerve and even blindness have resulted from an MRI examination in which the patients had metal fragments in the eye. The magnetic force can cause the metal fragment to spin, causing it to completely severe the optic nerve, resulting in blindness. Stainless steel aneurysm clips (safer titanium clips are now being used) to repair intracranial aneurysms have been dislodged or rotated in the strong MRI magnetic field, causing fatal hemorrhage in the brain.

To prevent such complications, patients are quizzed on three separate occasions about metal in the eye, metallic monitoring devices or aneurysm clips prior to allowing the patient to enter the room containing the magnetic scanner. Even with rigorous precautions by the technologists, accidents still happen.

Sometimes the patient is confused or senile and provides incorrect information. Sometimes a nurse, lab technician or transporter may enter the magnet room and have metal devices on them such as beepers, scissors, and pens that can accelerate with amazing speed and inflict severe puncture injuries.

"Therapy turned fatal" screamed the headline of an article describing the death of a fifty-nine-year-old beautician who was crushed to death when a 3,800-pound cancer treatment machine collapsed. That morning, as the radiation technologist was moving the 3,800-pound cobalt cancer-treatment machine to a distance of three feet over the woman's neck to treat a malignant tumor, the machine collapsed, crushing the woman's skull. It took the fire department more than two hours to move the mass of metal enough to remove her body. While doing that, they also had to contend with the radioactive cobalt source contained within the machine.

The radiation therapy machine was manufactured in Canada. The woman's death was the result of two large screws that had loosened. Before a warning could be issued about this risk, the same type of machine crushed another patient in China.

And this horror story is from the *American Medical News*: On the morning of March 21, a thirty-three-year-old oil field worker lay face down on a table beneath a linear accelerator radiation machine at a cancer center in Tyler, Texas. He was undergoing the last phase of radiation for a tumor on his shoulder. As the two technicians left the room, he felt at ease. From his previous sessions, he knew the radiation treatment to be a short, painless procedure.

One of the technicians turned on the accelerator machine at the computer console outside of the treatment room. The patient saw a bright flash of light, heard a frying sound and felt an electrical-shock-like pain shoot through his shoulder. Another one-second burst from the machine hit him in the neck, and he rolled across the table. Following the third burst, he jumped from the table and ran to the door, calling for help.

The technician had not seen his reaction to the treatment because the video monitor in the room was not plugged in and the intercom was out of order. The patient died of respiratory complications due to radiation exposure.

What happened to the thirty-three-year-old man—and to two others with similar experiences—is an example of what can go wrong in the high-tech world of modern medicine. It brings into question the role of doctors, technicians and computers when all three have overlapping responsibilities for administering patient care.

Although medical devices have saved countless lives, their use has also created the risk of serious injury or death. The sheer number of medical devices now on the market makes it unlikely that product-related injuries can ever be completely eliminated.

Fixing the Problems
Not WHO but WHY:

Do mistakes happen because doctors and nurses are confused or tired or misinformed? One of the big problems to overcome is this: Medicine continues to focus on *who* is at fault, while other fields try to focus on *why* the errors happened. Discovering "who" does nothing to fix the problem—and does nothing to understand the flawed process of "why" it happened.

Doctors and administrators in charge ask, "Who's the person that did it? Who do I blame? Give me a name." But the real question is: Why did it happen? And how can we prevent it from happening again? Slowly, health care has begun to understand this and has shifted its focus from the *person* to understanding and fixing the *process*.

In a *New York Times Magazine* article (June 15, 1997), the CEO of the prestigious Dana-Farber Cancer Institute in Boston, who understands this concept, said, "People don't make errors because they want to, or because they're bad people. Everybody makes errors. Every human being. What we need to focus on is how to best design our systems so that those errors are caught before they reach the patient."

The President's Advisory Commission listed error prevention as a top priority for health care quality improvement.

The cure for doctors' unreadable handwriting was to insist they type orders into a computer. One study found that the rate of serious medication errors fell by more than half on prescription-drug orders. In addition to providing better patient care, it saved the hospital money. Bad drug reactions in hospitalized patients cost a typical large hospital $5 million a year. And more than half of that cost is the result of errors.

Medical harm is not the result of ignorance, malice, laziness or greed. But today's American culture is characterized by anger, blame, guilt, fear, frustrations and distrust regarding health care errors.

Instead of a punitive approach blaming individuals, it is more important to use a systems approach. Shocking stories make great news. However, to fix the problems of mistakes, accidents and complications, it is important to understand the flaw in the system and correct it. A system has to be developed to see what went wrong and why—rather than a system of finger-pointing and blaming.

For example, a commercial airliner left the Detroit airport but failed to deploy the wing flaps before takeoff. The result was that everyone on that flight died during takeoff. Did the pilots make a mistake in failing to deploy the flaps? Yes. But rather than assigning blame, the more important issue is how to prevent flap mistakes from happening again.

An article in *USA Today*, "Medicine's Flying Lessons," shows how medicine is learning from the aviation industry about looking for a systems solution rather than looking for blame. Cockpit crews have protocols and checklists for takeoff, emergencies of equipment or passengers, and safety. Every crewperson is listened to when emergencies arise. There is no hierarchy at that moment, but rather a team approach to solving the problem.

However, traditionally the culture of the operating room works against warnings to surgeons or anesthesiologists. Nurses may be afraid to speak up or may not be listened to if they do. Medicine is now trying to apply the aviation method to decrease the 180,000 deaths that occur each year from medical errors. *Crew Resource Management (CRM)* is a training system used by the airlines. Pilots must listen to warnings from others in the cockpit.

Medical schools and residency programs are now beginning to use the CRM method to improve communications among surgeon, nurse and anesthesiologist in the OR. The method is also being applied to other areas in the hospital.

Open communication and shared responsibility are the key to eliminating medical errors.

CHAPTER NINE

Exams, Tests and Procedures

E very day, tens of thousands of procedures and tests are performed on both in-patients and outpatients. Catheters, tubes, probes and flexible fiber-optic scopes find their way into arteries, veins and every orifice of the body. And when there are no openings where needed, surgery makes one. Laparoscopy, arthroscopy, mediastinoscopy, central venous catheters and nephrostomy tubes all require that a new opening be made to accommodate the devices.

These procedures have allowed doctors to both diagnose and treat medical problems in ways that were never possible before. Medicine is changing at a rapid rate as newer technology becomes available. Lasers for surgery and imaging, flexible fiber-optic scopes, ultrafast CT scanners, powerful magnets for magnetic resonance imaging, PET (positron emission tomography) scanners, SPECT (single-photon emission computed tomography) scanners, Doppler ultrasound of vessels, antibody-tagged isotopes and drugs, balloon angioplasty of stenotic vessels and advanced microsurgery are just some of the recent advances in medicine.

The numbers are staggering. There are 3.5 million cardiac caths, 2.4 million angiograms, 60 million chest X rays, 100 million ultrasound scans and 26 million mammograms done in the United States each year. And each year more than 15 million Americans get prodded with flexible endoscopes.

Tens of thousands of hospital patients are wheeled out of their rooms each day for diagnostic tests, and they will most likely undergo one or more of the procedures discussed in the following sections. It should be

The control area is where digital images are monitored and processed during an arteriogram.

noted that as recently as thirty years ago, none of these procedures existed. They represent the most technological advancements of modern medicine. All of these procedures (excluding flexible fiber-optic endoscopy) are performed within the Radiology Department, an important section in the hospital with some of the most up-to-date technology available for diagnosing disease.

MRI Scan

MRI is the abbreviation for *magnetic resonance imaging*. The MRI scanner, more than any other medical device, personifies the most advanced technical development ever. Utilizing a powerful superconductive magnet in the range of 1.0 to 1.5 Tesla, a strong *rf* pulse is used to make the free hydrogen protons of the body resonate at varied frequencies. This allows amazing images of the body to be acquired in three dimensions, showing pathological processes as never before possible.

The modern MRI scanner is the most sophisticated diagnostic tool available today. Unlike the CT scanner, which uses ionizing radiation, MRI acquires images that are based on proton density and proton relaxation dynamics, and provides information that differs from other imaging

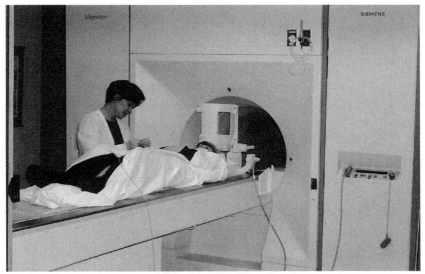

A patient is put inside the 1.5 Telsa MRI scanner.

modalities. Its major technological advantage is that it can characterize and discriminate among tissues using their physical and biochemical properties (water, iron, fat and extravascular blood). The MRI is a very demanding test and requires the most of the technologists: They must be well trained in cross-sectional anatomy and the physics of MRI scanning, and must be able to make important decisions regarding which pulse sequences to use and how to handle problems during the procedure.

The massive, futuristic appearance of the MRI scanner can be daunting to patients. As the patient steps into the scanner room, she sees a large machine, a small hole and long, dark, narrow tunnel. Because of the small bore of the magnet the patient must be placed in, some patients experience claustrophobia. Obese patients will not fit into the narrow opening and cannot be examined except in the "open magnets," a design that allows large patients to be studied. The magnetic coil is wound around the tunnel; the patient must be placed inside a long, confined tunnel ("gantry," or the metal frame that houses the coils). Large metal tanks containing liquid nitrogen and helium are behind the scanner; the extremely cold temperatures of these liquids (near absolute zero) create the superconductivity of the magnet.

269

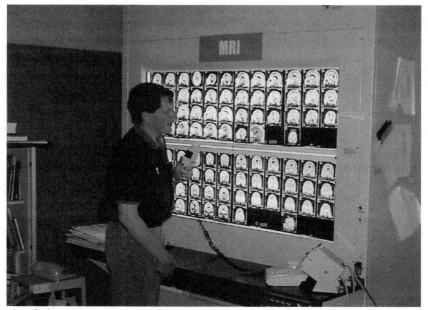

A radiologist reviews images from the MRI scan and dictates a diagnostic report based on the images.

Once the *rf* pulses are applied, there is a loud *knocking* sound inside the magnet. While the procedure is relatively comfortable and noninvasive, the combined effect of confined space inside the long narrow gantry, the loud repetitive knocking sound and the size of the device causes considerable anxiety and claustrophobia in a small percentage of patients. For these patients, sedation is often used to help them get through the procedure.

A newspaper staff writer described his experience during an MRI scan: ". . . they put you in what amounts to a dark coffin for an hour and bombard you with magnetic waves. . . ." He continues, "After they slide you in, they douse the lights. (In his frightened imagination) . . . the slightly muffled but still loud jackhammer sound was like rescue workers boring through the earth, using all their might to reach me before my oxygen ran out. . . ."

By the end of the article, he relates that in actuality, the technologists were very supportive he never felt the least bit anxious and the gantry was well-lighted and open at both ends, making the procedure not an unpleasant experience.

In his book *Critical Judgment*, best-selling author Michael Palmer describes the MRI procedure first through the eyes of a young doctor:

> *She had learned that there was a slight but significant rise in body temperature in patients undergoing the test, possibly caused by the intense radio-wave bombardment. . . . the temperature rise was it— except, of course, for the psychological trauma of lying in a metal tube for most of an hour, unable to move at all, surrounded by the echoing pings, hums and clangs of the charging and discharging electromagnet.*

And from the eyes of a patient:

> *The stretcher was wheeled into the place she had been told to expect—a gleaming, bright room with something like a huge space-ship in the middle, a hollow tube running through its center. She refused the technician girl's offer to help and scooted herself from the stretcher to a sliding bed attached to the hole in the ship. Then she allowed herself to be pushed into the cylinder. The banging and clanging of the magnet that she had been told to expect was scarcely blocked at all by the music. From someplace behind and above her, a fan started blowing. Oh, hell, she decided, forcing her muscles to relax. Let's just get it over with.*

Disregarding these vignettes and the somewhat ominous appearance of the MRI scanner, patient acceptability is high. It requires little patient preparation and is noninvasive.

CT Scan

CT is the abbreviation for *computed tomography*. An older term, *CAT scan*, is an abbreviation for *computed axial tomography*. These terms represent the same scanner and test; the name has been shortened from CAT to CT. The CT scanners are also a relatively new medical development. Unlike the MRI, which uses *rf* pulses and magnetic fields, the CT uses a narrow, focused beam of X rays. More than 30 million CT scans were performed last year. The CT is not as sensitive for detecting tissue variations as the MRI, but there are many advantages with CT.

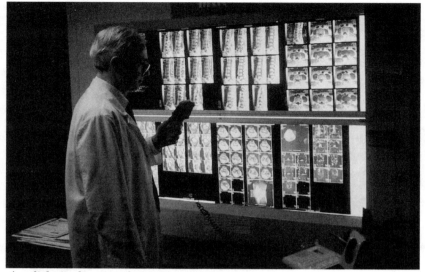

A radiologist dictates a diagnostic report on a scan.

The CT scanner in some ways looks similar to the MRI, but there are actually significant differences. There is a movable table and round gantry, and the patient moves through the middle of it, like the MRI. However, the opening of the CT gantry is much larger than the MRI, and there is no long dark tunnel. The "hole" that the patient's bed slides into has a wider diameter opening and is very short—not long and confining like the MRI.

Getting a CT scan is much faster than an MRI scan. The helical CT scans are now used to image coronary arteries and 3-D colonoscopy. CT scanners are the diagnostic tool of choice to evaluate trauma, especially head, abdomen and pelvic injuries.

Ultrasound

Unlike the CT scanners, which use a narrow beam of X rays, or the MRI scanners, which use magnets and *rf* pulses, ultrasound utilizes high-frequency sound waves to image the body. More than one hundred million ultrasound scans are performed annually throughout the world, second only to standard X rays. Because the sound waves are completely safe, with no known biological effects, ultrasound scans are the imaging tests of choice for evaluating the fetus during pregnancy.

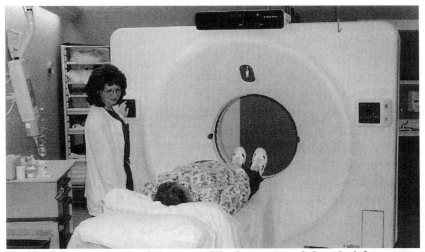

A patient is placed inside a CT scanner. The device suspended on the left is an electronic injector.

Because the body contains over 90 percent water, sound can be used to evaluate tissue density difference, much as sonar is used by ships to determine structures beneath the surface. Sound waves are sent out at a fixed frequency—usually in the 3 to 10 megahertz range—and as the sound waves bounce off tissue, the returning signal is converted into an image.

Ultrasound is used for a number of diagnostic situations besides pregnancy. Ultrasound is used to evaluate breasts with questionable findings on mammography; to evaluate the liver, gallbladder and bile ducts, the pancreas, and for pelvic evaluation of ovaries and the uterus. Doppler ultrasound allows the doctor to visualize blood flowing through vessels. It can be used to evaluate carotid artery disease, transient ischemic attacks (TIAs), suspected strokes and lower extremity veins for thrombosis.

Ultrasound is used to evaluate the brain of newborn babies, a safe, easy and noninvasive procedure that can be done at bedside. Echocardiography can also be used to evaluate the heart, measuring contraction of the heart and also allowing direct visualization of heart valves and wall motion.

Nuclear Medicine

Nuclear medicine uses radiation to evaluate various parts of the body. The radiation is essentially the same as that of X rays, but the photon

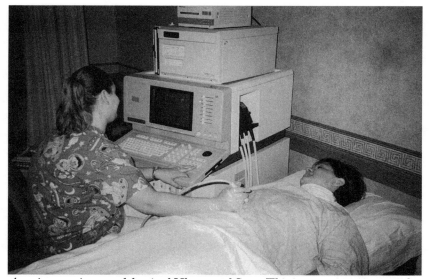

A patient receives an abdominal Ultrasound Scan. This is a non-invasive, painless procedure that utilizes sound waves to scan the patient.

radiation is called *gamma rays* instead of *X rays* because the radiation is caused by the decay of isotopes. Isotopes are injected into the veins of patients, and the isotope will deposit in various specific organs of the body, depending on what the isotope has been tagged to. As the isotope decays, gamma rays, which can be imaged with photon detectors, are produced.

Various materials are used for tagging the isotopes, which then are concentrated in the brain, the heart, bones, the stomach, the kidneys, the liver or other specific areas of the body. A *bone scan* is a very sensitive and easy means of evaluating the entire osseous skeleton for fractures, infection or tumor. While there are dozens of various diagnostic nuclear medicine scans that can be performed, only a few select types will be discussed.

One of the newer uses for isotopes is in the evaluation of the heart. *MUGA (multiple gated acquisitions)* scans are used to evaluate the *function* of the heart, how well it contracts, abnormalities of wall motion and the thickness of the myocardial wall. The MUGA scan of the heart measures the ejection fraction and reports this as a percentage (the amount of blood remaining in the heart versus the amount being pumped out with each contraction). If people are in chronic heart failure, or if patients are being considered for chemotherapy, the cardiologist wants to know how well the heart functions and contracts before giving drugs that might compromise an already poorly functioning heart.

MPI (myocardial perfusion imaging) scans are used to measure the blood flow to the heart. When a patient presents to the ER with chest pain, is it merely bad indigestion or is it a heart attack? A cardiac SPECT (*single photon emission computed tomogram*) MPI scan is a painless, nonsurgical test to evaluate blood flow to the heart and exclude or diagnose a myocardial infarction. The cardiac SPECT scan, known as *cardiolyte study*, evaluates the blood flow through thin sections of the heart and can diagnose ischemia or complete obstruction of blood with infarction. Cardiolyte is a compound tagged with isotope that can demonstrate the perfusion to the heart muscle.

After the cardiolyte isotope compound has been injected intravenously, thin-section scans are obtained with a camera designed to measure gamma rays.

As soon as an acute myocardial infarction is diagnosed, treatment begins immediately. Oxygen therapy is started to maximize tissue oxygenation, thrombolytic agents are given to dissolve coronary thrombus, and heparin or antiplatelet drugs are given to prevent new clots, or thrombus, from forming. Morphine is given to relieve pain and anxiety and decrease myocardial oxygen demands. When the patient is stabilized, either a coronary angioplasty or a coronary bypass graft surgery (CABG) will be performed if vessels are shown to be stenotic.

V/Q scans are pulmonary ventilation and perfusion scans, and are used to determine if the air ventilation and the blood perfusion to all areas of the lungs are normal. Blood clots from veins in the pelvis or legs travel through the heart to lodge in the pulmonary vessels. This condition is called a *PE*, or *pulmonary embolus*. There are approximately 650,000 cases of PE each year in the United States. If untreated, it carries a mortality rate of more than 30 percent. The V/Q scan measures both the ventilation and the perfusion of the lungs, and can detect if an embolus has occluded a vessel.

For the ventilation part of the study, the patient breathes an aerosol mixture containing tiny particles containing an isotope. For the perfusion, the isotope is injected into the veins, and its activity is measured in the lungs. Separate scans in various projections are obtained first with the ventilation phase and then with the perfusion phase.

DEXA Scan

DEXA scans (dual energy X-ray absorptiometry) are the newest and most accurate way to measure bone density (calcium content) and to diagnose osteoporosis. Osteoporosis is the overall loss of bone mass. The bones are therefore weaker, and fractures are much more likely to happen. Complications of hip fractures in the elderly is a very common cause of death. DEXA scans are now being ordered routinely as a screening procedure to diagnose osteoporosis and help prevent life-threatening hip fractures, as well as fractures in other parts of the body.

The DEXA uses a very minimal amount of X-ray radiation to measure the absorption of bone. The patient lies on a soft table while the scanner is passed over the spine, pelvis and hips. This is a safe, pleasant, noninvasive procedure that requires nothing of the patient except to lie comfortably still during the scan.

Interventional and Diagnostic Angiography

Angiography is a special diagnostic and therapeutic section of Radiology where angiograms are performed. There are many conditions that require that the arteries and veins of the body be examined in minute detail. For instance, if there has been a suspected PE, a pulmonary angiogram may be used to confirm the presence of a clot. Angiograms are used to show the increased vascularity of tumors, demonstrate clots, and detect stenotic or occluded vessels.

For any type of angiogram procedure, a catheter and guide wire are placed into a large vein, usually the groin or armpit, and advanced to the area of interest. Once in the right location, the guide wire is removed and contrast is injected to see the vessels. As the injection is being performed, X-ray images are acquired in rapid sequence to show the flow of contrast and blood.

The patient lies on an angio-table, the groin is numbed with local anesthetic, a small incision is made with a scalpel, and the catheter is guided into the vein. During the injection phase, the patient may feel a hot flushed or burning sensation. This is due to the rapid bolus of contrast causing some distension of vessels.

In addition to diagnostic angiograms, therapeutic or interventional angio procedures are now being performed. If a large clot is discovered, the catheter will be placed at the clot, and clot-dissolving drugs will be administered directly into the clot to dissolve it. If a vessel is found to be stenotic (narrowed), a balloon angioplasty will be performed to dilate it. If aneurysms are found, stents can be put in place through a catheter, preventing the need for major surgery. If a patient has massive gastro-intestinal bleeding, the bleeding site will be located, and then drugs or material will be injected to stop the bleeding. Catheters are also placed into certain organs or spaces of the body, such as kidneys or the abdominal cavity, to drain fluid.

Flexible Fiber-Optic Endoscopy

More than fifteen million Americans are prodded with flexible fiber-optic scopes each year, for both diagnostic evaluation and for surgical procedures. These long, flexible scopes with lights and cameras on the end can snake deep into the bronchi of the lungs, into the colon, the gastrointestinal tract or the bladder. Through these scopes, doctors can biopsy lung masses, take out gallbladders, remove colon polyps, biopsy tumors or explore the abdomen.

The advantage of fiber-optic endoscopic procedures is that it requires only a very small surgical incision, just large enough to allow passage of the tube (if not passed through a body orifice such as the mouth or the rectum). If surgery is performed, the recovery time is minimal and the patient can be an outpatient or be required to spend just a day or two in the hospital. This is both considerably cheaper and safer for the patient. And it allows direct visualization of areas of the body not before accessible without major surgery.

Depending on what type of endoscopy is being performed, the patient will receive an appropriate sedative, local anesthetic or general anesthesia. Once the drugs have been administered, the patient is relatively comfortable during the endoscopy and possible surgery through the scope. The recovery time is very short, and the patient can be sent home within hours or by the next day.

Types of Flexible Fiber-Optic Endoscopy

- **LAPAROSCOPY** scope is passed through the abdominal wall to evaluate the abdomen; used to perform some surgeries (chole-cystectomy)

- **ERPC** endoscopic retrograde pancreatico-cholangiography; used to visualize the pancreatic and bile ducts; minor surgery of the sphincter or ducts can be performed; stones can be snared and re-moved or strictures can be dilated
- **COLONOSCOPY** evaluation of the colon
- **ARTHROSCOPY** used to evaluate joints (most commonly the knee); surgery of the knee can be performed through the scope
- **BRONCHOSCOPY** the trachea and bronchi of the lungs can be as-sessed, and biopsies and cultures obtained
- **CYSTOSCOPY** used to evaluate the urinary bladder
- **CULDOSCOPY** used to evaluate the uterus and ovaries in women
- **LARYNGOSCOPY** used to evaluate the larynx and vocal cords
- **GASTROSCOPY** used to evaluate the stomach

Medical Jargon: Doctor-Slang Decoded

T his appendix lists terms, words and phrases that nurses and doctors use every day when talking to each other on the floor, in the OR or on the phone. They are usually shortened forms of words or phrases, and are universally understood by doctors, nurses and technical staff. If you were listening in the halls or on the phones, this is what you might hear.

When appropriate, we have used the word or phrase in a sentence the way it would be used.

BRONCH refers to fiber-optic bronchoscopy of the lungs. A pulmonologist or thoracic surgeon examines the tracheo-bronchial tree with a fiber-optic scope, and will biopsy or take cultures when appropriate.

- "The CT showed a mass, so I am going to *bronch* her tomorrow."

CABBAGE is the pronounced phrase for CABG, which means coronary artery bypass graft.

- "He had a *cabbage* six months ago and is still having severe chest pains."

CATH refers to an angiogram, also called *catheterization*.

- "His stress test was abnormal so we're going to *cath* him tomorrow."

CHEM SEVEN is a test that measures seven basic electrolytes and chemical compounds such as sodium, potassium and glucose in the bloodstream.

CLINIC PATIENT refers to nonpaying patients who have no private doctor and are on Welfare or Medicaid. The division is between private patients and clinic patients.

- "Why are they sending us all the *clinic patients*?"

COAG PANEL is an assessment of how well the blood is coagulating or clotting.

CODE OR CODED refers to either the actual CODE BLUE page or to patient's condition of complete cardiopulmonary arrest. This could be used two ways, meaning the *announcement* or the *condition*.

- "Call a *code*!" Here the person is asking for a CODE BLUE to be announced.
- "The guy in 612 just *coded*." This describes the patient's condition of cardiac arrest.
- "There's a *code* in the ER." This means that a patient has had cardio-pulmonary arrest and the code team is now in the process of trying to resuscitate him.

CRIT is short for hematocrit. A patient's blood count is measured and reported in two ways: the hemoglobin level and the hematocrit, or *crit*, which refers to the percentage of red blood cells. Blood is placed in a thin glass rod, spun in a centrifuge and read by the intern late at night when no lab techs are around.

CRUNCH OR BAD CRUNCH refers to a serious automobile accident in-volving victims with multiple injuries.

DIRTBALL is an unprofessional reference to a (filthy) street person.

FAILURE refers to congestive heart failure, also called *CHF*. This hap-pens because the heart isn't pumping efficiently, pressure builds up in the veins and fluid leaks out into the lungs.

FLATLINE refers to the straight line on a cardiac monitor when the heart stops; also called *asystole*.

GOMER is unprofessional reference to a very old patient.

IV PUSH is when a drug is put directly into the intravenous feed in a single dose (rather than a slower IV drip).

LABS refers to any laboratory studies that were done on that particular patient. The labs will vary from patient to patient, and from day to day, depending on what has been ordered.

- "Have the *labs* come back on Smith yet?"

LEAD POISONING refers to victim of multiple gunshot wounds.

LUNG-ER/CHRONIC LUNG-ER refers to people with severe emphysema or chronic lung disease. These people have difficulty breathing, sputum production and a barrel chest, and often breathe with pursed lips.

MI refers to myocardial infarction, also known as *heart attack*. *Myocardial* refers to the heart muscle, and *infarction* is a term for dead tissue.

- "The new admit in the *unit* has had an *MI* and now he's in *failure*."

NO CODE refers to a patient who will not be resuscitated if he has cardiac arrest. This is usually for terminal patients who are near death, or for patients in which there is no chance of survival.

- "Why did they order a scan? This guy's a *no code*."

PNEUMO short for pneumothorax, commonly known as "collapsed lung." Air gets trapped in the chest cavity and causes the lung to collapse. A large needle or tube is inserted into the chest cavity to allow the trapped air to escape and the lung to re-expand.

SCOPE refers to fiber-optic endoscopy; usually used in reference to endoscopy of the gastrointestinal tract.

- "She's still bleeding, so we're going to *scope* her tomorrow."

SCRIPT refers to a doctor's prescription, and usually refers to the paper pad on which the prescription was written.

- "Did you give her a *script* for Demerol?"

SCRUBBED OR SCRUB IN means that the doctor, nurse or scrub tech has put on gown, cap, mask and sterile gloves. The phrase *scrub in* usually means to join in or assist with the operation.

- "Are you going to *scrub in* with us on the case?"

SCRUBS refers to the (usually blue) scrub pants and shirts worn during surgery and during procedures, and often used as work clothes under a white coat by the staff. These can be cleaned and sterilized by the hospital laundry, and protect regular clothes from blood stains.

SINUS RHYTHM is a normal heartbeat with a regular rhythm.

SMEAR refers to a peripheral blood smear to examine blood cells. A drop of blood is placed on a slide and then smeared into a very thin layer. This allows the peripheral blood cells to be examined and counted.

- "What's her *smear* show?"

STIFF is unprofessional slang for a corpse. The term derived from the condition of rigor mortis, even though it now only refers to the condition of being dead.

TUBED OR TUBE THE PATIENT refers to inserting an endotracheal (breathing tube) into the trachea (windpipe) and then placing the patient on a ventilator; often performed as an emergency, may be done electively in someone slipping slowing into respiratory failure.

- "After he coded, we had to *tube* him."

THE UNIT refers to one of any ICUs in the hospital.

- "He's been transferred to the *unit*."
- "Is he still in the *unit*?"

V FIB   an erratic, ineffective heartbeat; the heart basically just quivers. When the heart is quivering, no blood is pumped, and the effect is the same as asystole.

- "Get me Lidocaine—he's in *v fib*!"

V TACH   a very rapid heartbeat; refers to ventricular tachycardia. Potentially dangerous because it can progress into ventricular fibrillation.

Understanding the Prescription Pad

On the following page is a sample blank prescription. The important features of the prescription include:

- Physician's name, address and office phone number
- DEA number: This number represents the doctor's drug license, issued by the Drug Enforcement Agency (DEA), which oversees the licensing and use of controlled substances. A doctor must have a valid DEA registration number in order to prescribe controlled drugs
- Date the prescription was written. If a prescription was written several months ago and not yet filled, the pharmacist will usually contact the physician's office to see if the prescription is still valid. The patient's condition may have changed in the meantime, or the patient may have started taking other drugs that would interfere with each other
- Patient's name and address
- Label: This tells the pharmacist whether to include a label with the prescription
- Refills: This also tells the pharmacist how many—if any—refills to include with the prescription
- Signature: The doctor must sign the prescription

The following written prescription is exactly like thousands of others written each day—except that it is actually legible. The doctor has written in the patient's name and the date, and has signed it. But what do all the words and abbreviations mean? See page 286 for a full definition.

RX "recipe"

DISP "dispense" this amount

SIG *signa* or *signature*; the directions for taking the recipe

Joseph Smith, M.D.

1234 OAK DRIVE
BROWNVILLE, MA
555-1234

DEA: AW00223344   Date:_____

Patient Name: _____

Patient Address: _____

Rx

Label
Refills: 1 2 3 4 5 6

_____M.D.

Sample blank prescription.

Joseph Smith, M.D.
1234 OAK DRIVE
BROWNVILLE, MA
555-1234

DEA: AW00223344   Date: *May 5, '01*

Patient Name: *Sophie LaRosa*

Patient Address: _____

Rx

Cypro 500 mg tabs

Disp: #20

Sig: take ii tab B.I.D.

Label
Refills: 1 (2) 3 4 5 6

_____ M.D.

Sample filled prescription.

Rx: This is the familiar symbol seen on every drugstore sign and on hundreds of packaged medications, remedies, syrups, sprays and tablets. Rx is short for *recipe*. Just a few decades ago, physicians would design medication for their patients. The formula would tell the pharmacist what to make up, and would include a gram of this, three drops of that and one teaspoon of something else. The pharmacist would then add the various components of the recipe to the mortar, and he would grind it up into a paste or fine powder with the pestle.

This was before mass production by huge drug companies, which now provide almost everything already made up by dosages and information on how often to take the drug. This information has been standardized and included in the *Physician's Desk Reference (PDR)*.

Disp: Gives instructions for the quantity of drug to dispense. This may define the size of a tube (in grams) and number of tubes to be given, the number of tablets, capsules, or volume of liquid medication to be dispensed.

Sig: These are the specific instructions the doctor wants the patient to have on how to take the prescribed drug. These instructions are called the *signa* or *signature*.

Some of the abbreviations included with the Sig include:
- how often to take the drug
- when to take the drug
- specific directions on taking the drug
- where to put the medication

Prescription Abbreviations:

How often or when to take medication:

bid	2 times a day (morning and night)
bin	twice a night
tid	take 3 times a day
qid	take 4 times a day
q	every
h	hour
q 4 h	take every 4 hours
qd	once every day
prn	as needed
hs	at bedtime

bih	take every other hour
m et n	morning and night
pc	after meals

Amount of medication to take:

u	unit
cap	capsule
tab	tablet
suppos	suppository
ss	take one-half (semi)
gtt	drop (gtts: drops)
tsp	teaspoon
tbsp	tablespoon (also T)
oz	ounce

How drug should be taken:

pr	per rectum
po	orally (by mouth)
pv	per vagina
epm	as directed (*ex modo prescripto*)
bib	drink
garg	gargle
IM	intramuscluar
IV	intravenous
sc	subcutaneously (injection)
ID	intradermal

Instructions or Description of Medication:

lot	lotion
lin	liniment
sol	solution
solv	dissolve
ppa	shake bottle first
agit	shake or stir before taking

Terminology of Medical Care and Health Care Regulations

As the health care environment continues to change, the terms associated with health care change also. Here is a glossary to help understand some of the terms.

ACCESS A patient's ability to obtain medical care. The ease of access is determined by components such as the availability of medical services and their acceptability to the patient, availability of insurance, the location of healthcare facilities, transportation, hours of operation, affordability and cost of care.

ACCREDITATION Approval by an authorizing agency for institutions and programs that meet or exceed a set of predetermined standards.

ACTIVITIES OF DAILY LIVING (ADLs) Activities performed as part of a person's daily routine of self-care, such as bathing, dressing, toileting and eating.

ACUTE CARE Hospital care given to patients who generally require a stay of up to seven days and that focuses on a physical or mental condition requiring immediate intervention and constant medical attention, equipment and personnel.

ACUTE CARE BED NEED METHODOLOGY A formula used to determine hospital bed needs.

ADMINISTRATIVE COSTS Costs related to activities such as utilization review, marketing, medical underwriting, commissions, premium collection, claims processing, insurer profit, quality assurance and risk management for purposes of insurance.

ADVANCE DIRECTIVE A document that patients complete to direct their medical care when they are unable to communicate their own wishes due to a medical condition. Living wills and durable powers of attorney are advance directives that are authorized by state law.

ADVANCED PRACTICE NURSE (APN) A registered nurse who is approved by the Board of Nursing to practice nursing in a specified area of advanced nursing practice. *APN* is an umbrella term given to a registered nurse who has met advanced educational and clinical practice requirements beyond the two to four years of basic nursing education required of all RNs. There are four types: (1) Certified Registered Nurse Anesthetist (CRNA); (2) Clinical Nurse Specialist (CNS); (3) Certified Nurse Practitioner (CNP); and (4) Certified Nurse Midwife (CNM).

ADVERSE SELECTION Among applicants for a given group or individual health insurance program, the tendency for those with an impaired health status, or who are prone to higher-than-average utilization of benefits, to be enrolled in disproportionate numbers in lower deductible plans.

AFTERCARE Services following hospitalization or rehabilitation, individualized for each patient's needs. Aftercare gradually phases the patient out of treatment while providing followup attention to prevent relapse.

ALLIED HEALTH PERSONNEL Specially trained and often licensed health workers other than physicians, dentists, optometrists, chiropractors, podiatrists and nurses. The term is sometimes used synonymously with *paramedical personnel*, all health workers who perform tasks that must otherwise be performed by a physician, or health workers who do not usually engage in independent practice.

ALLOPATHIC One of two schools of medicine that treats disease by inducing effects opposite to those produced by the disease. The other school of medicine is osteopathic.

ALLOWABLE COSTS Charges for services rendered or supplies furnished by a health provider that qualify as covered expenses for insurance purposes.

ALTERNATIVE DELIVERY An alternative to the traditional in-patient care system, such as ambulatory care, home health care and same-day surgery.

AMBULATORY CARE Care given to patients who do not require overnight hospitalization.

AMBULATORY SETTING An institutional health setting in which organized health services are provided on an outpatient basis, such as a surgery center, clinic or other outpatient facility. Ambulatory care settings also may be mobile units of service; e.g., mobile mammography or MRI.

AMERICAN ACCREDITATION HEALTHCARE COMMISSION (AAHC)/ URAC Formerly known as the Utilization Review Accreditation Commission, AAHC/URAC is an independent not-for-profit corporation that develops national standards for utilization review and managed-care organizations.

AMERICAN HEALTH CARE ASSOCIATION (AHCA) A trade association representing nursing homes and long-term care facilities in the United States; based in Washington, DC.

AMERICAN HOSPITAL ASSOCIATION (AHA) A national association that represents allopathic and osteopathic hospitals in the United States; based in Washington, DC, with operational offices in Chicago.

AMERICAN MEDICAL ASSOCIATION (AMA) A national association organized into local and regional societies that represent over 700,000 medical doctors in the United States; based in Chicago.

AMERICANS WITH DISABILITIES ACT (ADA) A federal law that prohibits employers of more than 25 employees from discriminating against any individual with a disability who can perform the essential functions, with or without accommodations, of the job that the individual holds or wants.

ANCILLARY A term used to describe additional services performed related to care, such as lab work, X ray and anesthesia.

ANTITRUST A situation in which a single entity, such as an integrated delivery system, controls enough of the practices in any one specialty in a relevant market to have monopoly power (i.e., the power to increase prices).

APPROVED HEALTH CARE FACILITY OR PROGRAM Facility or program that is licensed, certified or otherwise authorized pursuant to the laws of the state to provide health care and which is approved by a health plan to provide the care described in a contract.

ASSOCIATE DEGREE IN NURSING (ADN) A degree received after completing a two-year nursing education program at a college or university.

AVERAGE ADJUSTED PER CAPITA COST (AAPCC) Payment rates used by the Health Care Financing Administration to reimburse managed-care organizations for care delivered to Medicare enrollees.

AVERAGE LENGTH OF STAY (ALOS) A standard hospital statistic used to determine the average amount of time between admission and departure for patients in a diagnosis-related group (DRG), an age group, a specific hospital or other factors.

BACHELOR OF SCIENCE IN NURSING (BSN) Degree received after completing a four-year college or university program that qualifies a graduate nurse to take a national licensing exam to become a registered nurse.

BALANCE BILLING A provider's billing of a covered person directly for charges above the amount reimbursed by the health plan (i.e., the difference between billed charges and the amount paid). This may or may not be allowed, depending on the contractual arrangements between the parties.

BEHAVIORAL HEALTH CARE Mental health services, including services for alcohol and substance abuse.

BENEFICIARY A person designated by an insuring organization as eligible to receive insurance benefits.

BLUE CROSS AND BLUE SHIELD ASSOCIATION (BC/BS) An organization that offers information, consultation, representation and operational services for the Blue Cross and Blue Shield plan members across the country for purposes of providing insurance benefits.

BOARD CERTIFIED A clinician who has passed the national examination in a particular field. Board certification is available for most physician specialties, as well as for many allied medical professions.

BOUTIQUE HOSPITAL A limited service hospital designed to provide one medical specialty such as orthopedic or cardiac care.

BUREAU OF WORKERS' COMPENSATION (BWC) The state-operated insurance system that pays medical and lost-wage benefits to workers who are injured on the job.

CAPITATION (CAP) A stipulated dollar amount established to cover the cost of health care delivered for a person or group of persons. The term usually refers to a negotiated per capita rate to be paid periodically, usually monthly, to a health care provider. The provider is responsible for delivering or arranging for the delivery of all health services required by the covered person(s) under the conditions of the contract.

CARRIER An organization acting as an insurer for private plans or government programs.

CASE MIX INDEX A measure of the relative severity of medical conditions of a hospital's patients.

CENTERS FOR DISEASE CONTROL (CDC) An agency within the U.S. Department of Health and Human Services that serves as the central point for consolidation of disease control data, health promotion and public health programs. CDC is also known as the Centers for Disease Control and Prevention, and is based in Atlanta, Georgia

CERTIFICATE OF NEED (CON) A designation that hospitals had to obtain from the Department of Health to authorize an activity such as constructing or modifying hospitals, purchasing certain medical equipment or providing new health care services. This process was gradually phased out for most acute care hospital activities from 1995 through 1998 and replaced with quality data standards.

CHILDREN'S HEALTH INSURANCE PROGRAM (CHIP) A program administered by the state, funded partly by the federal government, which allows states to expand health coverage to uninsured low-income children not previously eligible for Medicaid.

CIVILIAN HEALTH AND MEDICAL PROGRAM OF THE UNIFORMED SERVICES (CHAMPUS) A program that provides funds to pay for treatment in private institutions for members of the uniformed services and their families.

CLINICAL LABORATORY INVOLVEMENT ACT (CLIA) A federal law designed to set national quality standards for laboratory testing. The law covers all laboratories that engage in testing for assessment, diagnosis, prevention or treatment purposes.

CO-INSURANCE A cost-sharing requirement under a health insurance policy that provides that the insured will assume a portion or percentage of the costs of covered services. After the deductible is paid, this provision obligates the subscriber to pay a certain percentage of any remaining medical bills, usually 20 percent.

CONTINUING MEDICAL EDUCATION (CME) The continuing education of practicing education (CME) physicians through refresher courses, medical journals and texts, educational programs and self-study courses. In some states, CME is required for continued licensure.

CO-PAYMENT A type of cost-sharing that requires the insured or subscriber to pay a specified flat dollar amount, usually on a per-unit-of-service basis, with the third-party payer reimbursing some portion of the remaining charges.

CREDENTIALING The process of reviewing a practitioner's academic, clinical and professional ability as demonstrated in the past to determine if criteria for clinical privileges are met.

DEDUCTIBLE   Out-of-pocket expenses that must be paid by health insurance subscriber before the insurer will begin reimbursing the subscriber for additional medical expenses.

DIAGNOSTIC-RELATED GROUP (DRG)   A hospital classification system that groups patients by common characteristics requiring treatment.

DISABILITY ASSISTANCE   A state-administered, state-funded program that provides cash assistance to individuals with physical or mental impairments, children not receiving other benefits and people sixty and over. The program also provides limited medical coverage of nonhospital medical services.

DISCHARGE PLANNING   The evaluation of patients' medical needs for appropriate care after discharge from an in-patient setting.

DISPROPORTIONATE SHARE HOSPITAL (DSH)   A hospital that provides care to a high number of patients who cannot afford to pay and/or do not have insurance.

DO NOT RESUSCITATE (DNR)   An advance directive that patients may make to forego cardiopulmonary resuscitation or other resuscitative efforts (see *advance directive*).

DOCTOR OF OSTEOPATHY (DO)   A licensed physician who is a graduate from an accredited school of osteopathic medicine.

DURABLE MEDICAL EQUIPMENT (DME)   Equipment that can stand repeated use, is primarily and customarily used to serve a medical purpose, generally is not useful to a person in the absence of illness or injury, and is appropriate for use at home, such as hospital beds, wheelchairs and oxygen equipment.

DURABLE POWER OF ATTORNEY   A document in which competent individuals can select other individuals to make decisions, including health care decisions, for them in the event they become incapacitated.

EMERGENCY MEDICAL SERVICES (EMS)   A system of health care professionals, facilities and equipment providing emergency care.

EMERGENCY MEDICAL TECHNICIAN (EMT)   A person certified to provide on-site or in-transit emergency medical treatment.

EMPLOYEE RETIREMENT INCOME SECURITY ACT (ERISA)   A federal law that exempts self-insured health plans from state laws governing health insurance, including contribution to risk pools, prohibitions against disease discrimination and other state health reforms.

ENVIRONMENTAL PROTECTION AGENCY (EPA) A federal and state agency responsible for programs to control air, water and noise pollution, solid waste disposal and other environmental concerns.

EXCLUSIONS Clauses in an insurance contract that deny coverage for select individuals, groups, locations, properties or risks.

FALSE CLAIMS ACT A federal law that imposes liability for treble damages and fines of $5,000 to $10,000 for knowingly submitting a false or fraudulent claim for payment to the federal government.

FARMERS HOME ADMINISTRATION (FHA) A division of the U.S. Department of Agriculture that guarantees hospital mortgages.

FEE FOR SERVICE A method in which physicians and other health care providers receive a fee for services performed.

FEE SCHEDULE A comprehensive listing of fees used by either a health care plan or the government to reimburse providers on a fee-for-service basis.

FOOD AND DRUG ADMINISTRATION (FDA) An agency within the federal government that is responsible for regulations pertaining to food and drugs sold in the United States.

FREESTANDING EMERGENCY MEDICAL SERVICE CENTER A health care facility that is physically separate from a hospital and whose primary purpose is the provision of immediate, short-term medical care for minor but urgent medical conditions. Also called *urgent care*.

FREESTANDING OUTPATIENT SURGICAL CENTER A health care facility, physically separate from a hospital, that provides prescheduled outpatient surgical services. Also called *surgi-center* or *ambulatory surgical facility*.

FULL-TIME EQUIVALENT (FTE) A standardized accounting of the numbers of full-time and part-time employees.

GATEKEEPER A primary care physician responsible for overseeing and coordinating all aspects of a patient's medical care and pre-authorizing specialty care.

GENERAL PRACTITIONER A physician whose practice is based on a broad understanding of all illnesses and who does not restrict his practice to any particular field of medicine.

GRADUATE MEDICAL EDUCATION (GME) Medical education as an intern, resident or fellow after graduating from a medical school.

GROUP INSURANCE   Any insurance policy or health services contract by which groups of employees (and often their dependents) are covered under a single policy or contract, issued by their employer or other group entity.

HEALTH CARE FINANCING ADMINISTRATION (HCFA)   An agency within the U.S. Department of Health and Human Services that is responsible for the administration of the Medicare and Medicaid programs.

HEALTH MAINTENANCE ORGANIZATION (HMO)   An entity that offers prepaid, comprehensive health coverage for both hospital and physician services, with specific health care providers using a fixed fee structure or capitated rates, membership and utilization, finance and descriptive information on health plan management.

HOME HEALTH AGENCY   An organization that provides medical, therapeutic or other health services in patients' homes.

HOSPICE   A facility or program that is licensed, certified or otherwise authorized by law to provide supportive care of the terminally ill.

HOSPITAL AFFILIATION   A contractual relationship between a health insurance plan and one or more hospitals whereby the hospital provides the in-patient benefits offered by the plan.

INDEPENDENT PRACTICE ASSOCIATION (IPA)   A health care delivery model in which an association of independent physicians contracts with health maintenance organizations and preferred provider organizations for physicians' services.

IN-PATIENT   An individual who has been admitted to a hospital for at least twenty-four hours.

INTEGRATED DELIVERY SYSTEM   Collaboration between physicians and hospitals for a variety of purposes. Some models of integration include physician-hospital organization, management-service organization, group practice without walls, integrated provider organization and medical foundation.

INTERMEDIATE CARE FACILITY   A facility providing a level of medical care that is less than the degree of care and treatment that a hospital or skilled nursing facility is designed to provide but greater than the level of room and board.

INTRACTABLE PAIN   Pain for which there is no cure.

JOINT COMMISSION ON ACCREDITATION OF HEALTHCARE ORGANIZATIONS (JCAHO)   Founded in 1951, the JCAHO evaluates and accredits health care organizations in the United States, including hospitals, health plans and other care organizations that provide home care, mental health care, laboratory, ambulatory care and long-term services.

JOINT VENTURE A loose form of affiliation, essentially contractual in nature, that preserves the prior legal identity of each party participating in the venture.

LENGTH OF STAY (LOS) The number of days a patient stays in a hospital or other health care facility.

LICENSED PRACTICAL NURSE (LPN) A graduate from a one-year vocational or technical nursing program who has been licensed by the state.

LICENSED SOCIAL WORKER (LSW) An individual who is licensed by the state to practice social work.

LIVING WILL A legal document generated by an individual to guide providers on the desired medical care in cases when the individual is unable to articulate her own wishes.

LONG-TERM CARE Care given to patients with chronic illnesses and who usually require a length of stay longer than thirty days.

LOW-LEVEL RADIOACTIVE WASTE Waste that has a low intensity of radioactivity, most of which decays to acceptable levels within a few months, but some of which contains radioactivity for hundreds of years.

MAGNETIC RESONANCE IMAGINING (MRI) A diagnostic technique that uses radio and magnetic waves, rather than radiation, to create images of body tissue and to monitor body chemistry.

MANAGED CARE A system of health care delivery that influences utilization and cost of services and often includes a capitated payment structure and a limited choice of health care providers.

MEDICAID A state-administered program funded partly by the federal government that provides health care services for certain low-income persons and certain aged, blind or disabled individuals. The program is approximately a 40/60 state/federal match.

MEDICAL CONSUMER PRICE INDEX An inflationary statistic that measures the cost of all purchased health care services.

MEDICAL DOCTOR (M.D.) A licensed physician who is a graduate of an accredited medical school and practices allopathic medicine.

MEDICARE A federally funded program that provides health insurance primarily for individuals entitled to Social Security who are age sixty-five or older.

MEDIGAP A policy guaranteeing to pay a Medicare beneficiary's co-insurance, deductible and co-payments and providing additional health plan or nonMedicare coverage for services up to a predefined benefit limit. In essence, the product pays for the portion of the cost of services not covered by Medicare.

MORBIDITY Incidence of illness and accidents in a defined group of individuals.

MORTALITY Incidence of death in a defined group of individuals.

NATIONAL BOARD OF MEDICAL EXAMINERS A nonprofit organization responsible for preparing and administering qualifying examinations for physicians.

NATIONAL CANCER REGISTRY A unit within the National Institutes of Health that provides updates on the latest cancer diseases, research and diagnosis.

NATIONAL INSTITUTES OF HEALTH A division within the U.S. Department of Health and Human Services that is responsible for most of the agency's medical research programs.

NUCLEAR REGULATORY COMMISSION (NRC) A federal commission created in 1974 to protect public health and safety by regulating civilian uses of nuclear materials.

OCCUPATIONAL SAFETY AND HEALTH ADMINISTRATION (OSHA) A federal agency within the U.S. Department of Labor that is responsible for setting standards to promote and enforce employee safety in the workplace.

OFFICE OF BUDGET AND MANAGEMENT (OBM) A state agency responsible for adopting and implementing financial policies for the administration of state programs.

OFFICE OF INSPECTOR GENERAL (OIG) The enforcement arm, within the United States, of the Department of Health and Human Services that oversees investigations of alleged health and human violations of Medicare and Medicaid laws, Services and rules.

OFFICE OF MANAGEMENT AND BUDGET (OMB) A federal agency responsible for providing fiscal accounting and budgeting services for the federal government.

OUTCOME MEASURES Assessments to gauge the results of treatment for a particular disease or condition. Outcome measures include the patient's perception of restoration of function, quality of life and functional status, as well as objective measures of mortality, morbidity and health status.

OUTLIER   A patient case that falls outside of the established norm for diagnosis-related groups.

OUTPATIENT   A person who receives health care services without being admitted to a hospital.

PARTICIPATING PROVIDER   A health care provider who has a contractual arrangement with a health care service contractor, HMO, PPO, IPA or other managed-care organization.

PATIENT SELF-DETERMINATION ACT   A federal law that requires health care facilities to determine if new patients have a living will and/or durable power of attorney for health care and to take patients' wishes into consideration in developing their treatment plans.

PAYER   A public or private organization that pays for or underwrites coverage for health care expenses.

PEER REVIEW   The evaluation of quality of total health care provided by medical staff with equivalent training.

PEER REVIEW ORGANIZATION   An entity established by the Tax Equity Organization and Fiscal Responsibility Act of 1982 (TEFRA) to review quality of care and appropriateness of admissions, readmissions and discharges for Medicare and Medicaid. These organizations are held responsible for maintaining and lowering admission rates, and reducing lengths of stay while ensuring against inadequate treatment.

PER MEMBER PER MONTH (PMPM)   The amount of money paid or received on a monthly basis for each individual enrolled in a managed-care plan, often referred to as *capitation*.

PHYSICIAN-HOSPITAL ORGANIZATION (PHO)   A legal entity formed and owned by one or more hospitals and physician groups in order to obtain payer contracts and to further mutual interests; one type of integrated delivery system.

POINT-OF-SERVICE (POS)   An insurance plan where members need not choose how to receive services until the time they need them, also known as an *open-ended HMO*.

POLITICAL ACTION COMMITTEE (PAC)   A group of people organized to collect and distribute contributions to political candidates.

PRE-ADMISSION TESTING   Patient tests performed on an outpatient basis prior to admission to the hospital.

PREFERRED PROVIDER ORGANIZATION (PPO) A panel of physicians, hospitals and other health care providers of services to an enrolled group for a fixed periodic payment.

PRENATAL CARE Services to pregnant women designed to ensure that both expectant mother and the newborn are in the best health. A lack of prenatal care early in the pregnancy is associated with low birth weight and infant mortality.

PREVENTIVE CARE Comprehensive care emphasizing priorities for prevention, early detection and early treatment of conditions, generally including routine physical examination and immunizations.

PRIMARY CARE Entry-level care that may include diagnostic, therapeutic or preventive services.

PROSPECTIVE PAYMENT SYSTEM (PPS) A method of financing health care that mandates payments in advance for the provision of services and is based on diagnostic-related groups.

PROVIDER A hospital, physician, group practice, nursing home, pharmacy or any individual or group of individuals that provides a health care service.

PUBLIC HEALTH SERVICE A federal agency responsible for public health services and programs, including biomedical research.

QUALITY ASSURANCE A formal set of activities to review and improve the quality of services provided. Quality assurance includes quality assessment and corrective actions to remedy any deficiencies identified in the quality of direct patient, administrative and support services.

RATE-SETTING The determination by a government body of rates a health care provider may charge private-pay patients.

RESOURCE-BASED RELATIVE VALUE SCALE (RBRVS) Medicare fee schedule for physician services that sets a uniform payment in each geographic area for most of the approximately seven thousand medical procedures.

RISK The chance or possibility of loss, often employed as a utilization control mechanism within the HMO setting. Risk is also defined in insurance terms as the possibility of loss associated with a given population.

ROUTINE NOTIFICATION A system being proposed at the state and national levels requiring hospitals to call a regional phone number when death is imminent to determine if organs are suitable for transplantation.

SELECTIVE CONTRACTING The practice of a managed-care organization (MCO) by which the MCO enters into participation agreements only with certain providers (and not with all providers who qualify) to provide health care services to health plan participants as members of the MCO's provider panel.

SKILLED NURSING FACILITY (SNF) A facility, either freestanding or part of a hospital, that accepts patients in need of rehabilitation and medical care that is of a lesser intensity than that received in the acute care setting of a hospital.

SOCIAL SECURITY ADMINISTRATION The administrative branch of the federal government established in 1935 to provide old age and survivor benefits.

STAFF MODEL HMO An HMO that delivers health services through a group in which physicians are salaried employees who treat HMO members exclusively.

STARK II The commonly used name for federal laws and regulations that ban physician referral to entities with which the physician has a financial relationship.

STOP LOSS The point at which a third party has reinsurance to protect against an overly large single claim or an excessively high aggregate claim during a given period of time. Large employers that self-insure may purchase reinsurance for stop loss purposes.

SUBACUTE CARE Care given to patients who require less than a thirty-day length of stay in a hospital and who have a more stable condition than those receiving acute care.

SUPPLEMENTAL MEDICAL INSURANCE Private health insurance, also called *insurance medigap*, designed to supplement Medicare benefits by covering certain health care costs that are not paid for by the Medicare program.

SUPPLEMENTAL SECURITY INCOME (SSI) A federal program of income support for low-income, aged, blind and disabled persons established by Title XVI of the Social Security Act. Qualification for SSI often is used to establish Medicaid eligibility.

SWING BEDS Acute care hospital beds that can also be used for long-term care.

TELEMEDICINE Health care consultation and education using telecommunication networks to transmit information.

TERTIARY CARE Highly specialized care given to patients who are in danger of disability or death.

TORT A negligent or intentional civil wrong, not arising out of a contract or statute, that injures someone in some way and for which the injured person may sue the wrongdoer for damages.

TRIAGE The process by which patients are sorted or classified according to the type and urgency of their conditions.

UNIFORM BILLING CODE OF 1992 (UB-92) A revised version of the UB-82, a federal directive requiring a hospital to follow specific billing procedures, itemizing all services included and billed for on each invoice, implemented October 1, 1993.

U.S. DEPARTMENT OF HEALTH AND HUMAN SERVICES (HHS) A department within the executive branch of the federal government responsible for Social Security and federal health programs in the civilian sector.

USUAL, CUSTOMARY AND REASONABLE CHARGES (UCR) Charges for health care services in a geographical area that are consistent with the charges of identical or similar providers in the same geographic area.

UTILIZATION The patterns of use of a service or type of service within a specified time, usually expressed in a rate per unit of population-at-risk for a given period (e.g., the number of hospital admissions per year per one thousand persons in a geographic area).

UTILIZATION REVIEW (UR) An evaluation of the necessity and appropriateness of the use of health care services, procedures and facilities.

VETERANS' ADMINISTRATION (VA) A federal agency responsible for veterans, including VA hospitals and veterans' benefits.

WELL-BABY CARE Services provided in the first year of a newborn's life to identify, treat and prevent health care problems.

WORKERS' COMPENSATION A state-mandated program that provides insurance for work-related injuries and disabilities.

Medical Terminology

M uch of our medical terminology comes from Latin and Greek, and common prefixes and suffixes are added to a central root to produce the impressive and confusing medical words or terms. Listed here are some of the basic roots, prefixes and suffixes.

Root:	*Meaning:*
cardio	heart
gastro	stomach
hemo	blood
hepatic	liver
laparo	in the abdomen
litho	stone
myo	muscle
oophor	ovary
osteo	bone
pneumo	lungs
reno	kidney

Prefix:	*Meaning:*
a- or an-	none or lack
anti-	against
auto-	self
hyper-	excessive
hypo-	deficient
iso-	equal
oligo-	too little
pachy-	thick
peri-	around
poly-	many

Suffix:	*Meaning:*
-ectomy	removing

-itis	inflammation
-megaly	enlarged
-oma	tumor
-osis	condition
-otomy	making a hole
-plasty	repairing
-rrhea	flow/discharge

Here are terms and words you might read in a patient's chart or hear doctors and nurses use in their day-to-day work:

ARRHYTHMIA refers to an abnormal heart rhythm, an EKG (ECG) pattern that may be innocent or lethal

ARTERIAL BLOOD GASES a blood test drawn from an artery, rather than the usual way from a vein. This is usually drawn from the radial artery at the wrist to assess levels of oxygen, CO_2, bicarbonate and the Ph levels of blood, which reflect both metabolic and respiratory events in the body.

ARTERIAL LINE a short plastic catheter placed into an artery, usually the radial artery at the wrist; not used to administer anything! Used to monitor blood pressure from moment to moment; used in very sick patients or in the OR to monitor patients undergoing major procedures, especially in those with heart disease

BOLUS is a rapid injection of IV fluid or medicine. A bolus injection is a very rapid injection, as opposed to the slow infusion method of IV drip.

CARDIOVERSION the use of a defibrillator machine with two pads, which also may provide a basic EKG lead; this allows the identification of abnormal rhythms and for immediate treatment with defibrillation or cardioversion; may start with 200 joules (electricity) and go as high as 350 on the third try with or without added cardiac drugs

CAUTERY electrocautery is used for dissection and coagulation; machine may be placed at different setting and set at cutting, coagulation or a blend of the two; the surgeon uses a spatula or needle tip

CENTRAL LINE a plastic catheter that is inserted below the collar bone or into the neck directly into large veins which flow to the heart; allows irritating medications and nutrients to be delivered where the fast blood flow of the central veins "whisk" off the drug before it clots the vein

COMA a state of unconsciousness where the victim is unaware of his surroundings; may be caused by head trauma, shock, severe infection, drugs or metabolic conditions such as uncontrolled diabetes

COMPRESSION BOOTS plastic wraps placed around the calves and attached to a machine that inflates the leg cuffs intermittently to milk blood out of the veins to discourage clots from forming (deep vein thrombosis or phlebitis)

DRAPES the sterile sheets and towels used to cover all but the prepped skin where an operation is to take place; the skin square is blocked off with towels held at the overlapping corners by towel clamps, and then everything else is draped with sterile sheets

EKG OR ECG (electrocardiogram) used to show typical QRS complex of the heart electrical signal and muscular contraction. This shows the heart rate and any arrhythmias; these conduction problems appear as abnormal patterns in the QRS complex ("blip").

ENDOTRACHEAL TUBE the common breathing tube placed into a patient's trachea, or windpipe, and through the vocal cords; attached to a ventilator to provide mechanical ventilation at a set rate and volume; also used for general anesthesia

"ETHER" SCREEN old term still used to describe the upper sterile sheet that is clipped to two IV poles to exclude the anesthesiologist from the sterile field

EXTUBATE to remove the endotracheal tube from a patient's trachea after weaning him off a mechanical ventilator; usually followed by facemask oxygen supplementation

HEMOSTAT the basic scissors-like instrument with a straight or curved tip with teeth on one end and ratchet (locking teeth) handles to permit grasping tissue; the basis for several types of surgical instruments

IV FLUID refers to any fluid administered by IV drip, usually saline, Lactated Ringers or other solutions used to replace lost blood and body fluids; administered by placing a plastic catheter into a vein; IV (intravenous) fluids are given to patients who cannot keep up their daily fluid needs of approximately two liters

LAPAROSCOPIC APPROACH refers to the use of tiny incisions to insert a trochar or sleeve into a body part or cavity; uses a video system with a camera mounted on a telescope; the small incision and scope replace the traditional large abdominal incision for direct visual and manual approach to surgical area

MULTI-ORGAN FAILURE the end result of severe disease seen in the ICU, a form of "final common pathway" with lung, heart and kidney failure requiring special cardiac medications, mechanical ventilation and dialysis; may also include coma; is usually fatal

OPEN SURGERY a large incision allowing direct hand manipulation and visualization of surgical area

OR TABLE mechanical or electrical, the narrow operating room table is built to accommodate side arms, stirrups and a wide band to anchor the patient and may be "broken" in the middle for positioning; may be moved in the room, for example angled to permit surgeon and assistant to both work from one side

OVERHEAD LIGHTS big, multibulb lights with a central receptacle for a sterile light handle placed by the scrub tech or surgeon; permits the lights, which are mounted on huge swivels from the ceiling, to be adjusted during the case

PEEP positive end-expiratory pressure; the pressure at the end of expiration is not permitted to return to zero in the lungs. The airway pressure may be 5 to 20cm H_2O and keeps the lungs inflated to improve the matching of blood flow to air exchange in the capillaries and air sacs, respectively.

PREP to get someone ready for surgery; may involve shaving the skin, taking a pre-op enema and antibiotics or washing the skin with antiseptic solution

SCALPEL razor-sharp cutting instrument, referred to in the OR as the "knife"; disposable blade with various-size handles

SHOCK STATES refer to low blood pressure, fast pulse, cold, clammy confused patient suffering from insufficient blood volume and pressure; caused by hemorrhage or other major body-fluid loss, heart attack, severe infection (sepsis) or allergic reaction (anaphylaxis)

STAPLING DEVICES disposable instruments which, when placed on tissue, fire single or staggered double rows of tiny titanium staples that serve in the place of sutures; used to remove lung tissue, resected bowel, appendix, stomach, etc; requires some sutures to support stapled connections

SUCTION to remove mucus from the trachea with a plastic catheter attached to a suction machine, to remove blood from a surgical cavity, or to remove air and fluid from the chest cavity

SWAN-GANZ CATHETER another monitoring catheter, a long flexible small-caliber tube inserted like a central line, but goes into the heart with a balloon into the pulmonary arteries to measure cardiac pressures and output; the measurements can help doctors decide what drugs to use and how much IV fluid to administer

TRANSFUSION THERAPY involves not only the provision of whole blood or packed red blood cells (the usual transfusions) but also *component therapy* using fresh frozen plasma, platelets and specific coagulation factors such as VIII or IX

UTI urinary tract infection; usually used as abbreviated UTI when describing condition in both written and spoken communication

VENTILATOR also called a *respirator*, it is the machine that provides artificial ventilator support; set for a range of rates and volumes, it also provides a number of breathing options such as partial or complete ventilation

WARMING BLANKET a special device used to keep a patient warm during surgery, on the floor or in the ICU; inflatable plastic configuration used in surgery ("Bare Hugger") sticks to the patient's skin and covers the "core" or chest area and is attached to a heating unit.

WEAN the process of reducing the number or volume of something from the patient as they can tolerate it. The patient may be weaned off certain dependent medications, or they may be weaned from a ventilator. In this case, it would be the transition from controlled mechanical ventilation to spontaneous patient breathing.

flawed curricula, 22
and hospitals, fusion, 19-20
proprietary, 12-14
Medical staff, and hospital administration, 158-160
Medical students. *See* Students
Medicine
early, European vs. colonial America, 9-10
See also Drugs
Mistakes, 144-150, 238-240
avoiding, in ER, 37-39
awareness during anesthesia, 243-245
ethical, 145, 150
misinterpreted orders, 250
technical, 145, 148-149
whos vs. whys, 265-266
wrong diagnosis, 254-255
wrong drugs, 245-247
wrong-site surgeries, 241-243
Morgue, 115-116
MRI scan, 268-271, 296
Multiple-organ failure, 185, 201, 305

Nightingale, Florence, 18-19
Nonphysician clinicians (NPCs), 166-171
Nuclear medicine, 273-276
Nurse(s), 160-166
APN, 289
circulating, 101, 103-104
ICU, 195-197
duties and opportunities, 162-164
types, 161-162, 296
Nurses' station, 209-211
Nursing process, 164-166

Operating room, 72, 84-88

basic components, 76
blood loss, 113-114
cardiac arrest, 114-115
case board, 110
corridors, 83-84
death, 115-116
layout, 74-78
locker room, 91-93
physical design, 81-82
rules of conduct, 103, 105-111
sensory perceptions, 87-88
specialty, 93
Orderlies, 172-173
Orders, misinterpreted, 250
Organs. *See* Vital organ function; individual names
Outpatient surgery. *See* Daystay surgery

PACU, 89-90, 116-118
Paging systems, 234
Patient
assessing, in ER, 39-41
critically ill, monitoring, 191-193
dependent on machine, 197-200
exposing, to assess illness or injury, 40
listening to, 127-130
positioning, during surgery, 74
reducing stress, in ICU, 178
Patient care
basic, for critically ill, 183
HMO guidelines for, 67-68
improved, 20, 26-27
Patient floors and rooms, 205-208
Patient identification
and in-hospital tracking, ER, 37-41
international coding system, 56
Patient's Bill of Rights, 26, 69
Pepper spray, 46-47

310

Permanently unconscious, defined, 62
Personnel, ER, 32
Pest houses, 9-10
Physicians. *See* Attending physicians,
    Intensivists, Interns, Primary
    care physicians, Residents,
    Surgeon
Point-of-service plans, 65, 298
Postanesthesia care unit. *See* PACU
Pre-certification, 60-61
Pre-operative holding unit, 82
Prescription pad, 283-287
Primary care physicians
    and HMOs, 66
    vs. specialist, 23
Promotion, residents', 143-144
Psychiatric emergencies, and lockdown
    units, 52
Pulmonary failure, 35-36

Reception area, ER, 29-30
Records
    patient-related, 224-225
    See also Medical records
Renal failure, 189-190
Research, medical, 20-21
Residents, 141
    four major responsibilities, 133
    junior and senior, 134-138
    overworked, 138-139
    promotion, 143-144
Respiratory distress or failure, 187
Rounds, types, 134
Routine admission, 59, 63

Scopes. *See* Endoscopy
Scrub sink alcove, 89-90
Scrub technician, 99-101
Security

hospital, 42-47, 253
    medical records, 225-231
Sepsis, 188-189, 260
Shock, 36, 305
    three kinds, 188
    See also Sepsis, Toxic shock
        syndrome
Short-stay surgical unit, 78
Short-term admission, 59-60, 63
Social workers, 172, 296
Staff
    medical, and hospital administra-
        tion, 158-160
    medical records department,
        219-222
Stepdown unit, 117, 205
Sterile processing department (SPD),
    90-91
Students
    medical, 126-130, 140-141
    premedical, 123-126, 140
Surgeon
    conflict with anesthesiologist, 97-98
    under stress, 106-108
Surgery
    basic principles, 73-74
    booking
        elective, 94
        levels of urgency, 94-95
    bumping booked cases, 95
    complications, 260-261
    distractions, 108-111
    elective, 77
    infection risks, 258
    patient positioning, 74
    rituals, 95-97
    teaching skills, 111-113
    wrong-site, 241-243
    See also Daystay surgery